T0325270

A DOCTOR'S LEGACY

A DOCTOR'S LEGACY

*A Memoir
of Merlin K. DuVal*

*Founding Dean of Arizona's
First Medical School*

• • •

As told to Linda Valdez

Foreword by Fred DuVal

• • •

ISBN: 9780615283937
Library of Congress Control Number: 2009924583

Printed in the United States of America
October, 2009
First Edition

Published by Legacy Publishing
Phoenix, AZ

Jacket and interior design by Renee Fullerton

DEDICATION

This book is dedicated to Merlin K. DuVal's
grandchildren and great-grandchildren.

As this book goes to press, the grandchildren are:

Adam Fenster
Allyson DuVal Klipa
Tiffany Fenster Burrell
Stephanie DuVal Henning
Case Fenster
Will DuVal
Montgomery "Monte" DuVal

As this book goes to press, the great-grandchildren are:

Keyo Fenster
Aleksandar Klipa
Lunden Fenster
Adriana Klipa

This book is also dedicated to all future descendants who want
to understand how one man used his intelligence, integrity and
talent to make a difference in the world and build a legacy that
continues to touch the lives of countless people.

• • •

ACKNOWLEDGEMENTS

We wish to acknowledge the help of the many people who contributed to the preparation of this book. In addition to those mentioned in the text, we owe special thanks to Dave Piper, Digital Resources Librarian, Arizona Health Sciences Library, University of Arizona; Linda O'Rourke, professor in surgery library science, University of Oklahoma Health Sciences Center; Kathy Whisman, University of Arizona Budget Office; Steve Nash, Executive Director, Pima County Medical Society; Rick Neeley, Director, Biomedical Communications, University of Arizona Health Sciences Center; Brian Bateman, Senior Director of Development for Major Gifts, University of Arizona College of Medicine; consultant Ryan Diercks and proofreader Anne Gully.

A portion of the proceeds from the sale of this book will be donated by the publishing company to:

Dr. Merlin K. "Monte" DuVal Memorial Med-Start Endowment
UA Foundation Development Office
UA College of Medicine
PO Box 245018
Tucson, AZ 85724-5018
530-626-2827

CONTENTS

Foreword

This book is a product of four things: a man who made enormous contributions to the world and the time he inhabited; a father becoming a grandfather whose grandchildren were deprived of the opportunity to learn from him; a modesty that wasn't evident early in his remarkable career but which grew commensurate with and counter to the accumulation of his achievements, resulting in family pressure urging him to complete this memoir; and an acquaintance – who became a valued family friend – who also happened to be a gifted and committed writer.

While I pressed for it the hardest, everyone in our family thought this book was an important effort and a good idea. That it would capture Dad's life story was good. That it would give him intellectual exercise and motivation to press on in his later years was also enticing. This book was intended to be – and will surely be – a gift to our family for generations. That it may also prove to be of great interest to University historians, doctors and those who muse about life's teachings, is a supplemental benefit

Here, in this text, his accomplishments become more profound with the passage of time and the test of history. Here his family biography and legacy becomes ever more meaningful for those of us sharing the honor of his name. And here we are called upon to reflect on the values he held dear and the ideas he thought important.

That he would lose his sight was a painful and cruel thing – but as is evident on these pages, he never lost his vision.

Much of the life-story he tells was known to the family, yet a remarkable amount of it was not. Upon each re-reading, the breadth and depth of Dad's achievements, and his intellectual range, grows ever more impressive. It was easy in the later years, as his time grew shorter and his love and his family commitment grew deeper, to think of him as we should: first and foremost as a loving father and grandfather. This book also reminds us how much more he was.

Fred DuVal
April, 2009
Phoenix, Arizona

• • •

Prologue

I knew Monte DuVal by reputation before I met him. As a long-time journalist in Arizona, I was well aware that if you wanted some insights into health care, you called Dr. DuVal. He could always put things in perspective. One day he called me. He asked if I ever took on side jobs. I said that would depend on the job. Then he asked me to help him write his memoirs. He said he wanted to put it all down on paper so his grandchildren would know who he was.

We began meeting on Fridays because I only worked four days a week. Sometimes we met in a borrowed conference room at the University of Arizona Health Sciences Center or in the hospital cafeteria. Sometimes he took the shuttle from Phoenix to Tucson. I'd pick him up at the corner of Park Avenue and 6th Street and we'd drive to a nearby restaurant or hotel lobby to talk for hours over endless cups of coffee. I only once made the four-hour round-trip to his home in Phoenix. He said it wasn't a good use of my time.

I was a bit surprised that a man of Monte's stature would consider my time more valuable than his. But I soon found out Monte was not predictable. This was a man who had faced down people of enormous ego and determination, advised at least four governors, testified before Congress many times, worked for one president and had his picture taken with another one. But when I met him at the shuttle, he'd be chatting up the driver as though they were friends from way back. He was a scientist, but he reminded me that medicine has it roots in the occult. He grew up embracing his father's anti-FDR conservatism, but teamed up with one of the most liberal members of the Arizona Legislature to work on expanding health care coverage for the poor. He was not an easy man to figure out.

One of our first interviews was at the Health Sciences Center, the monument he built with a surgeon's daring and a politician's practicality. Monte's son, Fred, suggested that walking those halls might jog some memories. It seemed like a good idea.

Monte told me he was legally blind due to macular degeneration, but that was easy to forget. He compensated for his blindness very well. With only light and shadow to guide him, he escorted me through the medical center with an air of complete confidence. Once or twice he told me that we were in unfamiliar territory, completely remodeled. But he never asked for directions and I never offered an opinion about which way to go. I let a blind man lead me because he had a pride and dignity that should not have to yield to something as mundane as eye disease. With Monte as my guide, I knew we'd get where we needed to go.

He moved with such purpose that few people challenged us as we wandered past the "Do not enter" signs into the non-public parts of the medical school and hospital. This was his domain. If someone did stop us, intimating that perhaps we were in restricted territory, Monte would simply say, "Thank you, we just wanted to have a look around." He never pulled rank, never said he was the man who had built the place. His sense of command was unmistakable, though. The person would back off. We'd look around unhindered. Before we left the area, Monte would stop by and thank the person for being so gracious. I suspect some of them had figured out who he was by then. But he never told anybody. He never played the role of Big Man on Campus, even though he had been the big man on every campus he ever walked.

We stopped at DuVal Auditorium, which had been named in his honor, and he showed me the oil painting done of him before he left the medical school. He said it might be worth mentioning in the book.

"What was it like to sit for a painting," I asked. It was an inane question, but I was hoping to get him to open up. Our conversation had been rather superficial, focused solely on the kind of information you can get off a resume. I needed him to trust me with something more personal or we weren't going to get very far.

"Oh, I have no idea," he said, "the artist worked from a picture."

Well, duh, I thought. Obviously, Dr. DuVal, the founding dean of a medical empire, would not have been able to sit still long enough to have a portrait done from life.

Later, I asked him how it felt to walk the halls of the hospital after so many years. I was still trying to reach beyond the monument and hear from the man. He answered by observing that the place seemed to be running smoothly and efficiently. There was no sentimentality. He'd built something to function well, and he was pleased to see that it was still doing so. Only later did I realize that the medical school was entirely the wrong place to try and move beyond his professional accomplishments into the realm of the heart and spirit. He'd been all business when he'd imagined those halls in exquisite detail, watched them grow into reality and supervised the teaching and healing that went on there. Those were his workaholic days.

These days, when he called the hospital administration office and asked to speak to one of the big shots, the secretaries sometimes asked, "How do you spell DuVal?" He seemed more amused than disappointed when he told me that. Given his expressed desire to create a medical school that did not rely on any one person for its identity, I imagine he was rather pleased to think that his school was grown up enough to forget him. Of course, the school did not forget. The medical school's library has an archive that includes massive books of news clippings in which Dr. DuVal is the main character. The librarians who preside over that special collection made me put on white gloves before I could touch those books.

There are other documents, carefully filed in box after box that Monte preserved in his home. It was not done out of ego – although he was quick to tell me he had plenty of that. It was done out of an appreciation of the enormity of what those papers represent. A medical school is a significant and important institution. Its history deserves respect. Yet Monte kept this in perspective, too. He'd say, "Here's a bunch of crap for you," when handing me a stack of files. They included onion-skin copies of letters he sent to deans of medical schools around the nation to solicit information that would help him design his medical school. The responses, on fine linen letterhead, are carefully stapled to those copies. Also in those files are some of the thousands of speeches he gave to audiences around the country. There are pages of notes where he refined his ideas about the role of doctors and medical schools in the context of a rapidly changing society.

"The human being who is afflicted by disease is as important an object for study, understanding and treatment as the pathology to which he succumbs." He wrote that in his tidy penmanship and bracketed it in red on one of those papers. "Human being" is underlined in red on that dog-eared and yellowing page. He wrote it years before people started saying such things.

It didn't bother him at all that many of the human beings at the medical school that day didn't know him. "Why should they?" he asked.

But he was certainly not anonymous. As we walked through the medical center, we'd hear a voice call out: "Dr. DuVal!" He would turn, look the person in the face, extend his hand and offer a warm greeting. He'd make gracious small talk that hinted at familiarity without revealing details until the person gave him a gushing goodbye.

"I have no idea who that was," Monte would tell me later in a slightly playful tone. "If I don't recognize the voice, I really have no way of knowing. I just keep talking and hope I'll pick up a clue from what they say."

It's a good bet that those he spoke to glowed for the rest of the day because a great man had taken the time to say hello in an unhurried way that reflected his cultured upbringing and genuine delight in his fellow human beings.

It was an education in graciousness to see him interact with people. But to cut down the distractions and make the best use of time, most of our interviews were conducted at my home. His wife Ruth would drop off Monte on her way to check on the progress of the house they were having built in Tucson's Academy Village, where a number of his retired former colleagues lived. Monte would take a seat in my living room and we'd talk as my tiny electronic voice recorder silently did its job on the table between us. Later, I would replay the interview and transcribe it. We did that through much of 2006. During the summer, my 15-year-old daughter would sometimes pass through on her way to the kitchen and Monte would greet her with a courtliness that was both flattering and a little startling. So few people take time to really greet each other these days. Monte didn't do the perfunctory "Hihowareyou?" If Monte asked how you were, it was because he wanted to know. He was fully prepared to listen to the answer. It made you feel special. It also made you feel like you had better come up with something more insightful than "Fineandyou?" Even teenagers were not immune to the persuasiveness of his expectations. I suspect my daughter sometimes listened in on our conversations from down the hall after she finished greeting Monte and returned to her room. I hope she did. He had a lot to say.

One Friday, he told me that he and Ruth had attended a performance of "Tuesdays With Morrie" the night before. We discussed the book, the theatrical adaptation and the fact that, unlike many performances, this one hadn't made him cry. It was odd because he had a long list of movies, books, poems and performances that did bring on the waterworks. This performance didn't touch him that way, and he wasn't sure why. It was clearly intended to, and most of the audience succumbed. Not Monte. He liked it, nevertheless. After he left, I reread the book and wondered if he'd brought it up because he was hoping for a similar approach in his memoirs.

Monte had entrusted me with the astonishing task of helping put his life on paper, and I wanted to make it exactly what he expected. Was he hoping for "Fridays with Monte"? The idea of copying the style of a best seller didn't thrill me. But if that was what he wanted, so be it. The next Friday, I asked Monte if he'd brought up "Tuesdays with Morrie" because he was hoping for a similar approach in his memoirs.

"No," he said, "that never occurred to me."

It was another "Well, duh!" moment. I'd been silly even to ask. The Mitch Albom story is about the last period of a dying man's life. Monte wasn't going to die anytime soon.

So throughout that year, the builders worked on the new house for Monte and Ruth, and Monte and I worked through the stories of his life. By now I had no trouble getting him to move beyond the resume. He loved talking about his concept of nobility, philosophy, liberty, God, the soul and assorted other mysteries. He could tease an idea to the heights of a 1960s bouffant hairdo and quote five or six notable philosophers on the way. It was not just stylish and educational. It was fun. If I didn't happen to know right off hand what Pierre LeCompte du Noüy contributed to the collective wisdom of humankind, Monte was more than glad to explain. He didn't do so in a superior or patronizing way, either. Knowledge was something to share. Generously. What's more, he understood that in a conversation, one of the primary responsibilities is to make the other person feel comfortable. Monte lamented the fact that so many people today act as though the goal of a discussion is to score points by diminishing the other person. He knew better. Conversation was something to share, too. It was supposed to enrich everyone involved.

Our rich conversations often veered into the news of the day and the deeper meaning of what was going on. His insight into politics was remarkable. I hated to do it, but I often had to bring him back to the mundane world of dates and events.

"We have to get through the broccoli," I would tell him.

He'd say how much more he enjoyed the discussions about ideas. I'd agree. But the events of his life were complex and they needed to be unwrapped and carefully sorted. They had to be told accurately. So we'd go back to talking about his college years or his internships or the days in Oklahoma.

Sometimes he'd bring me pictures. He showed me a portrait of his beautiful mother and shots of himself from his modeling days. I delighted in the wonderful, carefree young man he was when he posed for cigarette ads or the covers of romance books. Handsome doesn't half cover it. Neither does sparkling. He had star power. I'd tell him we should include this or that picture in the book, and he'd say, yes, let's keep it handy. I imagined we'd have months to work through the final details after he and Ruth moved to Tucson. I was looking forward to skipping a lot of the broccoli to savor the dry wine of his intellect as we poured over the first draft.

Of course, that didn't happen. Monte died before that year was out. It was sudden and unexpected, and I mourned him in a way that was astonishing, given the short time we'd known each other. But I wasn't entirely on my own when it came to finishing the book. We had discussed the basic format and the technique of alternating chapters between first-person and third-person narration. It made sense to do it that way because the creation of the medical school represented the most public part of his life. Using some third-person narration appealed to Monte for other reasons, too. He said he got tired of reading the "me, myself and I" in memoirs. It struck him as a bit narcissistic. But we needed some first person. After all, it was a memoir. We decided to put the more personal stories in his voice. Fortunately, I began with those first-person chapters and I wrote them out in sequence. They were completed before he died. With the help of his family, his notes, interviews with colleagues and friends and our long talks, I filled in the missing chapters. The result is the story of a remarkable man's life. He enhanced the stature of the University of Arizona, brought credit to Tucson, made Arizona an important place for medical education and helped put medical care within the reach of many, many low-income people. He also touched many lives, including mine, by demonstrating what one person can accomplish.

Linda Valdez

• • •

CHAPTER ONE

Destiny and a dusty piece of land

Along a busy stretch of Tucson's Campbell Avenue is a complex of buildings where life and hope intersect with death and misery. Night after day, week after week, lives are transformed in those buildings. Some people go there to fulfill a childhood dream and learn the special skills and secrets that can delay death and enhance life. Other people take their sick children there to be healed. It can be a place of joy and laughter. It can also be the last place a mother ever holds her baby. These buildings have seen the best and worst of human emotion. The walls echo ambition and achievement as well as despair and desperation. Yet despite the dramas going on inside, tens of thousands of people drive past every day without paying any attention. If they notice the buildings at all, they think, "Oh, there's university hospital."

Decades ago, other dramas played out on that site. In those days, people called the place the Magician's Palace. They knew that before a man named Merlin came to town, nothing was there except a lot of dust and rows of decrepit Quonset huts where the University of Arizona provided housing for married students.

Even the magician, who was really a man of science named Dr. Merlin K. DuVal, didn't envision a world-class medical school on that plot of land the first time he passed it. No grand music swelled when he went by. No light bulbs lit up above his head. As married students sweltered under metal roofs that absorbed more heat than the swamp coolers in their windows could dissipate, DuVal simply rode by in a car driven by university president Richard Harvill. Like the travelers in today's Tucson, neither paid much attention. They had other things on their minds.

Harvill was focused on whether the 39-year-old doctor he'd picked up from the airport was the right man to build a medical school in Tucson. The question of where in the city to locate that school was secondary. DuVal also thought about what it would be like to father a medical school in this Sun Belt city that showed more hope than accomplishment. But, unlike Harvill, he was trying not to think about that seductive possibility too much. After all, an Arizona medical school was more of an aspiration than a reality.

When DuVal walked across the tarmac at the Tucson airport and shook hands with Harvill the first time, it wasn't because he'd been asked to apply for a job. Harvill had called with a carefully worded invitation – a request, really – for DuVal to come and share his expertise about the needs of a medical school. Harvill had not been given the go-ahead to build a medical school. He was careful to make that clear, too. The university president said he was merely trying to educate himself in case – just in case – the university got the opportunity to go into medical education, something many universities were considering. That was all. He hoped DuVal could spare some time to talk about how things were done at the University of Oklahoma, where DuVal was assistant director of the Medical Center. That was all. This was about professional courtesy. An informational meeting. No strings. No expectations.

Of course, DuVal knew that wasn't all there was to it. He knew what was really going on. Harvill was doing more than making a few preparations for an opportunity that might – possibly – come his way. He was engaged in a pitched battle to make something happen. DuVal also knew that he was being sized up for the job of creating and running the medical school that Harvill was determined to have built at the University of Arizona. DuVal was one of several men with top reputations in medical education who were being flown to Tucson to meet with Harvill. None of them was told about the others. But all of them knew it or sensed it. It was a familiar courtship dance. A recruitment tango. And Harvill wasn't the only one who saw DuVal as a potential partner. Federal money was being made available for new medical schools, and other universities were looking for deans to start them.

DuVal was – although he would never have used the phrase – a hot commodity. Harvill had the good sense to treat him that way. When he arrived in Tucson, DuVal was met at the airport by Harvill himself, not some underling. What's more, Harvill took DuVal's suitcase and carried it to the car. It was the professional equivalent of a dozen red roses on the first date. DuVal was not willing to be swept off his feet, but he was flattered. Harvill was a man of considerable reputation, and he was clearly trying to impress his visitor. DuVal filed away this revealing bit of information. He kept it in the back of his mind, along with his own emerging dream of being able to do something that only a handful of men in the history of the United States had ever done: build a medical school from nothing.

• • •

DUVAL WAS A TALL, handsome man, who could make small talk seem big and leave his companions feeling more witty than they were. His charm looked effortless because he'd learned it without trying. It was in his genes. His parents regarded the social graces as among the necessities of life. DuVal had his father's sense of moral authority and his mother's impressive bearing. He could have easily followed his mother into a career as a model in New York City. DuVal did, in fact, earn money for college at modeling agencies that would have been happy to help him make a good living at it. He had presence. He filled up the room. Effortlessly.

But DuVal did not choose an effortless road. He wanted to make his lasting impressions through the force of his intellect, not the power of his smile. He enjoyed going well past small talk into topics that revealed the depth of his interests: science, philosophy, art, music, ballet and the human quest for understanding those things that are beyond understanding. He earned his reputation in medicine through hard work and demonstrated skill as both a surgeon and teacher. When he arrived in Tucson for that first meeting with Harvill, he came fully prepared to explain what it takes to train doctors because that's what Harvill had asked him to do. He had taken Harvill's request for information at face value and spent hours making notes after his day's work was done and his family was asleep. He would take pride in talking to Harvill about how the needs of a medical school differed from those of the rest of the university. He would enjoy explaining how medical education was changing and discussing how it should change even more. Harvill had asked him for a service, and he kept that request in the forefront of his mind when he met with the university president. It was an entirely worthwhile and valid goal on its own merits. If the possibility of becoming the founder of a medical school bubbled up in his brain, as it did in unguarded moments, DuVal would tamp it down.

He kept his focus.

It was this third attribute that was more important in DuVal's life than either his looks or his intelligence. It was DuVal's strength of will that let him build a professional relationship with Harvill and win the prize he was trying not to think about too much. He knew what he wanted. He knew that his life should count for something more than just an accumulation of goods and accolades. He valued service and honor over wealth and power. He wanted to do something that would advance humankind. You have to have a rather large ego to consider yourself worthy of such a goal, but DuVal never lacked ego.

He set his goals and pursued them with a surgeon's precision. He considered every task in relation to the larger purpose. If it needed to be done, it had to be done at the right time and in the right way. If it didn't matter, it wasn't on his agenda. If it did matter – if he made up his mind to do it – then his intention was iron. He did the job. He did it with integrity. He would have been judged enormously successful even if he hadn't spent so many nights working late. But he worked late anyway. It was a matter of honor. People could sense these things about him, and that made him both intimidating and inspiring. When DuVal was around, people stood up a little straighter and tried to do a little better. They hoped to measure up, and secretly suspected they never would meet his expectations.

As a young doctor, DuVal was offered the chance to join a private practice and make a great deal of money pampering grateful, wealthy patients. Instead, he followed the advice of an admired mentor, and went into teaching. He thought the goal of initiating students into mysteries of the body and the power a doctor has to heal the body was entirely worthy. Now he was deciding whether building a medical school on the desert was a logical next step.

As he and Harvill danced delicately around the real reason that

DuVal made repeated trips to Tucson, DuVal's attributes were adding up in Harvill's mind. All of it – the looks, the charm, the brains, the will and the ego – would be necessary to make a medical school happen in Tucson. Harvill was zeroing in on his man. But he didn't yet have his medical school. Before he died, DuVal would hear himself praised for the role he played in establishing the state's second medical school in Phoenix. But when he made his first trips to Tucson, it was doubtful if Harvill would ever be in a position to hire a dean for the state's first medical school.

It was clear that Arizona wanted a medical school. The state had been talking about building one since the late 1950s. Actually, "fighting" might be a better word for what was going on. This was not a blue-sky romp about needs and possibilities in a growing state. It was a down-and-dirty turf battle. The city fathers of Phoenix, Arizona's capitol and long the center of political power, thought they should have the first medical school. The city fathers of Tucson, the site of Arizona's first university, felt the same. Tucson is geographically prettier and has long had an air of intellectual and cultural superiority that still irritates the Phoenicians, who console themselves with the simple fact that everybody knows that the muscle and the money belong to Phoenix.

Many thought the state's first medical school belonged there, too. At least everybody in Phoenix thought that. On April 19, 1958, the banner headline on the front page of Phoenix's Arizona Republic screamed about the offer by a man named Walter McCune to put up $565,700 for a medical school at Arizona State College in Tempe, which is part of the metro Phoenix area.[1] Now called Arizona State University, it was not yet a full-fledged university like the one in Tucson. The idea being floated in Phoenix was to put the first two years of medical school in Tempe at a school named after McCune's mother. The rest of the training would be completed somewhere else in the country.

A few days later, an editorial in the Tucson Citizen pointed out the dangers to the University of Arizona of allowing Phoenix to claim the medical school.[2] Harvill – known around the state as Mr. Education because of the prominence of Tucson's University of Arizona – understood the stakes. He went to the Board of Regents, which governed the state's institutions of higher learning, and cautioned against making such an important decision in haste. The board not only agreed to give him some time, it authorized an independent study to look at the issue.

The battle began in earnest and was chronicled in the biggest papers in each city. The Arizona Republic in Phoenix blasted the regents for the study idea, which included bringing in an out-of-state group of experts to assess the situation and make recommendations. The editorial page of The Republic, the biggest paper in the state, said the regents should have authorized the "immediate establishment of a medical school."[3] In Tempe, of course.

A few months later, Tucson "exploded a bombshell"[4] at a regent's meeting, according to The Republic. The blast was in the form of an announcement that Tucson Medical Center had offered to give its $4.8 million, 133-acre hospital facility to the University of Arizona as an endowment for a Tucson-based medical school.[5]

Tucson could now make a case that it was the most cost effective option. Phoenix refused to be impressed. Arizona State President Homer Durham told his hometown paper that the independent consultant hired by the regents to do the study was bound to give the medical school to Tempe.

He was wrong.

Dr. Joseph P. Volker led the team of nationally known experts that prepared the report and delivered it in secret to the regents. The Volker report didn't just give an edge to Tucson, it gave that self-satisfied little city the entire enchilada.[6]

"The resources of Arizona State University will not equal those of the University of Arizona in the foreseeable future," the report said.[7] Volker also put to rest the idea of establishing a two-year medical school, saying that the need for a four-year medical college in Arizona was clear. Both of Tucson's papers, the Arizona Daily Star and the Tucson Citizen, reprinted the entire Volker report as a public service and distributed it widely.

Phoenix replied: So what?

The Board of Regents met to discuss what action to take on the Volker report. Gov. Paul Fannin looked down from his vantage point at the Capitol near downtown Phoenix and declared that Arizona had "more urgent needs"[8] than a medical school. Fannin had clout with the regents, but he was in the minority. The regents approved Tucson as the location for the state's first medical school.

Late in the summer of 1961, Harvill announced he would begin a nationwide search for someone to head the medical school, and DuVal made his first trip to the University of Arizona. But before his plane even touched down in Tucson, discussions began in Phoenix about how to make an end run around the regents. The idea was to refer the decision on a location for the medical school to a vote of the people. Phoenix knew it would win that vote easily because it was the state's leader in population and political clout. Citizens' committees were formed and breathless speeches were delivered at the state Capitol as lawmakers began pushing for a statewide election to rescind the regent's decision and move the medical school to Phoenix.

On May 19, 1962, the Board of Regents meeting bristled with talk of the issue. Regent John G. Babbitt made his case in favor of the Volker report's recommendations. He reminded his fellow regents that the state had secured $135,000 from the Commonwealth Fund of New York to pay for that report so that no local money would be involved and no charges of bias would result. Volker had been hired to chair the team of "internationally known medical leaders" from around the country because he had no ties to Arizona that might prejudice the study. The vote to hire him was unanimous, Babbitt reminded his fellow regents. He was the uncle of Bruce Babbitt, who was later to become governor of Arizona and Secretary of the Interior under President Bill Clinton.

"Now comes a small group in Maricopa County," John Babbitt said at the meeting, "asking for a new look or a fresh look at the Volker report and backing up their request with a bare threat that unless the regents kowtow to their wishes in this regard, they will initiate a measure to force the regents to build a medical school at Tempe and appropriate a half million dollars to start it. … It doesn't take much imagination to view the bitterness, sectionalism and disregard for the welfare of the state that will be engendered if this matter goes to the people. Apparently, however, the welfare of the state is not foremost in the minds of these people."[9]

Those eloquent sentiments reflected the clout Tucson had nurtured on the Board of Regents. Years earlier, William R. Mathews, publisher of the Arizona Daily Star, had used his considerable influence over Tucson representatives in the state Legislature on behalf of John Babbitt. At Mathews' urging, the Tucson legislative delegation had supported Babbitt for the post of senate president.[10] So even though he hailed from Flagstaff, Babbitt was sympathetic to the needs of Tucson. His support on this issue wasn't enough to solve the matter of the medical school in Tucson's favor, however.

It took water to do that.

• • •

IN THE WEST, people say that whiskey is for drinking and water is for fighting. It may be a cliché, but it is not a joke. In the early 1960s, Phoenix wanted Congress to approve funding the colossal water project called the Central Arizona Project, which was designed to channel Colorado River water hundreds of miles uphill to Phoenix. Without CAP water, Phoenix could not continue growing at breakneck speed. Tucson also saw growth as the key to its future, but Tucson used ground water at the time. It didn't link up to the CAP until decades later. Tucson didn't need the CAP then, but Phoenix very much needed Tucson's cooperation to win federal funding for the waterworks.

Discussions about the medical school had become so rancorous that the power brokers of Phoenix and Tucson were meeting in Casa Grande, a small city more or less halfway between the two, so that nobody would have a home field advantage. The Tucson contingent began to bring water into the conversation. Harold Ashton, then-president of the Tucson Chamber of Commerce, sent a letter to Sherman Hazeltine, then-president of the Phoenix Chamber of Commerce, warning that "irreparable damage" to Phoenix's relationship with the rest of the state might result if Phoenix forced a vote on the medical school and used its clout to get its way.[11] The letter said Phoenix needed to present a unified state front on such things as water development. Taking the medical school away from Tucson could, Ashton wrote, "alienate Phoenix and Maricopa County from other cities and counties in the state."

It was a serious threat to the future of Phoenix. City fathers in that thirsty city had to factor in the very real risks involved if Arizona failed to present a unified front when trying to get Congress to fund the Central Arizona Project.

Barely a month after Ashton's letter made news, full page ads appeared in the major papers in Tucson and Phoenix calling for peace. Signed by sixty-five top business concerns and leaders in both cities, the ads said "it is unwise for conscientious Arizonans to become party to the dangerous usurpation of the duties of the Board of Regents …"[12] In other words, drop the idea about a vote on the medical school because the business community was not going to support it. What's more, the top leaders in the state's business community were going to hold anyone accountable who did support it. The signers of that letter represented such a constellation of power that most people thought the fight was over.

A political cartoon by Reg Manning summed up the sentiment in a July 1, 1962, edition of The Arizona Republic. It showed Gov. Fannin as a saloon keeper presenting a bill to two gunslingers who were sitting at a table. One gunslinger was labeled "Tucson." His gun was labeled "To ram thru a med sch at UA." The other guy at the table was labeled "Phoenix." His gun was labeled "To force the med sch at ASU." Both guns were holstered and hanging on a wall, safely out of reach. Saloon keeper Fannin's speech bubble said: "Now we can work together on Arizona's really urgent problems." These problems were identified as "State reorganization, Colorado River Water, etc."

The fight wasn't over, of course, but it was enough of an armistice for Harvill. He seized the opportunity to move ahead. He made sure, however, that DuVal had no illusions about what was going on. Harvill made it clear that there was a very real risk of Phoenix undermining Tucson's plans. In addition to what Harvill told him, DuVal had cultivated his own sources in Arizona who had been sending him news clippings about the battles. He summed up his understanding of the situation in a letter to Harvill in February of 1962:

"… considerable impetus toward the solution will be derived simply by starting, even if it requires appointment of a dean to develop the plans for a medical school that has not been approved, using funds that have not yet been appropriated.

"There will be hazards in going this route, although you have presented your estimation of the risks with candor. Indeed, the position may be difficult to fill in the face of such a tenuous future. At the same time, if one waits to see two ducks in his gun sights in order to conserve his ammunition, he may never learn to fire his gun, and, meanwhile, go hungry."[13]

It was an extremely polite and eloquent way to tell Harvill he was up to a job that would frighten away lesser candidates. It was how these men did things. Today, the careful language and the exquisite formality of the letter seems as anachronistic as the carbon copy of it DuVal had in his files forty-five years later. But that's how these two highly cultured and well-educated men operated. Each had painstakingly built a reputation in his respective field. Each looked to the other to enhance those reputations.

So the courtship dance continued.

In March, DuVal sent Harvill a list of "persons to whom you should feel quite free to write in the event you need personal information on my behavior for your files."[14]

Some of the responses made DuVal sound custom-made for the particular political challenges facing a medical school in Tucson.

From J. Leland Gourley, assistant to Oklahoma Gov. James Howard Edmondson:

"Dr. DuVal has almost single-handedly been the salvation of the University of Oklahoma medical school, insofar as its relationships with the legislature and other public officials are concerned. Without sacrificing integrity, convictions or individuality, Dr. DuVal has become the best liked man in higher education, among political leaders in the state. ... while Dr. DuVal's primary motivations stem from altruism and a desire for worthwhile accomplishments, I think he also possesses another quality desirable for the position you have in mind – that is, a well-directed ambition."[15]

From Dr. Robert S. Ellis at the Oklahoma Allergy Clinic:

"I am chairman of the legislative committee of the alumni association and he is coordinator between the medical center and the legislature... I was amazed at his ability to convince legislators of our needs. He was able to gather facts, organize them, and present a concise picture of the problem very convincingly. Primarily through Dr. DuVal's efforts we were able to obtain funds for capital improvements from the legislature at a time when funds were practically nonexistent for this purpose."[16]

Harvill also heard of DuVal's skill as a teacher and a surgeon.

Ernest Lachman, professor and chairman of the University of Oklahoma Department of Anatomy, wrote that DuVal was a teacher who "excells by the clarity of his presentation, by his extemporaneous and original approach to the topic under discussion, and his ability to accommodate himself to any level of presentation from the elementary to the most advanced ... a brilliant medical educator who has given a great deal of thought to the philosophy of medical education and certainly can see beyond the confines of his specialty."[17]

As far as that specialty was concerned, Hugh G. Payne, executive vice president of the Oklahoma Medical Research Foundation, sent a six-page letter that included this assessment from someone who observed DuVal during those moments when he was least likely to realize he was being observed. Payne shared the observations of his niece, a surgical nurse who worked with DuVal more than a year.

When DuVal was performing surgery, according to the surgical nurse, the team "became sort of electrified and all performed to a high degree of efficiency. ... no other surgeon – full time on the medical school or part-time practitioners – could equal this great gift of Dr. DuVal's to inspire and charge up others to almost exceed themselves in many ways."[18]

By April, Harvill asked DuVal to bring his wife, Carol, for a visit to Tucson. Both men knew the implications. Things were getting serious. Harvill wrote to explain the hotel arrangements and the plans he'd made to have Mrs. DuVal tour the town. Once again, he took the time to do this personally instead of delegating the task. Yet Harvill was keeping his options open and he made sure DuVal knew it. The university president's letter, dated April 6, 1962, concluded:

"While, as you understand, I have not made any offer or come to any final decision, I am impressed by your qualifications for the particular situation here in Arizona. Unless you are willing to assume some degree of risk and are willing to help in an educational program during the next year or so that will be carried on along with some planning with architects and other specialized people, I believe that you should not give further consideration to the deanship. Personally, I am extremely optimistic and I am absolutely confident that we will be on our way toward the establishment of what will become the most outstanding medical school in all of the Southwest and the Mountain states within a comparatively few years."[19]

DuVal, whose first impression of Arizona had been to wonder how anybody could live in such a place, was beginning to see himself taking charge of the "particular situation" in Tucson. He liked the image of being the founding dean in a feisty, growing city that wanted a medical school badly enough to fight for it. He was also beginning to like the desert. He had planted cacti in Oklahoma. He was becoming restive in his job there. His response to Harvill's letter, dated April 8, 1962, reveals a man who wanted very much to impress a potential boss:

"The 'risk' that may indeed be involved in the situation is definitely not of primary concern to me. On the contrary, its existence is not only inherent in the challenge but is a substantial part of its appeal. My reservation has been entirely personal, and related only to the uncertainty I felt within myself with regard to the change in professional identification, from academic surgery to administration, which a consideration of the deanship necessarily required of me."[20]

The letters continued through the summer, as Arizona's desert heat was intensified by politics and a race for governor.

On Sept. 26, 1962, Harvill wrote to DuVal that "Governor Fannin got himself into a very difficult spot. He has been trying to stick to his guns in saying that the reason he voted, as a member of the Board of Regents, against the resolutions which a majority of the Board members favored (to accept the Volker report and build a med school in Tucson) was not because he objected to the location of the medical school at the University of Arizona in Tucson, but rather because he believes that we should not have a medical school at all at this time; that we cannot afford it. Mr. Mathews (publisher) of the Arizona Daily Star is taking him to task, more or less regularly, and he may be making a great mistake in doing so because many people will be with us on the medical school, but at the same time are with Fannin for Governor."[21]

Harvill went on to write that "I do not know of any political candidates running for state level offices who want the medical school issue to be injected into their campaigns. I have done a great deal of work in the Phoenix area and in other parts of the state and in my judgment, if we can keep this issue out of the political realm, we can get some action from the next legislature authorizing University of Arizona to expend money for planning."

Fannin was re-elected to his third two-year term as governor in November 1962. Despite Harvill's optimism, the next year's Legislature balked at appropriating the planning money. Harvill had the support of The Republic, which ran an editorial March 26, 1963, urging lawmakers "to rise above factionalism and approve the $160,000."[22] The funding bill had been stuck in the House, where Maricopa County had 40 out of 80 votes. It eventually passed with 46 votes.

Harvill seized the victory and vowed that no state money would be requested from the Legislature in the coming year for the medical school. He also said, "We will have a dean before a year passes."[23]

It didn't take that long. In September, Harvill offered DuVal the job. His salary would be $25,000 a year, which was one-eighth of the amount he'd been offered to join a posh private practice in New York City years earlier. It was also only slightly less than Harvill himself was making. According to the University of Arizona Budget Office, the president's salary was $27,000 that year.[24] But this wasn't about money. DuVal's salary was published in the local papers, which meant everybody in Tucson knew before he did. When he returned to Oklahoma to tell his family that they would be moving to Tucson so he could build a medical school, Carol asked him how much he would be making.

"I forgot to ask," he said to Carol. "I told him I wanted a parking place and a phone and he said he could accommodate that."[25]

DuVal's task would be to build a medical school with no funding from the state and no guarantee that the Legislature would ever willingly provide money to run the programs he established. At the same time, the University of Connecticut was interested in giving DuVal the deanship of the medical school it was building. Connecticut had set aside something on the order of $25 million to get started. The university there was discussing how to create a quality program while Arizona was still fighting about whether – and where – to build a medical school. Logically, Connecticut should have won the competition for DuVal.

Yet Tucson offered something more. DuVal explained it to himself and others in the most logical way. On the East Coast, DuVal reasoned, the most prestigious universities tended to be private ones. In the West, it was generally the public universities that had the top reputations. What's more, the University of Connecticut's school of medicine would be in competition with Harvard. No matter how well-funded, a public medical school in Connecticut would always be seen as the second choice. Arizona had no money, but it had energy and the school would be a flagship. There was also the aura of the West: wide open and full of possibilities. Here, a man could still make a mark. DuVal found it too intriguing to pass up.

During the years that Harvill had been recruiting him, DuVal had moved carefully and measured the opportunity against the risk. He was going into this challenge with full awareness of the delicate

diplomacy that would be necessary in order to succeed.
He started by making a large tactical mistake.

• • •

ON SEPT. 28, 1963, the newspapers were full of stories about
DuVal accepting the job as dean of the new medical school. All
over the state people were reading Harvill's quotes praising DuVal's
"profound understanding of medical sciences." By coincidence, DuVal
was in Phoenix at the time to fulfill a long-standing obligation as a
visiting professor at Maricopa County Hospital. DuVal had planned
to use the extended weekend visit to lecture on surgical techniques
involving the pancreas, something that had earned him professional
fame and respect. But with the news bubbling about his appointment,
nobody seemed to care much about pancreatic surgery. DuVal was
much more interesting for another reason. Instead of a discrete group
of surgeons at the hospital, he found himself in an auditorium before
what looked like the entire membership of the Maricopa County
Medical Association.[26] They wanted to hear from the man who would
head the state's first medical school – a school that would not be built
on their turf.

"I understand you are going to have to build a university hospital,"
said one of the doctors. "They say it will be 300 beds. Is that going
to be enough?"

With less-than-shrewd honesty, DuVal said, "No. As a matter of
fact, in real terms, it is not going to be enough."

It was a truthful response based on the experience in other medical
schools, not an expression of DuVal's intention to push for a bigger
hospital. But a reporter thought it was the most newsworthy thing to
come out of the meeting. When DuVal went down to the hotel lobby
the next morning, he saw the headline across the front of the Sunday
paper: "New Dean Says 300 Beds Insufficient."[27]

The phone rang not long after he returned to his room. It was
Harvill.

DuVal's new boss was polite and restrained, but there was no
mistaking the reason for the call. "You'll go back to Oklahoma City
today?" Harvill asked.

"Yes," said the new dean.

"Would it be convenient for you to come to Tucson on your way back to Oklahoma?" Harvill asked.

"Of course," said the new dean.

This time Harvill was a little more abrupt. "Try to get here by this afternoon because the Pima County Medical Association is going to have a meeting at the Pioneer Hotel, and they'd like very much to meet you."

Once again, Harvill met DuVal at the airport. They drove to the downtown hotel and sat in the bar for a drink. Harvill told him the news story had created "a little hysteria." The local doctors decided to gather in the hotel's ballroom because it was sufficiently large to accommodate all those interested.[28]

"You understand," Harvill told DuVal, "you have nothing to worry about. My concerns are the physicians in Maricopa County. Everybody here is very happy in Pima County."[29]

DuVal knew better. He understood that a medical school can be an enormous economic threat to local doctors. Medical school faculty members treat patients. That not only represents competition, it can feel like unfair competition because the doctors on a medical school faculty tend to get a lot of publicity. They represent the cutting edge of their fields. In addition, a teaching hospital takes patients that would otherwise go to local hospitals. The idea that the new dean of the medical school was an expansionist who was calling for a bigger teaching hospital on the day his appointment was announced would not be comforting to Tucson's medical professionals. The fact that the new dean had made his announcement in the rival territory of Phoenix, where the doctors would not face the competition of a medical school, would be even more galling.

"Dr. Harvill," he told his new boss, "you don't understand medical politics. You're going to find out it's the exact opposite... The proximity of a medical school to the practicing physicians in town is going to create a problem the likes of which you haven't seen before."

"In any case," Harvill replied, "I think we can meet people here and put them at ease."[30]

What followed was an hour-and-a-half of one of the "most unpleasant and tense" meetings DuVal had ever experienced. He fielded "what the hell do you mean?" questions from physicians he felt had sized him up as the enemy before they'd even formally met him. It was an awkward and confrontational introduction to the medical community, and it called for all the charm DuVal could muster. He tried to share his enthusiasm for the medical school. But it didn't take long for his audience to cut to the chase. What about the hospital? What about what you told the newspaper? How many beds do you think you need?

DuVal answered honestly, as he had done in Phoenix. But this time he made sure to provide a complete answer.

"If you base it strictly on the formula for the number of students we are expecting to have, we need a hospital with 350 to 400 beds," DuVal said. "But, on the other hand, we have no intention of doing that – we said we are going to build it with 300 beds and that's exactly what we are going to do."

DuVal also made it clear that he hoped to gain "permission" from community hospitals to use their facilities. In addition, he hoped the doctors in private practice would share their knowledge with the medical school in any capacity they felt appropriate. He'd welcome them as part-time instructors. He hoped to be able to share their expertise and to benefit from their advice. This was the beginning of what would be his long-term strategy to engage the entire community in the job of training doctors. He would have preferred to launch it under less tense circumstances. When he finished, DuVal and Harvill were asked to wait outside while the group talked in private.

Once again, Harvill and DuVal sat in the hotel bar. This time, however, Harvill didn't need anybody to explain how the local doctors felt. After fifteen or twenty minutes, a representative of the group came out to tell them that one of the members, Dr. Jim O'Hare, had made a motion that the entire body support the medical school and that each individual member contribute $1,000 to the cause.

The new dean had been well received.

DuVal not only appreciated the support at the time, he remembered it thirty years later. When O'Hare died in 1994, DuVal contacted Dr. James Dalen, who was then Dean of the UA Medical School, and said, "Get in touch with Mrs. O'Hare and tell her how important Jim had been to the medical school." Dalen wrote a "superb" letter to the widow and sent DuVal a copy of it, DuVal said.[31]

DuVal made good on his commitment to the local doctors. He went out of his way to maintain peace. First, he invited the Pima County Medical Society to give him suggestions for designing ways to integrate local doctors with the medical school. What emerged was a liaison committee that met regularly.

"Every single thought I had about the medical school – every single thought – I mean curriculum, I mean handling patients, I mean handling fees, and so forth, was discussed with them," DuVal said.[32] He listened to their reactions, and sometimes changed course.

One area of local anxiety had to do with the university's Student Health Service, which handled the health needs of students by paying consulting fees to local doctors who provided the medical care. The advent of a medical school could have changed that. It would have been a seamless and logical extension for the medical school faculty to step in and deliver services to students. But DuVal understood the concerns of local doctors who did not want to suffer the financial consequences of being displaced. He opted not to have the medical school become deeply involved with providing the health care needs of students.[33]

DuVal courted the local medical community with the same care, courtesy and professional skill that Harvill had used on him, and he did it for the same reason. The shared goal was to build a great medical school. That's not something one does in isolation. DuVal needed the community.

• • •

AFTER THE BATTLE with Phoenix, Tucson was ready to welcome DuVal and his family as heroes. Carol and their three children, David, 17, Barbara, 15, and Fred, 10, became instant celebrities. The Tucson Citizen ran a picture of Carol and the children putting books on the shelves of their new home in the El Encanto neighborhood.

"We feel like Alice in Wonderland," Carol told the reporter. "A few years ago, while we were still back in Oklahoma, my husband started a small indoor cactus garden with plants from Arizona. Now that we have moved to Tucson, the situation is reversed. The ocotillo and century plants in our front yard are enormous and we feel tiny by comparison."[34]

DuVal made his own contribution to the backyard. His first office as dean of the unbuilt medical school was three efficiency apartments in a building the university had taken over and was planning to demolish. When the destruction order was announced, DuVal decided to rescue the goldfish in a pond on the site. He took a lot of kidding for going out there in the middle of the night with a pail to catch them, but the fish thrived for years in a pond at the family's home.

The wonderland into which the DuVal family stepped was not the Sunbelt metropolis it has become. The university contributed an air of sophistication, but this was a small western town where "snowbirds" spent the winter and people with asthma and arthritis came for relief. The "UA medical school" was put in tenth place on the Arizona Daily Star's year-end round up of the most significant events of 1963. The establishment of a leash law for dogs made the No. 6 spot and a deadly explosion at a dry cleaning facility was No. 1. That's what the place was like.

The Star called the medical school "one of the biggest events in Tucson history." Star publisher Mathews launched a fundraising campaign called FAME or Founders for Arizona Medical Education. Business leaders kicked it off with televised fundraising events in Tucson and Phoenix, where Mathews' counterpart, Eugene Pulliam used The Republic to call for solidarity and push the process. FAME collected $3 million that was used to leverage federal funds and build the basic sciences building.

The list of donors read like a who's who of city power brokers: Tucson Realty, Holmes Tuttle Ford, Shamrock Dairy, Phelps Dodge Copper Co., Steinfeld's department store, the Sheet Metal Workers Union. Tucson businessman and Board of Regent's member Leon Levy called a contribution to the medical school "an investment in the future." J. Luther Davis, president of Tucson Gas and Electric, presented a check for $75,000 and said the medical school would be an "important factor in the growth and economy of Tucson."[35]

When photographers from the local papers shot pictures of DuVal receiving checks to build the medical school or speaking to a roomful of business leaders, they captured the image of a slim man in a well-cut dark suit with just the right amount of sleeve showing. Polished. Confident. Dignified. He looked every bit like the right man for a job the press called "epochal." It didn't hurt his image that he was prematurely gray.

"I felt extraordinarily challenged with the responsibility," DuVal would say decades later. "The idea that the president of the university would say 'go do it' and leave me alone was almost shockingly frightening. He had great confidence in me, for which I have been grateful all my life."[36]

Any doubts DuVal had were well hidden behind a finely polished presentation. Dan Capps, who was hired by DuVal to be the first administrator of the teaching hospital that has won international acclaim, saw DuVal as a race horse among the draught animals.[37] DuVal's East Coast manners made him look classy to the Westerners who wanted him to help transform their little pond into a bigger one.

Dr. Vince Fulginiti, who became the school's first head of the Department of Pediatrics, said DuVal had a clear vision of what he wanted the medical school to be. "He was absolutely convinced this was going to be the greatest thing since sliced bread and he made sure we understood that ... If you were in the room with him and heard him talk about the school, you would be convinced this was something you ought to support."[38]

But it wasn't just the movers and shakers who were impressed. Shortly after the family arrived in Tucson, DuVal drove up to the corner service station to set up an account. That was the nature of the time and place. There were corner service stations where the men who pumped your gas knew you by name, shared local gossip and extended credit to local customers. This gas station owner recognized DuVal from the publicity surrounding the medical school. He said they'd been collecting money in a jar from customers and employees to help get it going.

"We're on our second hundred dollars now, doc," the mechanic told DuVal, who repeated that story with pride many, many times. DuVal thought his new community was "fantastic," the community felt the same way about the dean of a medical school that had yet to be built.

There was a cache to the title "dean," and DuVal used it to charm people and win support for the medical school. He made his first hire shortly after he arrived. He and Dr. Philip Krutzsch did the grip-and-grin at a lot of cocktail parties. DuVal and Krutzsch had a running joke. "After we leave," they'd tell their hosts, "you can say you entertained the entire faculty of the medical school in your living room."[39] The aphorism hid a hard truth. DuVal was under pressure from Harvill to get the school up and running as fast as possible, but he was literally starting from nothing.

With himself and Krutzsch as the lone faculty members of a school that had not been built or funded, DuVal convinced the National Committee of Accreditation to issue the "letter of reasonable assurance" that was necessary to be eligible for federal matching money. The letter said the committee believed that the school would meet standards if it were built as described.

"They were taking a lot on faith," DuVal said.

• • •

THE COMMITTEE may have been favorably impressed, but battles with the folks up north weren't over. Phoenix was still smarting and rural Arizona was not entirely convinced, either. October 11, 1963, a rural town paper called the Winslow Mail ran an editorial that called the "unneeded Arizona medical college" an example of how "selfish interests have gone right ahead with a project for which the taxpayer will become the victim."[40] For years, there were efforts in the Legislature to relocate the school, limit its funding or otherwise sabotage its progress. Sometimes, DuVal himself created the controversy just by doing what he thought was best.

When the new dean went before the Board of Regents in September of 1963, they welcomed him with a question that might have been a bit of a trick: What do you want to do with the offer from Tucson Medical Center? DuVal knew the history, of course. He knew the politically smart course would be to accept the offer. After all, it had been integral to the early arguments in favor of putting the medical school in Tucson. DuVal did not take the safe route.

"Turn it down," the dean told the board that paid his salary as well as that of his boss.

All hell broke loose. DuVal watched Gov. Fannin become "livid" as he insisted that the offer of Tucson Medical Center had been instrumental in the decision on where to locate the school.[41] Regent O.D. Miller sternly reiterated that the offer of the hospital had tipped the economic balance in Tucson's favor.[42] How dare anyone suggest turning down that money-saving offer?

Harvill asked that DuVal be allowed to justify his position, and the new dean was once again standing before a hostile audience. He entered the argument from a position somewhere high above the old battlegrounds.

"We are convinced that there should be a healthy relationship between the medical student and the rest of the university," he said.

Who could argue with that?

Then DuVal explained that Tucson Medical Center had not been built as a teaching hospital so it would require extensive renovations to make it usable. That would cost money, possibly enough to offset any savings realized by accepting the offer. What's more, the basic sciences building where students would get their first two years of training should be close to the hospital where they would get their clinical instruction. The whole complex should be close to the university's main campus to allow "cross fertilization." He told the regents about medical schools that had been located distant from their home universities only to be moved closer to the main campus at great expense. What's more, federal money would be available at a matching ratio of two-to-one for construction of a new teaching hospital, but only at one-to-one for renovation. This, too, had to be considered before making a decision about which was the most cost-effective option. DuVal also pointed out that Tucson Medical Center was the city's biggest and best medical facility. It made no sense to take it out of the community's hands and turn it over to the state university.[43]

He won the argument so handily that he was subsequently invited to join Harvill when the university president went to Phoenix each year to make the case for the UA's budget.

DuVal did not win his preferred piece of real estate for the school, however.

He wanted the medical school to be located north of the existing campus and adjacent to it. But that northern boundary was – and is – marked by a major city arterial, Speedway Boulevard. DuVal began talking with members of the Tucson City Council to convince them to lower Speedway into a tunnel so that the campus could connect by pedestrian access to the new medical school. He wanted to put the medical school right on the other side of a park that would be built on top of that tunnel. But that piece of land was – and is – occupied by a busy McDonald's restaurant. Ronald wasn't inclined to give up this choice location. The plan was scrapped. Yet DuVal's vision of how the medical school should fit into the campus and the city is typical of how he thought about his new job. He wasn't just building a medical school, even though that task would be vast enough for most people. He was building something that would help define the university and the city. This was monumental. This was going to matter to the community, the state and the country for a very long time. That's how

DuVal saw it, and he had remarkable success in convincing others to see it that way, too, as the success in fundraising attests. But when it came to rebuilding a major city street, Tucson declined.

In later decades, as the campus continued to expand north of Speedway and the road became even more heavily traveled, the idea of a Speedway tunnel re-emerged. Cost, logistics and local opposition prevented it from happening. Subsequently, pedestrian walkways were built to allow students, faculty and university visitors to cross under Speedway. Had the community done what DuVal wanted when he suggested it, a more unified, pedestrian-friendly campus in the heart of the city might have been achieved decades ago.

Failing to win his first choice for a site, DuVal then pitched an idea for locating the medical school complex in the Tucson Mountains. He found the mountains west of the city to be so utterly beautiful that he thought such a site would make attracting top-notch faculty easier. But Harvill pointed out that the Tucson Mountains were no closer to the campus than Tucson Medical Center. DuVal bowed to some of the same arguments he had made to the regents.

Harvill had his own alternative. It was a 30-acre parcel four blocks from the campus that had an enormous advantage: the university already owned it. Euphemistically known as Polo Village because this Wild West state had tried that unlikely sport many years earlier, it was not even remotely pretty, let alone beautiful. For years, it had offered the sort of married student housing that made students recognize the value of remaining single. The 247 married students who lived in run-down Quonset huts on the site were no more enthusiastic about moving than McDonald's was. But they had considerably less clout.

Little by little, the Quonset huts disappeared as DuVal began building a medical school that would make Arizona the 42nd state to be able to train men and women to become doctors. He would rely entirely on donations and federal matching funds to create a health sciences complex that fits so seamlessly into the community that tens of thousands of people zoom by every day without giving it a second thought.

· · ·

CHAPTER TWO

My early years of privilege and parental pretext

I n September 1934, amidst the darkest days of the Depression, we looked at each other with curiosity as we came together at College High School in Montclair, New Jersey. Monte drew the most attention even then, particularly from among the girls who saw this remarkably handsome boy with easy manners, blue eyes and curly blonde hair. It was like that for all of his six years as a multi-sport athlete and student leader with top grades. Monte was frequently elected to school-wide Student Council posts, ultimately as president in his senior year, while I was class president in five of a possible twelve terms, including my senior year. I was never elected to Student Council, but I am now president-for-life thanks to Monte's proposal at one of our reunions.

He became captain and high scorer on every team, playing varsity basketball in his freshman year. Golf was the only leveler as several of us caddied and occasionally played together on local public courses, never that well, but always enthusiastically.

Monte moved in a social circle more sophisticated than the rest of us – from his success at dancing class to the rumored conquests at a time so contrastingly innocent with today. Yet, he was always ready with a concerned smile and quip as seven or eight boys gathered under an oak tree in front of school, rain, snow or shine in every day of our junior and senior years to brown-bag our lunch.

Graham "Pete" Harrison
Lifelong friend[44]

Pete's been a wonderful friend for so many years that I don't like to quarrel with his recollections. He got so much of it right, and he's such an accomplished person in his own life – he used his Harvard MBA to build a marvelous career that culminated with starting up an endowment for the Howard Hughes Medical Institute. I'm terribly fond of both Pete and his wife Joanne. I just wish he had been a bit more selective in his memory.

To be specific, I wish he hadn't brought up that stuff about my looks. I've never been comfortable with that because it tended to separate me from the other guys. I didn't want them to think I was a sissy. My parents made it worse, especially my mother. She would introduce me as her "handsome son." I found it awkward and embarrassing that she would say this in front of other people. I thought she should let them make up their own minds what they thought of me. What's more, I used to wonder how it made my younger brother, William Kirkland, feel. She didn't introduce Bill that way.

It is typical of our family that I never asked Bill, and he certainly never told me, what he thought about this. He was only two years younger than I, but we weren't close in any other sense. I was inclined to be outgoing and extroverted; he was shy. I was athletic; he wasn't. Many siblings swing between sharing their deepest secrets and fighting with equal gusto. We did neither. I can tell you that I greatly respect what he did with his life. Like our paternal grandfather, Bill became a minister, first working in Geneva with the World Council of Churches to relocate displaced persons and eventually in the Manhattan offices of the Presbyterian Church, where he was instrumental in establishing non-profit relief agencies, like the Heifer Project International. We did have one thing in common: we both married our childhood sweethearts. But as children, we shared little except for a rather distant, but respectful, relationship with each other and our parents.

I can't tell you much about what my parents were like, either. I didn't really know them. We weren't close in the intensely personal way many families are today, but I have every indication that they were both devoted to caring for their children the best way they knew how.

• • •

MY FATHER, Merlin Kearfott DuVal, was a stock broker for Merrill Lynch. He commuted daily to New York City from our comfortable bedroom community in New Jersey. I can trace Dad's family tree all the way back to an 11th century castle in a French town call Laval, just south of Normandy Beach. It was the home of Mareen Duvall.[45] Born in 1625, he is the oldest known ancestor of my family. An activist who got in trouble during the Jacobean uprising, he was sent to America in 1651. He settled in Calvert County, Maryland, now known as Anne Arundel County. Many years later, Judge Gabriel Duvall, an associate justice of the U.S. Supreme Court, dropped the second "l" and capitalized the "V" in his last name. That's how DuVal became my father's last name.

Dad's grandfather, Robert William Kearfott was born in 1828. He was married on June 5, 1855, to 18-year-old Anna Dunham. There is a suggestion that she was his boss' daughter, but I don't know that for sure. They lived in Baltimore, Maryland, and had three children: Corinne Louisa Kearfott, who was born on March 25, 1856; Thornton Pierceall Kearfott, who was born on October 3, 1859, and died of scarlet fever in 1862; and William Dunham Kearfott, who was born on January 12, 1864. The family moved to West Virginia, where Mr. Kearfott reportedly died of sunstroke on the unlikely occasion of Christmas Eve 1864. His widow, Anna, moved to Richmond and became friends with General and Mrs. Robert E. Lee. In 1870, she moved to Philadelphia for a short time and then to Washington, D.C. to work for the U.S. Pension Office. She died in 1917, in Montclair, N.J., at the home of her son, William, who had become a marine engineer and entomologist. He and his wife, Mary Rowan Jackson, were married in 1893. They had two children: Thornton Campbell Kearfott was born in 1894 and died in an automobile accident in 1918; I don't know when Mary Tuley Kearfott was born or what became of her. She was last known to be living in New York City.

The eldest child of Robert Kearfott and Anna Dunham was my paternal grandmother, Corinne Louisa Kearfott. In 1875, she married Rev. Frederick Beale DuVal. He was born in Bladensburg, Maryland, on May 31, 1847, and subsequently graduated from Princeton Theological to become a Presbyterian minister.

The couple had four of their nine children while he was minister at the Wilmington Delaware Church. They were: Genevieve, born October 3, 1876; Lina Dunham, born October 14, 1877; Lorraine E., born September 30, 1879; and Frederick C., born August 24, 1882.

In 1884, the family moved to Westminster Presbyterian Church in

Toledo, Ohio, where, on June 5, 1885, twin brothers Edward William and Robert were born. Robert died in infancy. On August 10, 1886, Anna Corinne was born.

Two years later, in 1888, the family moved to Winnipeg, Canada, where my grandfather took over the Knox Church. Two more children were born there: Paul G. on October 8, 1893, and my father, Merlin Kearfott on October 1, 1897.

The name, Merlin, embodies the hopes that were placed on Dad as an infant. The Rev. DuVal wanted a doctor in the family. The president of the French Academy of Sciences at the time was a Dr. Merlin, and my grandfather apparently thought the name would influence my father's choice of career. It didn't. My father rejected the profession as well as the name. Throughout his adult life, my father was called Mike.

When my father was about 13, Rev. DuVal became moderator of the Presbyterian Church of Canada. That same year, just as my father was entering the labyrinth of adolescence, his mother died. When Dad was only 17, Canada and England had entered World War I, and he enlisted. He was sent to France, where so many young men of his generation learned the horrors of war and the wonders of Paris. Dad was wounded relatively early in the war, recovered and returned to duty. He came back to Canada after the armistice and married my mother, Margaret Smith.

I don't know much about my mother's ancestry. She was born in Guelph, Ontario, Canada, on June 25, 1898, and I believe she met my father at the University of Manitoba in Winnepeg. She was a remarkably beautiful woman and extremely accomplished. Before she moved to the United States with my father around 1919, she had earned accolades as Canada's national figure skating champion. Her success in this arena led to one of my earliest – and utterly inglorious – memories.

I recall a brittle winter evening when my mother and father took me to an outdoor ice skating pond. My father had played hockey in Toronto, so this probably seemed to both of them like a completely delightful way to spend an evening. I don't know how old I was, but I have a memory of them fitting my small feet with a pair of skates and welcoming me to the ice with the apparent expectation that their skating skills had been inherited by me – or maybe even genetically honed. Their hopes were dashed. My ankles buckled and my knees gave no indication that each was separate from the other. I remember seeing those around me skating happily and with confidence. I felt only shame and embarrassment. They never took me skating again, and I never tried it on my own.

My mother was also deeply involved in music and insisted both Bill and I take music lessons while we were growing up in Montclair, N.J. Here, again, I proved something of a disappointment. My piano teacher's son, Herman Hupfeld, wrote the classic, "As Time Goes By," but the best I ever did was get a local dance band to perform one of my compositions. But I don't believe I demonstrated the level of musical inclinations Mother had hoped for, although I did major in music as an undergraduate. By that time, though, my mother was not terribly involved in my life. When I was a child, I remember her as an accomplished actress in the local theater. She no doubt would have approved of my performances decades later in Tucson when I took the stage to ask for donations during breaks in the plays produced by the Arizona Civic Theatre (later Arizona Theatre Company) that my first wife, Carol, and I helped initiate.

Mother attracted a wide circle of accomplished and sophisticated friends. She appeared in many musical operettas and musical comedies as I was growing up. She introduced a popular song called, "Have You Ever Been Lonely?" by Peter DeRose and George Brown, and her picture was on the front cover of the sheet music. She became a photographer's model when I was in my teens.

She and my father gave a long leash to my brother and me. We were expected to behave in a way that would reflect well on the family, but we were not expected to provide a great deal of detail about our daily activities. If I was home when my father arrived back from New York, he might say, "How did school go today?" I would reply "fine," and that was the extent of the interaction. My mother was attentive to those things she felt she needed to be maternal about, but I do not have a strong memory of a deep mother and child relationship.

We almost always had a formal dinner together. My father, who smoked a pack of cigarettes a day and enjoyed a Scotch and soda before the evening meal, would often expound on the failings of President Franklin Delano Roosevelt as our housekeeper, Mrs. Catherine Manning, served us in the dining room. Dad was quite conservative, and an avid FDR hater. He maintained our upper-middle class lifestyle at great personal sacrifice, and had no use for a liberal president who specialized in creating government programs to help those who were having trouble helping themselves.

My parents stayed busy with their own lives and social activities. They had lots of friends, entertaining frequently or attending the entertainments of others. Mother played bridge, father played golf. There was a great deal of socializing in a smart and sophisticated way. My daughter Barbara says they were on the edge of the F. Scott Fitzgerald and Zelda crowd. I never knew about that, but Barbara was close to my mother before Mother died so she may know more about this than I do.

What I do know is that we spent little time together as a family when I was growing up. Nor did my brother and I do things together very often. Yet there were treasured family times, and I hold these recollections dear even after a lifetime of building my own memories. Thanksgiving was one of the high points of the year. On that day, we all got up early, put on warm clothes and went to the local high school to watch the football championship. Dad enjoyed that. We would go home and prepare a big turkey dinner. Those were wonderful days.

Christmas was another delight. Every year until I went away to college, my parents would hang two stockings by the fireplace, one for me and one for Bill. We'd run to get them as soon as we woke up on Christmas morning and jump onto our mother's bed to open the presents that were hidden inside the stockings. Later, Dad would play Santa in front of a big tree. These were generous Christmases full of presents and drama. Dad would pass the gifts out one at a time and everybody watched as each gift was opened. He used the occasion for a bit of political commentary, labeling the presents "To Merlin, from Anna" or "To Bill, from Elliot." The names referred to FDR's children and signaled Dad's attitude about the president's largesse. Some of the presents were also from Santa. Before he handed anything out, though, Dad would give a speech all of my children have heard me deliver. He'd say, "You understand, of course, that if you put this off a day, you'll have all this to look forward to tomorrow." He did his best to thwart our instant impulses, but it never worked. It didn't work with my children, either.

In the afternoon, we would eat turkey dinner, but not always as a family. Sometimes friends would come over. Sometimes my parents would go out and leave Bill and me on our own. It was Christmas morning that was special. That's when we were always together.

I realize that in today's era of helicopter parents, who can't stop hovering over their children, the family I describe may seem odd. Clearly, it was not warm and fuzzy. My own childhood may, indeed, have provided too poor a model for my own duties as a father. I sadly admit that I was not as engaged as a parent as I have seen my children become with their own children. Perhaps my parents' manner had something to do with that. But I did not grow up feeling deprived in the slightest. My father always treated my brother and me in a warm and decent manner. I had utter respect for him. My mother took us to classical music concerts in New York City to hear such greats as Walter Damrosch and Andre Kostelanetz conduct. She made sure we were exposed to those things that she thought were important for a cultured, well-rounded life. It was not until many years later that I realized my relationship with my parents had many shortcomings. I was unable to identify them – or miss them – at the time because I had no other example against which to measure my childhood.

I was seven years old on Black Friday, 1929. The stock market crash had a seismic impact on my father and mother, but I knew nothing about that until nearly 40 years later. I remember overhearing conversations about what some of the people who worked with my father had done. He expressed extreme irritation over the fact that colleagues had just washed their hands of the whole thing, kept the money they made and said to hell with the rest of the world. There was also talk of those who jumped out of windows. But for the most part, my brother and I felt little real consequences of the event that shook the foundations of the country and ushered in the era of FDR that my father so loathed. Dad went on being a stock broker. We went on looking like the upper middle class family we had always been. Everything appeared the same, even though everything had changed. The appearance of comfort had become something of an illusion. But for Bill and me, the transition was seamless, a fact that helps illustrate how isolated we were from our parents' lives.

I went on attending nearby Edgemont School, which was close enough that I could walk there and back every day from the time I started kindergarten until I finished sixth grade. The route didn't change, but my awareness of the world beyond Montclair expanded in the early spring of 1932. That's when the baby of Charles and Anne Morrow Lindbergh was kidnapped from their home. They lived only 30 to 40 miles from Montclair. The national press went wild, of course, because Lindbergh was such a public figure, having made the first, solo non-stop flight across the Atlantic Ocean five years earlier. But our local press played it up even bigger. It was in the very air of the community. There was no way you could ignore it during those ten long weeks when they searched for the baby. Even before the child's body was found, I had become aware of dangers in the world that I could never have imagined. Our peaceful, bedroom community could not remain innocent of this terrible thing that had happened virtually down the street. People speculated about who could have done it, and shuddered with the realization that their own homes also had second-story windows against which someone could lean a ladder and enter their seemingly safe and secure world.

I wasn't the only one who felt an enormous relief the day it was announced that a carpenter named Bruno Richard Hauptmann had been arrested. The entire community let out a collective sigh and the interest in the case caved immediately. The guilty party had been arrested, justice would be served, and that was enough for Montclair. Many have subsequently questioned whether Hauptmann received a fair trial in the highly sensitized atmosphere of the times. I don't know the answer to that question, but at the time, I think Montclair was terribly eager for a satisfactory end to the story. Hauptmann's conviction provided that closure. In fact, for some, his arrest itself might have been enough to make them feel they were finished with an ugly and disturbing event. He was executed in 1936.

The Lindbergh kidnapping is one of the most vivid specific memories of my grade-school years. But on the whole, I remember those times as wonderful days filled with friends and excitement. This is when I learned that for a few cents one could build a personal radio that needed no energy source. I was hooked on my crystal set, which enabled me to hear transmissions of the Amos 'n' Andy Show, Jack Armstrong, All-American Boy, The Shadow and the Lone Ranger.

The melodramatic heroics of those radio shows were stirring, but the real drama was going on under my own roof – and without my knowledge. To explain this, I have to jump ahead several decades to the time of my father's death after a massive stroke left him completely incapacitated. That was in 1965. I was delivering a speech as dean of the UA College of Medicine when I received the news of his stroke. I immediately flew back to Montclair. My brother returned from Manhattan. Dad died on June 3, 1965.

Bill and I believed we knew exactly who our parents were and how they lived. If asked, either of us would have told of a slightly formal, but utterly gracious upbringing in an atmosphere infused with the love of beauty and sophistication that we learned from our mother, and the respect for achievement and privilege that came from my father's hard work and success in New York.

But when my brother and I attempted to help our mother straighten out our father's estate, we were appalled to find out the net value of his assets amounted to about $22,000, primarily from a life insurance policy. It was incongruous with the lifestyle we'd known.

"Gee, Mom," I immediately said, "I would have thought Dad would have allotted a lot more for you than that."

"Well," she said with great reluctance, "let me tell you about your dad."

The story she told is one I have told all my children because I think it is a story of a man who acted with great honor. But I had a gut feeling that my mother would rather have kept the secret. I sensed a slight embarrassment on her part that her husband was being revealed to his children as a man who did not properly provide for his widow. But there was also pride in her voice.

She told us that, as a stock broker, our father had naturally given advice to many clients. To avoid any appearance of conflict of interest, he'd never purchased for himself any of the stock he recommended. In 1929, everybody with money in the market sustained huge losses, including my father's clients. As I said, my father was appalled by the fact that many of his friends and colleagues declared bankruptcy and walked away from the losses. He did something different. He tried to make his clients whole again. Throughout the rest of his working life, he slowly and progressively paid back every one of his clients for the losses they had sustained. It cost him his legacy to his wife.

I might have guessed that there was less to our family fortune than there appeared to be. When it was time for me to enter college, I made a tour of the Ivy League schools with my good friend, Jim Towson, and his father, who was my Sunday school teacher at Central Presbyterian Church. I decided on Dartmouth College in Hanover, New Hampshire. Dad made it clear that he would undertake whatever was necessary to make it possible for me to go there. He immediately sought – and won – major financial aid, which probably saved him from going further into debt. He never suggested I abandon my dream and attend the state school. I never imagined how essential it was to my family that Dad secure that financial aid. I worked all through college, but I believed that was because I was expected to provide for my own needs. Dad never said a word about financial problems. He moved through his days with great confidence and gave the outward appearance of someone who was doing quite well.

When my brother and I saw behind that façade, we found the truth utterly amazing. But we were also busy men with families and demanding careers. Our most immediate concern was assuring that our mother would be able to live in comfort. We needed to determine how much we would have to contribute to her support. After finding that our father had left her with so little, we supposed she would require substantial assistance. As it turned out, she also surprised us. Once again, my brother and I learned that our parents were much more complicated than we'd imagined. Mother needed little financial help because she already had a successful modeling career. What appeared for years to have been merely an extension of her interest in art and beauty turned out to be Mother's way of contributing to the maintenance of our family. Mother had begun modeling in the late 1930s to bring in additional income. She was very successful because of her stunning looks, grace and presence. She mostly posed for photo ads for clothes, but she also appeared for years in the Sunday paper, wearing a bathing suit and extolling the virtues of retiring in Florida. She worked for both Harry Conover and John Robert Powers, going into New York – as my father did – to work. Mother helped support the family in a way that kept the focus on the kind of style and accomplishments that were fully accepted in the society in which she and my father moved. She worked without drawing attention to the fact that she was bringing home needed money. She continued modeling after Dad's death and made a satisfactory living at it. She didn't need financial help from her grown sons.

I never discussed my father's secret with my mother or my brother after hearing the story. Initially, it was hard enough to believe that Dad had done such an extraordinary thing, let alone to begin to understand why he had done it. After reflection, I realized my dad had a streak in him that had gone unappreciated by me. My reaction remains: Wow, why would somebody do that?

Consider the facts. After Black Friday, there were a great many people in the United States who had lost some equity in the stock market. Many books have been written by those who sought to explain the disaster and assign guilt. Certainly the fault was not with one single stock broker. The idea that there was one stock broker – one nut – out there who was trying to pay people back was a little bit hard to take. I would have accepted any explanation my dad offered. But I won't create one. That wouldn't be fair. I admire my father greatly and I am not about to second-guess him. I've wondered about the wisdom of what he did. But I always back away from making judgments about it. He called the shots the way he saw them. Being treated as warmly by him as I was, there is no way I can look back and impose my feelings about his choices. I won't pass a negative judgment.

I never saw anything about my dad that was other than modest. I think he was proud, but he never exhibited the downside of an ego, the hubris, the immodesty. I'm much more apt to do that than my dad ever was. During my life, I have occasionally wrestled with the meaning of the word integrity. I have never found a better example than the one my dad provided. That's as far as I will go in categorizing what he did.

I didn't ask my mother how she felt about it or how it affected their lives. Did he consult her? I don't know. Did they decide together to keep this remarkable endeavor from their children? I don't know. I don't even know how or when she became aware that the image of their upper-middle class lifestyle would have to be carefully maintained so that no one – not even their children – would suspect it was an illusion. I wish I had asked her some of these questions when I had the chance. But that isn't the kind of family we were. We did not share the details of our daily lives, much less the kind of intensely personal thoughts and conversations that must have surrounded these decisions.

● ● ●

MY FATHER'S DEATH was a time of great discovery in another way, too. My mother gave me something the day we went through his effects that reveals both the interest she had in my well being and the distance she kept from her eldest son. She came across it as we were going through the "important papers" that every family keeps hidden somewhere. She handed it to me and simply said: "You might find this interesting." It was a horoscope dated October 12, 1922, my birthday, it read, in part:

"Blending the Sun in Libra and the Moon in Cancer representing the individual and personal character, it may be judged that you have an ambitious and very sensitive nature and are inclined to worry yourself unnecessarily at times. You will have much creativity and will not be anxious to change your pursuits frequently. You have an inclination to embark on business pursuits and will meet with fair success. You will be anxious about those you love and your intuitions and perceptions will be very good when turned to domestic uses. You will be eager to come before the public and you will have much success in this direction. ...

"Scorpio was rising at the moment of birth. It makes one forceful and decided. You will know your own mind and you are very emphatic in your ideas and opinions. Irresoluteness is not one of the weaknesses of this sign. It gives tremendous ability. Perhaps too much pride and too much willingness to fight. Not sufficiently conciliatory toward those who differ with you and inclined to be somewhat masterful. You will have a taste for things occult and secret. This would make you a very good doctor, and it is brought out by the Sun being in the twelfth house, which rules large institutions, such as hospitals. The planet Jupiter, which is the financial ruler of this chart is also there, therefore, such a profession is fine for this chart and a protection against troubles. ...

"Mercury, the ruler of the mind, is in the sign of Libra: it makes him studious; it makes the mind neat and orderly; it gives an appreciation of art and literature; it makes a very persuasive orator. It is the ruler representing gain through loss of others – once more it signifies the doctor. Mercury is the planet of money. Law would be the second best vocation because of an uncanny faculty of being able to solve a problem."

Of course, I could not have known of those predictions when I was growing up and making the decisions that would lead to my becoming a physician and later the founding dean of a medical school and teaching hospital. It wasn't until I was well into adulthood and firmly settled into a life of medicine that Mother gave the horoscope to me. What's more, I have no idea why she commissioned an astrologer to prepare a reading based on the exact moment of my birth; I never asked her. She may have had friends who told her this would be a good idea. I do not know if she gave it any significance, or if she had a reading prepared for my brother. I wish I had asked those questions, but I didn't. So, again, I won't speculate.

My first reaction was to wonder why anybody would pay attention to such stuff, particularly my mother, who had never shown an interest in astrology. But when I read it, I was deeply impressed. There's a lot in there that is pretty close to the mark. It is a little frightening, maybe awesome, to use today's word. I cannot ignore the way this horoscope seems to predict my life in many ways, but I'm not sure what to think about it beyond simply marveling at the uncommon accuracy.

I can say that neither she nor my father ever encouraged me to become a physician. The only push I got in that direction came from our housekeeper, Mrs. Manning. She lived on the fourth floor of our home in Montclair with her son, who was rarely seen, and the insinuation of a husband, who was never in the picture. Mrs. Manning was a housekeeper in the true sense of the word. She cooked and served the meals, cleaned the house and acted as a full-time babysitter for Bill and me. She was the one who laid out our breakfast and prepared the lunches we took to school. In our formal home, Mrs. Manning apparently fulfilled her role in maintaining a smooth running household to my parent's satisfaction because I never heard them complain.

It was Mrs. Manning who told me repeatedly as I was growing up that if I wanted to get ahead in the world, I should be a physician. She never saw fruit from the seed she planted because she left our family the same time I went off to college, which is when my parents sold the house and moved into an apartment. I never saw her again. But as I grew up, she was as indelible a part of that community of 19,000 to 20,000 as the men who delivered bread and milk to the kitchen or the knife sharpeners and shoemakers who regularly made the rounds in those shaded neighborhoods of graceful, comfortable homes.

Some of the credit for my choice of a career also goes to our family doctor, who was a bit rough around the edges, but damned confident about what he did. My mother took me to him one time when I split my lip badly. He very matter-of-factly said it had to be stitched, and proceeded to stitch it, efficiently and without anesthesia. He explained that he'd have to stick me two or three times to give me the anesthetic, so there was no point. In two or three sticks, he had the wound sewed

up and I was on my way home. I liked him. I have always admired
and respected competence. By the time I was in high school, I had
firmly decided that I would be a physician.

That brings us back to Pete and his recollections of our days
together. He got a couple of other things wrong, but he certainly
nailed the feeling of the place. The camaraderie of that school stuck.
We still have reunions every five years, and they are well attended by
all who are able to make the trip. That oak tree he mentioned had a
rock retaining wall around it, and we used to gather there for lunch.
We called ourselves the Quinque Club because we thought that was
Latin for seven. By the time we realized it means five, we were used
to the name so we kept it.

We had some challenges in French, too. During a class play, my
friend Don Hawes and I were supposed to be Ferdinand the bull. We
were inside the damnedest costume, a burlap bag with horns. Pete had
a rope and he was supposed lasso the thing. He kept missing during
rehearsal and saying, "Oh, shit!" The French and Spanish teachers
were watching from the upper row of the amphitheater, which had
been built by FDR's Works Progress Administration. They cautioned
him about his language in a way that characterizes the school better
than any description I could offer.

"We don't say 'shit,'" the French teacher told him. "We say
'merde.'"

Don't ask me which end of the bull I played.

Our school was located on the campus of the Montclair State
Teachers College, a little over two miles from my home. When I
finished the sixth grade, there were two choices: the nearby public
school and College High School, where the professors taught small
classes of students while those studying to be teachers sat in the back
of the class and learned by example. My parents wanted me to go to
this select and elite school, which I did. I entered the seventh grade
class of 29 students, 18 girls and 11 boys. My classmates giggled
when I introduced myself as Merlin. It didn't take them long to dub
me Monte, after the villain, Monte DuVal, from the Jack Armstrong
radio show I loved. The nickname stuck throughout my life.

Many of our teachers wrote textbooks that were used across the
country. Before the books were reprinted, they would offer us five
cents for every mistake we found. I made some spending money that
way, particularly with the algebra texts.

Among the life-long friends I met at that school was Carol Nickerson, who became my first wife on June 21, 1944. Her father, Paul Nickerson, was an English professor at the Teachers College. The Nickerson family lived only a few blocks from the school, and I very quickly began walking Carol home. Often we would just stop on the way to sit and talk. We became childhood sweethearts and spent as much time together as her parents would allow.

This would be a good place to deal with what Pete called "rumored conquests." There may have been rumors, I won't challenge my good friend's memory. But he's making me sound like a Romeo. I think all women are beautiful, so maybe that's where he got the idea. But after I met Carol, I never looked at another girl.

As we got older, Carol and I would often go into New York City together to hear the big bands. Her parents were Christian Scientists, and her father was suitably strict with his daughter. He had his doubts about letting his daughter go off to New York with a young man (maybe he'd heard those "rumors"). But we won his confidence and went many times.

On one occasion, I told my father we were going to the Paramount Theater in Times Square to hear a singer named Frank Sinatra. Dad gave a "huh!" and said, "Let me tell you a story."

He told about riding a train bound for Los Angeles. In Kansas City, a sleeper was added to the back of the train and Dad wound up sharing it with a young man who said he was an actor. His name was John Wayne. "We had a helluva fine time," Dad said, "we drank and ate all the way to Los Angeles. When we got there, Wayne said, 'It's been great, stay in touch.' I went to my hotel room and was ready to pack it in when the phone rang. It was Wayne and he said, 'I'd like very much to take you to see a new young singer.' So we met for drinks and heard this Frank Sinatra."

Dad said "huh!" again, and the story was over. I got the impression he hadn't been too impressed with Frank Sinatra. I think my mother would have been, though. She was much more musical.

These were years of great excitement, and we were in a particularly good place to view the dramas unfolding in the world. In 1937, one of the largest dirigibles ever built, the Hindenburg, exploded not far from Montclair. The airship's hydrogen gas ignited a fire that killed many people who were so near the end of the journey from Germany to Lakehurst, New Jersey. The pictures of that disaster are etched in my memory. Clearly they had a similarly powerful effect worldwide because the explosion of the Hindenburg was the beginning of the end of travel by dirigible.

In 1939, Carol and I witnessed the beginning of something that has marked our culture in ways that some might argue were also disastrous. One of the gee-whiz exhibits at the New York World's Fair was a demonstration television. Carol and I saw each other on a TV screen. We also attended a live broadcast featuring Benny Goodman. He's long been a favorite of mine. His picture hangs in my study along with one of Frank Sinatra, the man who left Dad feeling less than overwhelmed.

It was about the time of the World's Fair that Carol's father first invited me to join the family at their vacation cottage on the coast of Maine. They called it the Nubble because it was built on a rocky outcropping about 50 yards off the eastern side of Bustins Island in Casco Bay. The eight-sided house had two stories. Downstairs was a living area and a kitchen with an old-fashioned icebox that was kept cool by large blocks of ice that were delivered twice a week from an icehouse on the island. Upstairs were two bedrooms and a room that had a bathtub and a commode. It was flushed each night with pails of bay water that were hauled up the stairs and dumped into the commode until the contents were washed out to sea. Light was provided by kerosene lamps. At low tide, you could walk to the Nubble. At high tide, you needed a boat. Carol and I continued to visit the Nubble long after we were married.

• • •

DURING HIGH SCHOOL, I was paid 11 cents an hour to dip ice cream. It was a fun job that gave me the opportunity to talk to lots of people, but the wage was pitifully low even for the times. "You know you are being taken advantage of, don't you?" my father said. And I probably did know. But I enjoyed working in one of the tiny roadside cottages where Mr. and Mrs. Bonds sold the ice cream they made in their home. They were Christian Scientists, like Carol's family. Pete says I served ice cream to an "inordinate" amount of girl customers, but I really don't remember it that way. He could be right. I did enjoy talking to all the people who came by, though.

The ice cream "cottages" were really just small booths that faced the road. The Bonds had several of them around town. Whenever they wanted to open a new one, all the workers and the family's children would nail it up and paint it – yellow, with a green roof and a big "Bonds Ice Cream" sign. Only one person at a time worked in each booth. My booth was located at the foot of a hill that led to Teachers College. One of the Bonds would deliver the ice cream packed in great big cans. At the end of the shift, they expected the workers to scrape down the sides and flatten the ice cream so they could measure how much had been sold. That way they could make sure the salesmen weren't eating the profits. They were frugal to the point of penny-pinching, but very good business people.

One of my most enduring – and embarrassing – lessons was administered on that job. I never told my parents, but I have shared the story with all of my children because I think it can teach a great deal.

It happened on an evening when the cottage probably shouldn't even have been open. Rain was pouring so hard that it must have been tough to see the 60-square-foot structure from the road, let alone the sign advertising ice cream. But somebody saw it. A car pulled up to the curb and started honking. Usually, customers would walk the 20 feet from the curb to the front of the cottage to place the order and wait while I dipped the ice cream. Now the rain was pouring so hard I could barely see to the curb. Somebody obviously wanted me to walk out there, take the order, return to the cottage to dip the ice cream and then return to the car in the pouring rain. I thought that was a bit much to ask for 11 cents an hour. Who needs ice cream in the rain, for crying out loud? So I did nothing. When the honking stopped, the sound of the rain seemed louder than before. Still I did nothing. Maybe they'll just drive away, I thought.

Unfortunately, that's not what happened.

After a minute or two, the passenger door opened and someone came slowly around the car. It was a young man – no one I had ever seen in our town – and he stuttered forward stiffly. Each leg was encased in a heavy brace down its entire length and he used crutches to help him cross the wet ground. Everything about the scene was heavy: the weight of the hardware on his legs, the rain, the slow, plodding way he moved – and the way I felt. Particularly the way I felt. When he finally reached the cottage, he placed an order that I filled without saying a word. He paid and hobbled back to the car, where someone else who had not been willing to get wet was waiting to drive them away.

I was devastated. To this day I wish I had not been so selfish and unkind. I still can't believe I behaved as arrogantly as I was that night. I am still learning from that lesson.

• • •

An edifice for medical education

D r. DuVal had done his homework. As always. He'd formed strong opinions about how things should be. As always. He was ready to explain why others might want to see things his way. As always.

So when he joined the architects to talk about the design for the health sciences building of the University of Arizona's new medical school, he came with an armful of books and a lesson. (That, too, was not unusual.) He flipped open a book and showed them a picture of the Palace of the Medici in Florence, then the Vatican, then some villas in Tuscany.

"This could only be Italy," he said.

Another book. A streetscape in a quaint Bavarian village, crazy Ludwig's castle.

"This could only be Germany," he said.

The tour continued around the globe with architecture so linked to its location that DuVal's prompts were hardly necessary. The architects could have been forgiven for wondering where he was going with this. Did he want to put the Versailles Palace on that dusty plot of land on North Campbell Avenue? Did he want Big Ben presiding over the new medical school?

He got to the point, as he always did, in his own time, and only after building a solid foundation with carefully chosen words. DuVal held up a picture of Tucson's Veterans Administration Hospital, which was built in the late-1920s in an unmistakable Spanish mission style.

It was, he told the architects, the handsomest hospital-type building he'd seen. It was graceful, sprawling, unhurried, with colors that look like a summer sunset. DuVal had been struck by the impression the building gave from the street. It had a distinctive look, an Arizona look – and DuVal was falling in love with the desert. Years later he would describe it as almost a religious feeling to come to a land he saw as terribly violent – with its harsh climate, well-armed plants and venomous animals dueling for survival under a merciless sun – yet cathedral-like with its dramatic skies, its bigness and its stillness. A place like this deserved very special architecture. The Spanish-Renaissance style of the veteran's hospital could also be found in the Benedictine Monastery on North Country Club Road and the tile-domed county courthouse in downtown. All had been designed by Tucson architect Roy Place, who died in 1950. All looked as though they belonged in the desert landscape. Proud. Patient. Enduring. The new medical school should offer a similar sense of place, a similar feeling of architectural majesty, DuVal thought. Of course, the building would house a top-notch academic and medical facility and offer convenience and efficiency to all who used it. That was function. But DuVal also wanted a medical school that said something to the people who passed by on the street. It should have a presence that reflected the heritage of a desert city: the stark, yet beguiling landscape, the deep Native American roots, the memory of being a Mexican frontier, the brash, inexplicable optimism of the settlers who made it a U.S. territory.

"You look at this," he told the architects as he held up the picture of the VA Hospital, "and you know right away this has got to be in Tucson. The architecture says Tucson. That's how the medical school should be."[46]

What followed were nervous chuckles, polite nods and, subsequently, a design for the basic sciences building that was 100 percent contemporary. It was utterly and completely in keeping with a time when Tucson was far more interested in plowing ahead than pondering its past. In that sense, DuVal got just what he'd wanted. The architecture definitely said "Tucson," it just didn't say it with the nod to history DuVal was hoping for.

DuVal didn't kick. He did wonder if the architects had gone to university president Harvill with his idea and been told: To hell with what he wants, just build something we can afford. But he didn't wonder for long about what happened after his lecture on the architectural characteristics of the world's great cities. There were so many other things to engage his time, and so many other areas where he knew he wouldn't be able to compromise. So he was prepared to be flexible in some things. He praised the plans produced by the architect firm of Friedman & Jobusch, who'd won the contract to do the design, and moved on to other tasks. Such graciousness came naturally to DuVal – besides, the exterior of the building was less important than what would be happening inside. DuVal was getting the features he wanted inside the basic sciences building.

In this realm, he had more than an aesthetic sense and a respect for tradition, he had expertise and a surgeon's eye for efficiency. He'd been working in hospitals all his adult life. He knew what made things easier and what didn't. He knew the importance of efficiency and the folly of wasted steps. Yet this was not a man who based decisions solely on personal experience. He did some more homework.

And he made sure everybody knew it.

In November of 1964, DuVal told the campus paper, The Arizona Wildcat, that the medical college was in a "period of gestation" and that he was traveling around the country to measure the way other medical schools were constructed.[47] He wanted to see what worked and what didn't. He also wanted the Arizona taxpayers who were footing the bill for his salary to know he wasn't wasting their money. He told the reporter that he kept a check list on the wall by his closet so he didn't lose time when preparing for these trips. It was a habit he would keep for the rest of his life. The list told him what to throw in his suitcase, cutting down the time needed to pack.

"I stop at home on the way to the airport, pick up what I need and go," he told the reporter.

Not too many men in his position would have bothered sharing such intimate details about their personal habits, but DuVal was building more than a medical school. He was building a legacy for himself and the community. This was about pride and honor. If doing it right meant his workday extended late into the night, then that's what it meant. Finishing each day's tasks was not simply an option, it was an unshirkable duty. Later in life, he would say that this sense of obligation was almost a sickness; he couldn't help it. DuVal's commitment made him a driven man, and Arizona got the benefit.

After touring four medical schools and corresponding with the deans of others, he found the story was always the same. Success led to growth, and growth could make a mess of anybody's good plan. Expansions too often created awkwardness. Functions that belonged together, such as outpatient clinics and the records room for those clinics, might wind up separated. The original building often wound up buried under layers of additions that did not flow in any logical order. Departments that interacted on a regular basis became isolated from one another so that getting from here to there could only be accomplished by detouring through someplace else, adding time and inconvenience to routine chores. The daily interaction among teachers, students and patients became more cumbersome than it should be. This progression from brand-new to bursting-at-the-seams was a common theme. What's worse, the need for expansion often emerged very shortly after a school was opened. The cost, inefficiencies and inconvenience of renovations looked like just the sort of thing a new dean should try to avoid. The answer was to design for expansion. To achieve that simple, yet elusive, goal, DuVal did something else that probably made the architects shake their heads. He went to the toy store and bought a couple of net containers of children's building blocks.

For weeks, those blocks went home with him and were carted back to work. He labeled some of them for relative size and function. Operating rooms take a certain amount of space; they could be represented by blue blocks. Laboratories and patient facilities could be represented by yellow and red. He began to arrange and rearrange the blocks with consideration for which areas needed to go together, and what those areas would need when they outgrew the space he was providing. He didn't just envision the building horizontally, he designed it vertically. The library was in the center, a core that was accessible on different levels. Departments representing the different basic sciences might be on different floors, but offices of the heads of departments were located within a single corridor that made it easy for them to get together while keeping their departments close at hand.

He thought of other things, too. The basic sciences building where instruction takes place would be on the south side of the site, closest to the main campus. The hospital would be on the north end, so that ambulances and other traffic would enter as far away as possible from the hustle and bustle of student activities. For the hospital, he rejected long corridors in the pediatrics ward, and created a circular plan that put the nurses' station in the center, with rooms arrayed around it. This saved the nurses a lot of steps and made it easier to keep an eye on the sick children. The concept is common today because of its efficiency. In the cafeteria, he wanted to do away with lines, so he came up with the idea of having different stations for different kinds of foods. Today, this, too, is common, but it wasn't then. It resulted from a clever and busy man's respect for time – his time and other people's. In a medical school and teaching hospital, everybody's in a hurry. Why should you have to stand in line for a main course when all you want is a salad?

He relied on Krutzsch for help in designing the research laboratories – "I didn't know a research laboratory from a tobacco shop," DuVal said. Together they designed a medical school that has been expanded many times, but remains functional and efficient. Early on, DuVal also hired librarian, David Bishop, because he knew it takes time to put together the kind of collection needed by medical students and their professors. The books were stored in rented space in the back of a vacant downtown store, and, later, in several Quonset huts at Polo Village that had been spared demolition for just that purpose.

• • •

ONCE HE KNEW the general configuration of the complex, DuVal put the blocks away and began working with the architects on every square foot of the design. Dickie Houston, director and vice president of the physical plant department for the University of Arizona, was also in on the planning sessions. When the design for the basic sciences building was finished, he went up to DuVal with a barely concealed grin.

"Monte," he said, "I've watched deans give instructions to architects for years. They say what they want and go away. But you stuck with it. I've got to congratulate you. I've never seen a dean who knew exactly what he wanted and where everything should be. This is the most complicated building I've ever seen and you had an answer for everything."

"Why thank you, Dick," DuVal replied, "But I've lived in these buildings. I don't think I deserve that compliment."

"But you overlooked one thing," Houston said.

"What was that, Dickie," DuVal asked. Had he missed something that was going to require long and costly modifications of the plan?

"You forgot the clocks," Houston said, no longer concealing his smile. "You need to have a clock on the wall of every classroom to sound the bell at 10 minutes to the hour so the kids know when the class is over."

DuVal was relieved and amused. "That's not the way we do things in medical school. You can't watch a clock when you are in the middle of a lab."

Houston walked out broken hearted, DuVal would recall with a smile. He'd tried and failed to trip up the new dean. It was, as Humphrey Bogart might have said, the beginning of a beautiful friendship. Decades later, DuVal would recount the story of the clocks with deep emotion and real appreciation for Houston: "I was crazy about that man. He was a superb friend."[48]

DuVal's early teaching challenges at the school involved other lessons in the differences between how things are done on a college campus and how they are done in a medical school. He had many conversations with Harvill about this. The success of the medical school would ultimately hinge on whether the university president came to appreciate that it wasn't just the complexity of the buildings that set this endeavor apart from the rest of the campus. There were intrinsic differences. The University of Arizona had a superb college of engineering that graduates wonderful engineers, he told Harvill, but the students don't actually produce buildings. The same was true throughout the university. Students were learning to meet society's needs, but they were not yet meeting those needs.

Conversely, colleges of medicine are part of the health-care delivery system in the United States. They serve the public directly. The stakes are higher. What's more, what works for the college of engineering might cause real problems in a college of medicine. For example, a system of central purchasing for the entire university is fiscally sound and efficient. But if you have a patient who needs a transfusion of a rare blood type, you can't write out an order in triplicate and wait six weeks for delivery. In addition, medical school faculty members work year-round. That's only one of many reasons they demand a higher salary. Even the administrative assistants who support the medical school need specialized knowledge of medical terminology and practices. They, too, command higher pay.

The conversations paid off. Harvill not only grasped the unique needs of the medical school, he relied on DuVal to communicate those needs when it was time to make annual budget requests to the regents and Legislature. DuVal would go along and take questions. Harvill's trust in DuVal was evident from the beginning. He left the new dean in charge of everything that had to do with the medical center complex, which ultimately included the college of medicine and the colleges of nursing and pharmacy.

"That he placed this much confidence in me, permitting me to oversee all of the designs, planning and execution of the construction and ultimate establishment of an academic medical center involving multimillions of dollars I interpreted as a great compliment even as it exhibited the strength of his character and commitment to the institution," DuVal would later recall.

DuVal did what was necessary to make sure that confidence was not misplaced. He spent a lot of time on the road in those days, traveling around the state to continue building enthusiasm for the medical school. There were also trips designed to raise the national profile of the emerging school.

"I would work on the medical school all day, then go to some banquet or private dinner and then go to the airport and get on the redeye at midnight. I would get to Washington at 9 or 9:30 in time for a 10 o'clock meeting. Work there all day until 4:30 or 5 and run to the airport and fly home," DuVal recalled. "I can't tell you how many times I did that."

• • •

HARVILL WANTED THE SCHOOL up and running as fast as possible. When DuVal told him the school could be ready for the first students in the fall of 1968, Harvill said, "You're going to have to move faster than that." The university president knew that the sooner the school opened, the harder it would be for the powers in Maricopa County to decide it ought to be in Phoenix after all. His concerns were legitimate. Even after the medical school enrolled its first students in 1967, the Legislature was discussing ways of moving the last two years, the clinical instruction, up to Phoenix.

But DuVal had been paying attention to the politics. He moved to preempt Maricopa's ambitions even as he was designing the basic sciences building. The issue that caught his attention would have seemed remote to many people: Maricopa County was discussing where to put the new county hospital. DuVal recognized that the location mattered a great deal. If the new Maricopa County hospital were built near Arizona State University in Tempe, it would become a direct threat to the Tucson campus. That's because the Maricopa County hospital would likely be finished before the teaching hospital in Tucson could be completed. The new Maricopa facility could be used to argue in favor of moving the clinical years of medical training from Tucson to Tempe, where many people still thought the entire medical school should be located. DuVal needed to counter the idea of putting Maricopa's new hospital in Papago Park, near Arizona State University. He didn't need to draw attention or controversy by speaking out himself. So he called a friend who was in a position of power in Maricopa County medical circles. In the course of the conversation, DuVal planted a seed. Didn't it make sense, he asked his friend, to locate the new Maricopa Medical Center in the center of Phoenix? That way, it would be near both the existing state mental hospital and the most population-dense part of the entire county. If it went to the adjacent, much smaller, college town of Tempe, the facility would be far from the people most likely to need it.

The logic was impeccable. The seed grew with no further help from DuVal. The importance of locating the new hospital near the urban center became a primary consideration. Maricopa County's new hospital was built in central Phoenix, and completed in 1969. The timing would have been ideal if the goal had been to move the clinical years of Tucson's medical school to Maricopa County. But because the county hospital was far from ASU, the new facility could not be effectively used as an argument for shifting important functions of the medical school from the University of Arizona to Arizona State University.[49]

DuVal was not done playing architect.

He also had to design the medical school's relationship with the main campus. For example, should the medical school duplicate existing campus departments in the basic sciences? DuVal saw efficiency in establishing single, campus wide departments of such disciplines as anatomy, physiology and microbiology. Yet there were also the issues raised by the inherently different nature of a medical school. He did more homework.

DuVal wrote to Dr. George Aagaard, who was dean of the

Washington University School of Medicine, on April 22, 1964: "As you well know, plans are progressing slowly for the development for our school of medicine here in Arizona. We are currently giving maximum attention to the question of how best to integrate the basic science divisions of the College of Medicine with those on the parent University campus. ..."[50]

He asked about the efficiency of the shared department of biological sciences at Washington, and closed in a style that was typical of a man who never forgot his manners: "Thanks enormously for letting me intrude on your time in this way and I will look forward to hearing from you."

The detailed response explained exactly why the University of Washington medical school did not share a division of biological sciences with the main campus. DuVal's followup read: "Thanks immensely ... This was precisely the information I needed."

He wrote to the University of Chicago, where the umbrella Division of Biological Sciences included the school of medicine. He wrote to Northwestern University, where the organizational structure was in a process of change.

In a letter to Dr. John A.D. Cooper, Dean of Sciences at Northwestern University, on May 11, 1964, DuVal wrote: "We have made no decision on the campus of the University of Arizona with regard to how the problem of the health sciences should be handled. However, since the University is now at approximately 18,000 students, and is adding a medical school, we have decided that a pretty thorough look at administrative structures elsewhere would be a desirable step at this time."[51]

DuVal drew charts on yellow legal pads detailing how different schools handled this issue. He was deep into collecting this information when he got an invitation to Harvill's office and a set of marching orders.

"I'd like to have you separate yourself from the campus and create whatever you need out there as a separate, and in effect, autonomous set of buildings and departments and so forth and not attempt to integrate those particular activities with those on the campus," Harvill said.[52]

DuVal had been leaning the other way. But he accepted his boss' direction without dispute. It was one of the rare times that Harvill exercised his authority over the design of the medical school.

For the most part, DuVal's ideas and intellect shaped the school.

Harvill wanted the University of Arizona to be among the nation's top-tier schools, and that meant it had to have a medical school. Once he won the battle to put the medical school on his campus, Harvill hired the man he thought could make it happen. Then he bucked the details over to DuVal. He did not communicate any particular concept or philosophy of how he thought the medical school should be.[53] That part was up to the new dean, and, in addition to having some strong ideas, the new dean was self-confident enough to make up a lot of things as he went along.

When it came to recruiting, he had to be creative. DuVal started assembling his faculty from a relatively small pool of talent at a time when well over a dozen other new colleges of medicine were also trying to hook the best prospects. The big name schools had a reputation they could use to leverage faculty. DuVal didn't. Nor did he have a faculty from which to form a committee that could identify candidates. The other common way of finding talent was to hire a headhunter. DuVal saw that as a complete waste of time and money. He was short on both those commodities. So he relied on networking before that idea became a cliché. He began contacting friends, colleagues and associates around the country. His Rolodex went back to people he'd known in high school and spanned doctors and professors at dozens of universities and hospitals. He started dialing. He'd say, for instance, that he was looking for a pediatrician and he'd outline the qualifications. As colleagues provided names, DuVal began compiling lists. It wasn't long before he noticed that some names appeared on just about everybody's list. From those names, he selected the two or three people to call for interviews. If he was leaning toward one candidate, he'd schedule that person to come to town last so there would be less time between the job interview and the job offer. After all, if the candidate was hot, DuVal didn't want some other new dean to make the first offer.

• • •

DUVAL TRIED TO MEET every candidate's plane, just as Dr. Harvill had met him at the airport. He carried their bags, too. In Harvill's case, the gesture could be characterized as stooping to conquer. In DuVal's case, it was more a practical matter. There were no lower level functionaries who could be assigned the job. DuVal not only did it all, he devised a way to do it better than anyone else. From the airport, the candidates were taken on a trip that was written up in the local paper and dubbed "The DuVal Tour." The idea behind it was crisp: A person's comfort level with a new community is a function of how long it takes that person to become familiar with the geography. DuVal wanted candidates to feel comfortable enough to say yes if he decided to pop the question. He took them first to one of Tucson's fine old hotels, the Lodge on the Desert. Built of adobe in the 1930s, its big rooms had fireplaces and stout wooden furniture reminiscent of an old Spanish hacienda. Desert gardens and graceful courtyards made it as geographically distinctive as DuVal had wanted the medical school architecture to be. It was run by his friend and neighbor, Schuyler Lininger, who was a big supporter of the medical school. He gave DuVal's guests a warm, Western welcome. After chatting with Lininger and dropping off the candidate's luggage, DuVal drove the candidate up to "A" Mountain, which was then at the west edge of a city that has since grown all around it. The little mountain remains a favorite place to take in the panorama, close enough to downtown to see detail and just high enough to provide a dramatic view. Tucson is in a valley surrounded by much bigger mountains that provide dramatic vistas in every direction. The Santa Catalina Mountains are to the north and the Rincon Mountains are in the east. To the south, on the kind of clear day that was common back then, you could see all the way to Mexico.

DuVal would drive up the road that coils steeply up and around "A" Mountain, and past the parking lot favored by weekend lovers. He stopped at a place where the road widens just enough for a car to pull off. From there, he could show the lay of the land and the location of pertinent landmarks: the airport, the hotel, the university, the site of the medical school. The candidate could see where everything was and put it in context later as they drove around. This provided the sense of familiarity and comfort DuVal was seeking. But there was more.

Standing by a rock wall at the edge of a cliff, DuVal would light up a cigarette and talk about how you could drive up the Santa Catalina Mountains and reach the ski resort on Mount Lemmon in an hour. Much of the recruiting had to be done in the sweltering heat of a Tucson summer, so DuVal could effectively point out that no matter how uncomfortable it was on the desert floor, a cool pine forest was just a short drive away. At the foot of the Santa Catalina Mountains, you could see what was left of a rapidly disappearing ribbon of green that marked the location of the Rillito River. Although groundwater pumping had left it dry except in the rainy season, the Rillito still held enough water just below the surface to support some massive cottonwood trees. Those who missed the more traditional seasons of cold-weather climates could walk under those trees in the autumn and hear the fallen yellow leaves crackle underfoot.

On the other side of "A" Mountain – out of sight and behind them to the west – were the Tucson Mountains, home of the world renowned Arizona-Sonora Desert Museum. DuVal would talk about that, too, and explain its unique approach as a "living" museum where the plants and animals native to the region were on display in a natural setting. DuVal used Chamber of Commerce superlatives that were convincing because they were heartfelt: He saw this place as marvelous and spectacular. It was the best place to be. The future was happening here. Believe it. Building a medical school was the best task a person could undertake. Believe that, too. Be part of it. Who wouldn't want that chance? Who wouldn't want to be on this dynamic, silver-haired man's team?

With the city stretching out below and a flawless blue sky above, the potential looked endless. For people from cold, grey places, it was a stunner. Under that open sky, DuVal would talk about his plans for a top-notch medical school that would rise in the middle of this still-small Sun Belt city. It was clear that he had every intention of helping to shape this city's growth. What candidate wouldn't wonder whether he, too, could create something of value in this remarkable place?

The pair would then get back in the car for a drive through downtown and over to the university campus. It was just a drive by. They didn't stop. DuVal just wanted to show off the stately red-brick dorms and classrooms that surround the wooden Old Main building, with its wide steps, rambling second-story porch and deep sense of frontier heritage. Then DuVal drove up Campbell Avenue and past the site of the new medical school. DuVal still didn't stop. Not yet. He drove up to River Road, which was nearly the northern edge of the city in those days. He stopped at St. Philip's in the Hills Episcopal Church, not out of any religious affiliation with the church, but because the setting itself was another take on desert architecture. Built on a site that included massive mesquite trees, the church offers a remarkable view of the Catalina Mountains. From this close, you could see the pine and fir-studded ridges that ripple toward the mountain top. It's a fantastic view. It was also the gateway to foothills living, which is the stuff of Sunset Magazine spreads. The gracious houses on large desert lots were farther away from the bustle of the city in those days, but they were no less desirable for an elegant lifestyle than they are now. DuVal, who chose to live in the city, nevertheless understood the appeal this real estate had for some prospective faculty members. The tour went east on River Road to Swan Road and then turned south to cross the Rillito on the way back to town. Going south along this road, the visitor missed the view of rusted cars and other junk that had been punched into the north side of the Rillito River to stabilize the banks. That was part of Tucson, too. But it wasn't a big selling point, so DuVal made sure no one saw it.

Carol played a large part in hosting spouses, making the same get-acquainted tour with the wives if the interview went to the next level. It was her job to show them what was good about the desert, but sometimes the task was impossible. Women from greener places were often unshakably unimpressed with Tucson. In those cases, Carol would tell her husband not to expect the candidate to accept an offer. She was always right. If the wife was not ready to trade hydrangeas for prickly pears, there would be no deal.[54]

On the first evening of a couple's recruitment visit, the DuVals would host the candidate in their home, while the DuVal children kept to their rooms. On the second night, Carol and DuVal and Phil Krutzsch and his wife, Dorothy, would join candidate and spouse in a private dining room at a local restaurant. Chemistry mattered greatly. DuVal believed that if you hit it off with someone immediately, you were going to be compatible over the long term. A River Road restaurant named El Corral offered thick steaks and a private room that invited conversation. If a candidate was not really in the running after the first night's dinner, DuVal would take the couple to a noisier restaurant that offered live Mariachi music. This gave the visitors a chance to appreciate some Southern Arizona atmosphere. The noise spared the DuVals from answering questions about the city from candidates who weren't going to be invited to join the faculty.[55]

DuVal was looking for people who shared a definite philosophy about what a medical school should be. He wanted a generalist orientation. He didn't want the head of pediatrics, for instance, who wanted subsections of pediatric neurology, pediatric gastrology, etc. Until the school was financially stable, he didn't want the faculty "replicating itself like metal coat hangers in a closet."[56] It was also important that the candidate be willing to put the best interests of the institution above personal goals. He wanted people who could help him design a curriculum with the interests of the institution in mind. He planned to give his department heads a great deal of autonomy, so he needed people who would not use that independence to put the needs of individual departments above what was beneficial to the medical school as a whole. DuVal's philosophy of what a medical school should be also included involving the community and its doctors in the process of training new doctors.

One of his more radical ideas never took flight. He wanted to establish a committee of non-physician community members to interview medical school applicants and make admissions decisions. These lay people would be given a list of names and told that the medical school faculty had determined that anyone on that list could make it through medical school. The committee would be asked to conduct the interviews and decide which applicants got the limited slots in the next medical school class. Committee members would essentially pick their future doctors. DuVal thought the community would get the kind of doctors it needed that way. But selecting students was a traditional faculty prerogative, and DuVal's faculty was not willing to give it up. He went along with their decision not to use a community selection process, but he continued to think it represented a better way to produce doctors who would be in tune with the community.

He also wanted the students to be part of a more human-oriented process. His ladder down from the Ivory Tower called for a better balance between research and student education, with the emphasis on the students. He hired faculty to teach, not win research grants. DuVal's emphasis was on the institution he was building and the students he would be teaching. The focus would not be on courting research grants; it would be on training doctors.

Dr. Jack Layton was recruited early as head of the department of pathology. Layton left a very good position at the University of Iowa for Arizona because of the remarkable opportunity to grow professionally, and because he shared DuVal's idea of what a medical school should be. He never regretted the move. In fact, forty years later, long after each man had retired, Layton would still call DuVal every year on May 1, the anniversary of the day he was hired, to express his appreciation. The bond was about more than just two professionals who shared a long history. These men made history and became good friends in the process.

"Monte was a very dynamic person with strong opinions," Layton would recall many years later. "He really had the institution's well being at heart. As a result, he collected around him a group of department heads who were well established people at major universities, all prominent nationally. He was able to bring them to Tucson and explain his vision ... and they were able to recruit – almost without exception – those who were interested in having a medical school that took college graduates and put them in positions with an eye toward practicing medicine, not doing research."[57]

• • •

DUVAL BELIEVED that if you are going to tap the public well – as would be the case in a medical school attached to a state university – you should keep your focus on the public good. That meant producing doctors who would take care of the public. If the faculty was too reliant on outside research grants, then the job of teaching could become secondary because the funding for that research was not coming from the state of Arizona. Their primary focus would be on satisfying the requirements of the grant, not teaching students. In the early years of the state's first medical school, DuVal didn't want any split allegiances. He wanted a faculty that was focused on teaching, and he made that clear.

DuVal also believed in the importance of well-trained family doctors with broad experience, and he faulted the contemporary medical school curriculum for the declining interest in this important area. DuVal wanted very much to ensure the new medical school had a strong department of family practice. But family practice didn't look exciting when medical students compared it with the drama of transplanting a kidney, for example. It was not glamorous. In fact, at the time some medical writers were speculating that what was then called "general practice" was outdated and should go by the wayside. DuVal was among those who felt it needed to be redefined and rejuvenated. His challenge was to find a way to do that in Arizona's new medical school.

He again began by asking questions and reaching out to his network of colleagues, friends and acquaintances. Again, he kept a careful record of the correspondence that helped his thinking evolve. On July 2, 1964, he wrote to Dr. Karl Voldeng of Phoenix: "There can be no doubt that men who are doing family practice are making a real contribution. This does seem to be worth preserving. I also am aware that many patients want to have a personal physician. This being so, it seems to me to be incumbent on medical schools to deliver a program of medical education which will prepare a man to be just that, a personal physician. Incidentally, like you, I prefer the name personal physician to that of either family doctor or general practitioner.

"Your comments about establishing a separate department of general practice made interesting reading. While this might be an acceptable route, I have a built-in reservation about this since, in those institutions where a department of general practice does exist, it does not function the way it is supposed to. I think the reason is a fairly simple one. If you attempt to give general practice equal status with that of any individual specialty, then you have one person representing general practice sitting around the table as it were, discussing curriculum with as many as ten or fifteen other men, each of whom represents one specialty. The man representing general practice, even though he is a department chairman, is overwhelmed by this much competition. ..."[58]

Nearly a year later, DuVal was still pondering this challenge, but his thinking had changed about how one might build status into the specialty of family practice. By now he was not only thinking about a separate department of family medicine, he was picturing it as being physically separated from the medical school campus.

On March 1, 1965, DuVal wrote to Dr. Robert Price at the Encanto Medical and Surgical Clinic in Phoenix: "You made reference to the use of a large out-patient clinic ... to help young medical students become familiar with the practice of ambulatory medicine, and with this small circle of 'families' which would be his for the period of his experience in that clinic. This is, of course, a very sound idea and one which is most appealing to me."[59]

In a subsequent letter, DuVal shows why he was able to charm so many people as he honed his ideas and worked them into reality. He closed this letter by telling Dr. Price: "Keep thinking. As long as you are, and as long as you communicate your thoughts to me, I can stay in business."[60]

DuVal began with a goal, did his homework and designed a plan. He would establish a family practice specialty away from the medical school in a clinic. It would serve indigent and other neighborhood patients. It would provide medical students with the real world experience delivering medical care where it was needed to a group of patients. It wouldn't be brain surgery, but it would offer the inherently exciting and rewarding opportunity to touch the lives of people where they lived, to know entire families and to see the positive changes that regular medical care could bring to those families. The clinic would provide those young doctors with the satisfaction of knowing that many of their patients would not be getting care if it weren't for the clinic.

This neighborhood clinic concept had been developed in Chicago by Dr. Herbert Abrams. DuVal recruited Abrams in 1968, and Abrams subsequently set up and ran El Rio Santa Cruz Neighborhood Health Center. DuVal talked the county into letting him use a facility that had formerly served as a school for delinquent girls. The center used a federal grant to become the first in the southwest to provide all-encompassing care to low-income residents. It was the Department of Family and Community Medicine, and it developed a stature and independence that made it attractive to medical students, just as DuVal had hoped. El Rio provided student doctors with an opportunity to learn about family practice medicine by becoming a part of the community they served.

Abrams was widely praised for offering a model of how to distribute health care to disadvantaged communities, but he also answered the challenge of redefining general practice medicine for the modern age. Abrams explained it at the time: "We are entering a new age where we are taking a long look at the effect of the environment – the whole social and physical environment – on health. More and more we are realizing the largest effect on health is environmental, not hereditary.

"Therefore, the doctor needs to be involved with the family and the community, and we've got a resource that will bring the student into the community. That's what we are working on here."[61] It was dynamic and exciting – even in comparison with some of the more traditionally glamorous specialties.

DuVal's relationship with Abrams and many other faculty members was similar to his own relationship with Harvill. "I left him alone and he would not usually bring me problems," DuVal said of Abrams. "He would bring me things he wanted to achieve."

Abrams became a neighbor of the DuVals and, like so many others, a lifelong close friend. DuVal was there to eulogize Abrams in September of 2006 during a memorial at University Medical Center's DuVal Auditorium.

The auditorium, named for DuVal years after it was built, was another carefully thought out aspect of the medical school. When the teaching hospital was designed, DuVal insisted that the auditorium be close to the front entrance. That way, it could be used for public lectures, movies and presentations, further integrating the medical school into the community it served.

• • •

WHEN THE MEDICAL SCHOOL opened, it was, by anybody's definition, very much DuVal's college. His quest for innovation and efficiency was epitomized by multi-disciplinary labs that were widely praised in the state newspapers. The labs would be "home base" for students. Instead of wasting time lugging books from class to class, students would remain in their labs and teachers would come to them to teach anatomy, bio-chemistry, physiology, pathology, microbiology and pharmacology.

"In the old type of medical school," DuVal told the Phoenix Gazette in November 1967, "the student goes from room to room and building to building. The result is, five-sixths of the school plant is vacant and unused all the time." Such waste was not part of DuVal's plan.[62]

But it was a story in his hometown paper, Tucson's Arizona Daily Star, that really captured what DuVal had done: "The University of Arizona College of Medicine – the first medical school started with private funds on a tax-supported campus – is a reality."[63]

Thirty-two students – twenty-six men and six women – had been chosen from more than 600 applicants. They would be arriving to start classes on September 11 – only one day after the faculty moved into the new building.

With money raised by the FAME campaign, DuVal had leveraged a $4.2 million federal grant and built the basic sciences building. Dr. William N. Hubbard Jr., president of the Association of American

Medical Colleges, praised DuVal for the "remarkable, if not unique achievement" of enrolling the first class only a year-and-a-half after groundbreaking.[64]

DuVal would have gently and meticulously corrected anyone who said the school was solely the product of his vision. In the same methodical way he tried to make the case for a geographically appropriate design, he would have listed the names of the people who helped him produce a medical school in the modern building that rose on the site. It would have been a long list that included every Arizonan who sent in a $5 donation. "The support we had in starting the medical school here really was such that a guy would have to be a horse's ass not to have been successful," DuVal said.[65]

• • •

CHAPTER FOUR

My college years
of poetry, world war and healing

*Education is the ability to listen to almost anything without losing
your temper or your self-confidence.*

Robert Frost

In addition to good will, good manners, a good education and a
respect for the finer things in life, my parents equipped me with
a heavy, fur-lined coat for my years at Dartmouth College in
Hanover, New Hampshire. It's hard to say which of those gifts was most
helpful, although locals are entirely correct in referring to the area's two
seasons as winter and August. Snow was heavy and the temperature
– sometimes slipping to 40 degrees Fahrenheit below zero – kept the
ground crunchy underfoot much of the year. When the thaw finally
came, the ground got so muddy that the director of the physical plant
put down wooden planks for us to walk on. These "duckboards" were
both greatly appreciated and mercilessly ridiculed by the students.

Jim Towson, the son of my former Sunday school teacher, was
my roommate in a dormitory on campus. We got along famously,
no doubt because we so rarely saw each other. Don't get me wrong;
Jim was a dear friend. But our interests and academics kept us going,
often in opposite directions.

I had been a regular at Central Presbyterian Church in Montclair,
where Jim's father taught us about the Bible and I passed the plate

during services, but I did not attend church regularly after I went away to college. I can't say whether this was the result of an epiphany or simply natural evolution for a young man with too many other things to do. I will say that I had begun to lay down the foundations of a philosophy on which I continue to build. I was – and am – interested in religion and the role it plays in the world, but I was – and remain – unimpressed with the implicit contract of most religions, which requires one to live according to some theological construct in exchange for a feeling of security and comfort. I would prefer that people take personal responsibility for what they do rather than beat their chests and beg to be granted forgiveness for their transgressions. I don't like paraphernalia and trappings of organized religion, either. Much of the symbolism makes me uncomfortable. The idea behind the Eucharist borders on being unhealthy. Bluntly put, it's cannibalistic. Not my cup of tea, so to speak. I do admire people whose beliefs are sincere, even if I disagree with them. But I don't admire duplicity, and I see a great deal of that in the practice of organized religion. For example: How can someone say they value life – even the life of the unborn – and yet own a gun? A gun has only one purpose, and that is to end life. How can you be pro-life and support the death penalty? That is fraudulent. How can you believe that humans were given dominion over the Earth and then use that power to mistreat animals and despoil the environment? It makes no sense.

• • •

I ACCEPT the existence of God. But it is a mistake to cast that presence in our image and describe it with personal pronouns. God is not someone to whom you pray and he, she or it "hears" and pays attention. It is incomprehensible that any such entity would burden itself with my – or your – petty problems. But let me say that if such an idea gives some people comfort, I can respect their choice. Just don't force it on me.

The order, harmony and magnificence that surround us are beyond human creation. They demand reverence – that feeling one has in the presence of the transcendent. In quiet moments occupied only by thoughts of this subject, I have concluded that there is at least one common element that could explain all that we see, hear, feel, know or understand. That is energy. I see God as energy. Except for mass, there's nothing in the universe that cannot be explained by energy.

Does the energy think? Plan? Clearly, the universe is too logically ordered to be explained by chance, but I have a hard time taking the next step and attributing the order to a "mindful" energy. I cannot visualize God as either rewarding or punishing individuals for their behavior. That comes too close to implying a person-like God is behind it all. I'm not prepared to go that far. My good friend, Stan Jones, an Episcopal minister, buys expensive telescopes to scan the heavens. I tease him about it.

"You're not going to find God out there, Stan," I tell him. "God is not to be found with a telescope."

Organized religion is often credited with providing a check on harmful behavior and instilling a moral sense. But moral sense can also come from growing up in a civilized society where you learn the advantages of self-restraint. In such a society, "free" people are willing to give up some of their "liberty" for the sake of everyone's good – including their own. They stop at red lights. They refrain from yelling "fire" in a crowded theater. They willingly trade a little of their liberty in exchange for order. I believe such liberty is inborn, innate. It cannot be taken away. But constraints can be placed on one's freedom to exercise that liberty. I prefer for those constraints to be the result of personal choice that comes from a desire to be part of a moral, civilized society rather than the result of religion. After all, the overwhelming majority of wars have been the result of one religion pitting itself against another. The personal choice that constrains liberty for the good of all can be shaped by a government. That, of course, raises problems defining the role of government.

When the Pilgrims first arrived in what we now call America, they were seeking refuge from an environment characterized by two forms of oppression on their liberties: religion and royalty. The subsequent American Revolution was a formal statement of the principle that people should be allowed the same privileges as royalty.

This is evident from the words of three men. George Mason, the author of the 1776 Virginia Declaration of Rights, said, "All men are born equally free and independent." This was subsequently distorted by Thomas Jefferson into the famous "all men are created equal," which, of course, is nonsense. One of my all-time favorite books, "American Scripture: Making the Declaration of Independence," by Pauline Maier, discusses how Jefferson reworked Mason's phrase to make it easier to enunciate in a public setting. In the process, he changed a statement that is arguably true to one that is obviously false. Jefferson went on in the Declaration of Independence to set the tone for the American philosophy by including a right to "life, liberty and the pursuit of happiness." Finally, John Adams set the tone for governance when he said the United States was to have a "government of law, and not of men." This triad of philosophies was responsible for producing one of the greatest societies in all of history and populating the most powerful superpower in the world.

No superpower, no matter how powerful, has been able to achieve permanence or sustainability. This forces us to address the question of what might cause American dominance to end. My inclination is to believe that our strength is also our weakness. That which made us strong may be destroying us by recreating the 17th and 18th century conditions that prompted our revolution in the first place. I refer to the progressive development of governance by individuals rather than by law, and by the displacement of democracy by religion. After all, life, liberty and the pursuit of happiness is a prescription for individual strength rather than being oriented to the strength of our society.

This raises grand and interesting questions that I am not going to answer here in a story about my life. But to know me, you have to know that I care deeply about such things. My life is a constant quest to understand. I read a lot as a result, and enjoy the kind of conversations that poke at ideas hard enough to make them squirm and give up their secrets.

• • •

WHEN I WAS at Dartmouth, the world was inhaling some dizzying questions about religion, the role of government and the need for restraint – moral or legal – on the behavior of those in power. Our professors – like those today – no doubt sought to stretch our minds enough to accommodate some of the answers. But I can't say we spent all our time pondering the great issues. We were young. We were away from parental oversight. There were a lot of other things to do. I can't even say I stayed away from church because I had carefully thought things through. But I was thinking about them, reading about philosophy and religion, just as I do today. The difference is that I am much more humble these days. And no doubt wiser, if that's not too contradictory.

As part of the freshman class at Dartmouth in 1940, I was full of myself, as are most young people, and utterly in love with the idea of having the chance to bloom in that beautiful setting.

As it is now, Dartmouth's glorious green was surrounded by gracious, colonial-era buildings that were constructed by people who anticipated that they would be used for a very long time. Dartmouth was built to last. The campus, one of the oldest in the country, was a mixture of stability, nobility and a spirit of academic excellence. But mostly, there was a sense of expectation. Great things were expected of those of us lucky enough to attend Dartmouth. Whether we were there because of financial aid – as in my case – or family means, we all knew our privilege included promise. The world would be what we made it. Or so we thought.

I enrolled as a pre-med student and was given the somewhat surprising advice by Dr. Rolf Syvertsen, dean of the medical school, to focus on the liberal arts as an undergraduate. He said my future was to be a life of science, so I should take advantage of the opportunity to broaden and balance my education with other things. I chose music. I loved the studies and I gave them as much energy as I could, but there were a lot of other demands on my time.

Carol was in Russell Sage College in Troy, New York, and we visited each other often. I bought a thoroughly used Model A Ford for $25. It made the 130-odd-mile trip far easier, but not necessarily comfortable. The car had no seats, so we sat on orange crates. I used it for three years and sold it for a profit to someone willing to pay $35. E-Bay recently advertised a picture – Just a picture! – of a 1930 Model A for $26. The asking price for a restored version of a 1929 Model A was $22,900 on e-Bay, so I could have made even more if I'd kept that car all these years.

In a class of slightly more than 700, I was elected Dartmouth's President of the Vigilantes, a group that was supposed to keep the freshmen in line. Later, I was vice president of Green Key, a group that monitored social events on campus. Unlike high school, where I remained mostly on solid ground, I took up swimming at Dartmouth, earning my letter in the 220- and 440-yard freestyle. I did not ski, despite the vast opportunities to do so in the area, because my swimming coach told me he'd throw me off the team if he caught me on skis. I attended football, basketball and hockey games whenever possible.

I never returned home to live after I left for college. I had to work to support myself and earn spending money during the summers. I began by waiting tables at Rood's Eating Club, a dining hall that catered to the better-off students. I also washed dishes for Dartmouth dining hall. For the better part of four years, I worked beside Clark MacGregor. We scrimed dirty dishes. That's what we called it: scriming. It involved using a big brush and a tub of sudsy water to scrape dirty dishes before loading them onto the conveyor belt that took them through a huge dishwashing machine. Eventually, Clark and I worked our way up to waiting tables in that dining hall.

Clark eventually served in the U.S. House as a Republican representing Minnesota. He worked in the Nixon administration during the Watergate break-in, but remained unsullied by the scandal. He died in 2003. I was terribly fond of him.

After my freshman year, I remained in Hanover during the summer of 1941. I lived in the Dartmouth Boat House on the Connecticut River, sharing my quarters with some canoes, a few rowboats and racks of sculling shells. During the day, I taught swimming classes and worked as a lifeguard at Hanover's Storrs Pond.

Around this time, I began doing something that was then viewed as sophisticated and appealing. Rather than being seen as a habit, with all the pejorative connotations that word has today, it was viewed as a moment's relaxation, a well-earned break, a swell accompaniment to any activity. Getting hooked was easy. The major cigarette manufacturers took advantage of college students to promote their products. They sent out enormous quantities of cigarettes in sample packs that could be handed out to friends. I signed on to be a distributor and immediately started smoking – unfiltered Lucky Strikes – a (bad) habit I kept for almost 45 years.

During those summer evenings, I would go to hear Robert Frost read his poems at Dartmouth library's Sanborn House. He was a man of remarkable talent, winning the Pulitzer Prize four times in his lifetime. It was a thrill to hear this incredible man recite his poetry in such an intimate setting. It is no exaggeration to say my friends and I were hypnotized by him. He sometimes read new works to us, not to hear our critiques, of course. But I believe he was watching our reactions. On many of these occasions, my tears flowed freely because of the beauty of his words.

While we are on the subject of tears, I may as well get this out of the way. I cry at ballets, symphonies and plays. Not all of them, by any means. It has to be a performance of extraordinary beauty or superb talent to touch me. I also cry at some movies. I say this without reservation. Perhaps I even say it in my own defense. Much of the story of my life is dominated by drive and ambition. I was totally absorbed in my first career in surgery. You always belong to other people in that role, always on call and always responsible for someone's life. When I got the invitation to start the medical school, I was awed. The task was all-consuming and more than a little bit frightening. There was no question that my work came first. In that regard, I was no different from any other man of my generation and status. But looking back I can see my attitude toward my career was all-consuming. I was totally preoccupied. I couldn't let go, even on vacation. I carried heavy responsibilities. That Alpha-male, double type-A personality was all my children knew as they grew up. All three of them say I changed after I had a heart attack in the mid-1970s. They say I became a mellower, more caring person. Perhaps they are right. But I had a sentimental side long before I became the workaholic they remember. And I took a great deal of ribbing for it during college.

As a sophomore, I was chosen to be a member of Phi Kappa Psi and moved into the fraternity house. Although fraternities these days often make the news because of deaths or criminal behavior resulting from excessive drinking, we are talking about very different times during the 1940s. Phi Kappa Psi was established as a service organization dedicated to helping others. This wasn't Animal House. But it wasn't a group of young men who regarded themselves as wimps and sob sisters, either. One evening, my fraternity brothers and I went across the street to the Nugget Theater to see "Lassie Come Home." The theater was crowded, so we wound up down in the first or second row. We had to look up to the screen, and we were close enough so the light reflected off our faces. There was no hiding in the dark. When that dog made it back across Scotland – or wherever the hell it was – to be with the little boy, I just broke out in tears. I sobbed out loud, so even darkness wouldn't have helped. I think my frat brothers all wanted to get up, walk away and not admit any association with me. I never lived it down. Or changed. I still cry at movies. Unashamedly.

It is typical of my approach to life that I have tried to figure out why. What is the theme in motion pictures that taps into my sentimentality? I've decided it is demonstrations of nobility that get to me. Lassie, for instance, did exactly the right thing. That's how I would describe nobility: doing just the right thing in a way that serves the best interests of everyone involved. An edge of selflessness helps, too, because in order to be noble an action has to serve something bigger than self-interest. The dog was limping and exhausted after her long journey, but she was determined not to let the boy down.

It's like that when the French sing "La Marseillaise" to defy the Nazis in the movie "Casablanca." Although the theme of that entire movie is nobility, there are particular vignettes that get to me as much or more than the famous ending. One is the singing of that French anthem. Another is when Humphrey Bogart's character rigs the roulette wheel to pay off for the young couple. I tear up every time. When Dorothy gets back home from Oz. When Walter Huston laughs as the gold dust blows away at the end of "Treasure of the Sierra Madre."

Some things are exactly right.

• • •

ROBERT FROST'S "Nothing Gold Can Stay" wasn't about my sophomore year. He wrote it many years earlier. But it would have been exactly right for my time at Dartmouth:

> *Nature's first green is gold,*
> *Her hardest hue to hold.*
> *Her early leaf's a flower;*
> *But only so an hour.*
> *Then leaf subsides to leaf.*
> *So Eden sank to grief,*
> *So dawn goes down to day.*
> *Nothing gold can stay.*

On Dec. 7, 1941, the Japanese bombed Pearl Harbor, and the golden promise of our college years took on a more gritty hue. Like the rest of the nation, we reeled from the blow. I was among those who enlisted immediately, choosing the U.S. Naval submarine service. After a physical in Boston, I was enrolled in the service and sent back to college. As a pre-med student, I was worth more to my country in school than on the battlefield. The U.S. government was apparently expecting a long war, and wanted to ensure the supply of future doctors. I and others like me were transferred to the V-12 program, where we wore uniforms and added military training to our college activities.

In the weeks, months and years after Pearl Harbor, the nation settled into a new reality and so did Dartmouth. Our summer vacations were eliminated and the curriculum was compacted. I was expected to finish my four-year undergraduate degree and the first two years of medical school at Dartmouth in four years, which I did.

In my sophomore year, just as in my freshman year, nearly everything I did instead of studying generated income to help with my living expenses. My mother, who had begun modeling, suggested I give that a try. She said it would pay better than the odd jobs I'd been doing, and she was certainly right. I earned $25 an hour – the price of a used Model A! – on weekends and other times when I could take a train into New York City. I did a lot of what was called pulp-and-paper work, which was used to illustrate modern romance stories. I did ads for cereal, toothpaste, breath mints and Chesterfield cigarettes. In one of those, I was a Navy pilot leaning against his fighter plane and obviously enjoying his richly deserved smoke. Chesterfield used that one for a big ad that ran at the back of the subway car. On trips to the city, I would sit near it and wait for people to react. They didn't; I was just kidding myself. I had not become recognizably famous yet, but I had become big. One of my ads was featured high above Times Square, where I puffed circles of "smoke" over the crowd of people on the sidewalks below. Not one of them thought to complain about second-hand smoke.

I moved out of the frat house in my senior year and into the house across from the Hanover Inn that was reserved for members of the Casque and Gauntlet, an honorary society to which I had been elected. At the end of the year, commencement exercises for the Class of 1944 were cancelled because of the war, and our diplomas were mailed to us. Our class did not receive public recognition until its 50th reunion in 1994.

Carol also graduated in 1944, and we were married immediately. Her step-grandfather, Rev. Joseph Price, officiated at the ceremony in Upper Montclair. We honeymooned on the Nubble, in the cottage where I had spent many vacations with her family. I had long known that Carol was pretty, intelligent and downright nifty, but I was to find out that she was also willing to do whatever was necessary to make our family a success. I give her credit for how well our children turned out.

The only time I infracted one of Dean Syvertsen's rules was when I got married. As medical school dean, he strongly recommended that his students remain single throughout their training. It was a good thing he didn't hold it against me for breaking that rule. At the time, Dartmouth only offered the first two years of medical school, so I had to win admittance to a different medical school to complete my training. I needed a great deal of help from Dr. Syvertsen to do that.

I wanted to go to Cornell University Medical College in New York City. But I was not the most attractive candidate. I finished 21st academically out of 22 medical students at Dartmouth. Cornell offered four years of medical school and consequently had its own crop of students ready to enter the third year. Cornell could be selective about accepting transfer students – and it was. Two of my classmates from Dartmouth were accepted. My application was rejected. Twice. After my second rejection, Dean Syvertsen got on the phone with Cornell and made an argument on my behalf. I have no idea what he said to them, but I was accepted – though Cornell made it quite clear to me that I was being admitted with great reluctance. Dr. Syvertsen championed my cause despite the fact that I had broken his rule about marriage. He was known for caring deeply for all his students and acting as though he had a personal responsibility for their success. I was the beneficiary of this generous philosophy.

• • •

SO WE WENT to New York City, Carol and I, as husband and wife. It was hardly the first time we'd been there. We went there often while growing up and during college. We knew the excitement of the city, the crowds, the outdoor vendors hawking eggs in wire baskets under laundry that flew like flags above the sidewalk. The sounds, the smells, the intensity. Our senses had been enlivened by all that before. But New York City had always been a place to go for a day or an evening. This time, it was to be home. What's more, it was to be a home where Carol would work while I studied to become a physician.

We found an apartment two blocks from the medical school and New York Hospital. It was owned by a retired ear, nose and throat man from Czechoslovakia who was unpleasant personally and not particularly meticulous about maintaining his property. Our small railroad flat at 609 East 69th Street was on the first floor. It had a front door that opened onto the street and a back door that led to an open space behind the building. This shotgun-setup is where such apartments get the description "railroad." In between these doors, there were a great many cockroaches. We cleaned the place up and sealed the holes we could find, but the roaches continued to be a problem. Carol insisted they must have a horde somewhere, and one night we decided to go looking for it.

After poking about, tapping walls and looking in likely places, we found it in the kitchen. The apartment was furnished with an old refrigerator that had a sort of lid or shell that could be lifted to reveal the insulation. The lid did not offer access to the interior of the refrigerator so there was little reason to open it, and we never had. That night we pried it up and found the stuff of nightmares and B-grade horror movies. What seemed like millions of roaches began pouring out. They came in swarms spilled onto the floor and spread out in ugly, brown waves. Carol screamed and I didn't behave any better. It was just awful, but we had to act. Using a broom to smash them and a can of bug spray to slow them down, we whacked and sprayed until the river of roaches stopped flowing. By the time we were through, the nest was empty and our roach problem was considerably reduced. But, as I said, the landlord was not particularly meticulous and we always had a few of the bugs slipping in through cracks in the walls while we lived there. To this day when I talk about it, I refer to the railroad flat with roaches and the image is as crisp as the crunch of a bug underfoot.

Carol took a job on the obstetrics ward of the hospital. It included a lot of paperwork and the particularly unhappy task of carrying the dead babies down to the morgue. Her pay was adequate to the needs of two people living in a railroad flat. But just barely. I spent all day in classes and all night studying. Carol captured the essence of the time when she took a picture of me sound asleep over a medical book. I'm sure she saw me that way many times. We didn't have much time or money to spend together. On weekends, if we could come up with the change on Saturday night, we'd buy the early edition of the Sunday New York Times and read it in bed until we fell asleep. There were weekends, however, when we couldn't even put together enough to buy the paper.

Part of my early training at Cornell included serving "externships" at other hospitals. I was assigned to the emergency room at Bellevue Hospital in lower New York City. As the oldest public hospital in the country, Bellevue is part of a genre of hospitals that share certain characteristics. These safety-net, or charity hospitals, were enormous institutions that relied heavily on medical residents to deliver care to the patients. There was slim oversight by the medical staff, most of whom volunteered some hours each week to run the clinics or guide the residents. In those days, physicians considered such charity work to be part of their responsibility to the community. Without the willing participation of these doctors, the poor would have lacked medical care. Bellevue was a dynamic place with a large emergency room where patients with gunshot wounds were treated as the police stood waiting to arrest them, and people who had tried to commit suicide by jumping out of upper-story windows competed for attention with accident victims. These were the routine cases.

Saturday, July 28, 1945, was not routine. That morning, Lt. Colonel William Smith was piloting a U.S. Army B-25 to Newark. It was foggy. When he dropped down to try and regain visibility, he found himself in the middle of Manhattan. At 9:49 a.m., he crashed his plane into the Empire State Building. The fuel tank exploded and sent flames roaring through halls and stairwells between the 70th and 80th floors. Bellevue was one of the area hospitals that got word to prepare for a large number of casualties. When the ambulances screamed off to the scene, the emergency medical staff was on board. I was left alone to wait for them to return with patients whose injuries would be profound.

As the ambulances began to return, the first ones carried firemen with burns and minor injuries. Then I received a woman elevator operator with extensive injuries. Betty Lou Oliver had been badly burned by the crash and subsequently plunged from the 75th floor to the sub-basement when the elevator cable snapped. Rescuers had to cut a hole in the elevator car to get her out. She was in spinal shock and her legs were pushed up through her pelvis nearly to her arm pits. She survived, in part, because the emergency brakes on the elevator cushioned her fall. But the care she received at Bellevue is also responsible for the fact that she was able to later marry, become a mother and have her name entered in the Guinness Book of World Records for "Longest fall survived in an elevator." I never saw her after she left the hospital, but we read about her progress in the paper.

The New York Times ran a dramatic photo of the crash on the front page. You can find it on the Internet. The story of the plane that crashed into the Empire State Building has been carefully documented. Yet when terrorists crashed jets into the Twin Towers on Sept. 11, 2001, many commentators insisted there was no precedent. Of course, there are tremendous differences between the 1945 crash and the attack of 2001. The biggest difference is that the 1945 incident was not intentional. But the fact that it happened and was well recorded should not have been ignored by those who write the first draft of modern history. I called several columnists at The Arizona Republic to point this out, but they weren't particularly interested. People often prefer to disregard inconvenient facts.

I was learning that, along with a great many other things, as I finished medical school and began my internships.

• • •

ONE OF THOSE LESSONS was given by an Australian woman named Elizabeth Kenny, who earned the title "Sister" for her service in her nation's military as a nurse. Sister Kenny developed her own method of treating poliomyelitis using hot woolen packs to relieve the muscle spasms, combined with massage and activity to rehabilitate the limbs. Those she treated had better success regaining the use of their limbs than those who received the standard care for the day, which was based on the belief that deformities would result if strong muscles worked against those paralyzed by polio. As a consequence of that belief, physicians would immobilize the affected part of the body in splints, braces, plaster of Paris or other devices that some have likened to implements of Medieval torture. Sister Kenny came along to tell the learned doctors they were wrong, and the learned doctors didn't initially appreciate the lesson.

You have to realize – or remember – that in the 1940s, it wasn't just the war and its aftermath that made fear an unwelcome guest in many homes. Polio was both dreaded and denied. Unlike today, when the word "polio" is most often paired with the word "vaccine," the disease was not yet tamed. It was a destructive and indiscriminate force. Beaches were closed, state fairs cancelled and large gatherings were discouraged during epidemics for fear of the spread of a poorly understood disease known as infantile paralysis. Strong, active children could be left crippled for life by polio. One of the most dreaded diseases of childhood, it also struck adults. President Franklin Roosevelt was an example of the consequences of this disease – and of the national state of denial. Throughout his presidency, the press conspired with him to hide the fact that polio had left him in a wheelchair.

Sister Kenny's method of treating polio was also greeted with denial. She found more open-minded physicians in the United States than in her home country of Australia, where she was initially ridiculed. But resistance remained even in this country, despite evidence that her technique was effective. I attended a relatively small meeting in a New York City hospital in the mid-1940s where she discussed her findings. Some physicians were highly skeptical that they could learn anything from a nurse. Enough of them were open to the results she achieved to listen, and eventually her method was adopted almost universally. It provided far better outcomes for patients.

But my lesson didn't end with Sister Kenny's success at convincing the medical profession that she had something to say. Although she earned great fame and became the subject of a movie in 1946 called "Sister Kenny" starring Rosalind Russell, she was not an undisputed heroine in my eyes. She diminished her own reputation by exhibiting the kind of denial that had initially greeted her own discovery. Physicians recognized polio as a disease of the central nervous system even before they had the good sense to consider the value of Sister Kenny's treatment. They had the training, insights and ability to correctly make that assessment. Sister Kenny, possibly because of her success in treating the muscles involved, insisted it was a disease of the muscles. She did not have medical training or the knowledge of the way the human body works to make that assessment. But she stuck to it. Despite mounting evidence that the doctors were right about how polio attacked the body, she refused to change her mind and continued to loudly deny what medical science was affirming. She'd proven the doctors wrong once, and was arrogant enough to believe she could do it again. Her obstinacy tarnished her success.

I'd like to say I learned that lesson well and never made the same mistake. But, as you will see, it would be a lie.

• • •

Margaret Smith   Merlin "Mike" DuVal

Margaret Victoria Smith wed Merlin Kearfott DuVal Sr. October 1, 1921.

Two-and-a-half month old Monte
with his father

With his mother

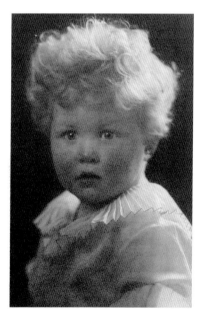

At 18 months old

A day at the New Jersey shore

Monte and
his younger
brother, Bill

An accomplished singer, Margaret introduced "Have You Ever Been Lonely."

Margaret was a figure skating champion in Canada, an actress in New Jersey theater productions and a successful New York model.

Born in Canada, Merlin Sr., know as Mike, served in WW I, and after moving to the U.S., became an investment broker and a member of the New York Stock Exchange.

Monte with his parents.

Wins Camp Award

Montclair Times Photo.

Even as a young teen, Monte excelled.

Monte and Carol graduated from College High School, Montclair, NJ, in 1940.

From La Campanilla 1940, yearbook for College High School:

Monte is truly the fair-haired lad of the Class of '40 not only in appearance, but in action as well. Though his tousled hair sets feminine hearts aflutter, it is in other fields that his conquests are more widely recognized. Captain and high-scorer of the Pony basketeers and center on the undefeated football team, are two of the athletic laurels he has garnered at C.H.S. His personlity has often been turned to the class's advantage whenever tickets must be sold, or ads solicted. His popularity is school-wide, for he has been twice elected vice-president of the Student Council in his junior year, and twice president in his senior.

As a sophomore at Dartmouth, Monte was president of the Vigilantes, a group that was "supposed to keep the freshmen in line."

PLAYING 2ND FIDDLE BECAUSE OF DRY SCALP?

5 DROPS A DAY CAN CHECK IT...

KEEP YOUR HAIR HANDSOME, WELL-GROOMED!

As a college student in the early 1940s, Monte earned $25 an hour working as a photographer's model in New York City by posing for romance magazine illustrations and for products including Life Savers, Vaseline Hair Tonic and Chesterfield cigarettes.

They Keep on Scoring—Right on to Victory
Each stenciled flag means another enemy plane destroyed. So hats off to the daring and skill of our Navy fliers and to the superb performance of their fighter planes.

They keep on Scoring for MILDER BETTER TASTE

The proof is that where a cigarette counts most, Chesterfields are winning more smokers every day.

The world's best cigarette tobaccos, plus an important manufacturing secret give to Chesterfield that special *Mildness* and *Better Taste*. This secret is Chesterfield's *Right Combination* of these tobaccos . . . just the right amount of each kind blended with all the others makes Chesterfield the cigarette that really satisfies.

★★ BUY ★★
WAR BONDS
STAMPS

CHESTERFIELD

THE CIGARETTE THAT GIVES SMOKERS
WHAT THEY WANT *They Satisfy*

Monte met Carol Nickerson in seventh grade, and they were married June 21, 1944.

Baby David followed in his grandmother's and father's footsteps by working as a photographer's model.

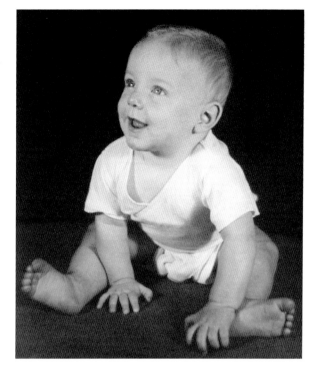

Barbara's love for ballet began early.

Even as a young child, Fred made his voice heard.

David, Barbara and Fred

1954

1955

1960

1964

The first full time faculty at the University of Oklahoma Department of Surgery: standing—Drs. William Richardson, G. Rainey Williams; seated, Drs. Gilbert Campbell, Merlin DuVal, Jr., Rene Menguy and John Schilling.

1963

'WHERE CAN THEY ALL FIT?'

—Citizen Photo by Jon Kamman

Mrs. Merlin K. DuVal Jr. watches as son Fred, 10, looks for a place to put some more books. His sister, Barbara, 15, and brother, David, 17, stand by with a few more volumes. They are getting settled in their new home while their father tours to raise funds for the University medical school.

February 7, 1964. Reprinted with permission of the Tucson Citizen

The DuVal family in their back yard in Tucson's El Encanto neighborhood, 1969

University of Arizona Special Collections / University Photograph Collection / Arizona Medical Center

The statue of Hippocrates, carved from white marble in Greece and given to the school, was a crowning glory of the new College of Medicine.

"The Big Three" during the early days of the College of Medicine — Drs. Phil Krutzsch and Oscar Thorup along with Monte.

University President Richard Harvill, Arizona Daily Star Publisher William Mathews, and Monte dig in at the groundbreaking for the clinical sciences building and teaching hospital, July 15, 1968.

University of Arizona Special Collections / University Photograph Collection / Arizona Medical Center

Also at the groundbreaking for University Hospital— Dr. Oscar Thorup, Jack McGee of Del Webb, Monte, Hospital Administrator Daniel Capps and Dr. Jack Layton.

Dean Merlin (Monte) DuVal welcomes the first class and founding faculty members, 1967
The University of Arizona
College of Medicine
Class of 1971

The first graduating class started a tradition — The Senior Follies — and portrayed Monte as The Silver Fox.

Monte crashed the Follies disguised as a hippie.

CHAPTER FIVE

Teaching medicine in an unsettled era

Protesting was a way of life on college campuses in the late 1960s. Some of it was heartfelt and necessary. Some of it was an exercise in excess and vulgarity. To the dismay of almost everybody's grandmother, good manners and personal hygiene were among the things being protested.

As Arizona's first class of medical school students began their long journey in 1967, DuVal was a master of the conventional world that was the subject of a great deal of this protest. His establishment credentials were a measure of his success and a natural consequence of his upbringing. Every previous experience had provided the perfect antecedent to his current position. He was the epitome of a highly educated, hard-driving executive, and an example of just the sort of ordered and reasoned approach the protesters were railing against. He was a celebrity in his new hometown and an awe-inspiring figure to his children. He and Carol were deeply involved in the cultural and artistic life of the community. This was exactly the person his parents had bred him to be – and the last person you would expect to be sympathetic to the malcontents.

DuVal was thriving in his establishment role as the social conventions he negotiated with such ease were being relentlessly slapped upside the head. His response was not conventional. It set him apart from many other men of his generation. His way of dealing with the upheaval also allowed him to shape a medical school that was entirely ready for a changing world.

It started with disgust. At one point, a group of students took over the University of Arizona's administration building and confronted President Harvill. Along with their screams and epithets, they produced a letter with their demands. DuVal found it appalling, not for what it said, but for how it made the statement. The letter's language was foul, its grammar deplorable, its content an indictment of the education the students had received before ever arriving on Harvill's campus. Harvill responded with a letter that was published in the campus newspaper. DuVal was impressed with its reasonableness, its sanity and its civility.

"How could you compose yourself so rapidly after receiving that insulting letter?" DuVal asked Harvill. "How could you respond in such a decent manner?"

Harvill's response: "Monte, when tensions and emotions are running high, it is important not to pay attention to the words one hears but rather the message that is being conveyed."[66]

DuVal remembered that lesson when his own department heads began telling him about a few students who questioned the way things were being done. There were two main complaints. One involved the dress code. The other involved the sacrifice of live animals for teaching purposes. To some professors, any student demand represented an unacceptable confrontation. Students were there to learn, not to challenge the authority of their teachers. They were supposed to be awed by the opportunity to get an education. The competition to get into medical school was so tough that those who were admitted should feel privileged just to be there. They should act accordingly. It was not their place to make demands. When DuVal was in medical school, students were not seen as having the capacity to even dream up something that their professors had not already carefully considered, resolved and put to rest. They were "just students," and they treated their betters with humility and respect. He had no reason to expect less from his students.

But DuVal didn't dismiss student unrest as inappropriate or meet it with outrage. He recognized that this was part of a larger discontent. Increasingly, patients were expressing dissatisfaction with how they were treated. The non-medical community, which helped pay to educate doctors, was beginning to ask questions about how well the medical profession was meeting the needs of society. DuVal didn't dismiss those concerns, either. He listened to the message, and he urged his colleagues to do the same.

"These students hold the view that if passing every course in today's medical school will result in the production of a physician with the same value system and technology that we have, then they're not so sure they want it," DuVal told his faculty. "The student is saying: 'I'm not sure I want your kind of success. Who is a doctor? What is a doctor? Are you one? What is the evidence that I must pass each course you give in order to become a doctor? Passing those courses obviously didn't equip you to meet the needs of society.'"[67]

• • •

DUVAL SENSED SOMETHING in this discontent that could not be ignored and should not be denied. This man of patrician birth, scrupulous education, enormous intellect and flawless manners allowed his ideas to be challenged. He listened to his students, even though their message was unsettling.

"There was wisdom in what they were saying," DuVal recalled decades later. "I understood that people were angry in the so-called era of the 60s. I felt many of their points were valid."[68]

The result was change. Some of it lasted and some of it didn't. Because some students needed to work during medical school, students were given more time to finish the required courses. They could leave for a semester and come back. DuVal did away with animal dissections in cases where the lesson could be taught from a film of the process. The job of redefining a dress code was essentially handed over to the students. They were told that if they wanted to wear their hair down to there and dress like hippies, that was their choice – unless a patient complained. DuVal reminded them that part of their training involved direct contact with patients, and that it was important for patients to respect the person who provided their medical care.

"Keep that in mind," he told them, "then set your own limits."

He didn't hear any complaints from patients. The furor over the dress code evaporated. He knew his students.

DuVal taught anatomy classes so he would have regular contact with students. It was important to him that they know their dean had taken the same classes they were taking, had endured the same grueling schedule, and had achieved respect as a skilled diagnostician and gifted surgeon long before he was put in the exalted position of teaching others. DuVal wanted them to respect the demands of the education they were receiving and see where it could lead. He also offered students a chance to take a block of time and shadow a faculty member or someone in the administration. He included himself in the offer so students could see things from the other side.

These were kids – even though they preferred to think of themselves as young adults. They were receptive to skilled handling by a man who saw the job of turning them into doctors as an almost sacred duty.

It was sacred, yes, but not necessarily stuffy. During the end-of-year follies, the students parodied DuVal as ubiquitous and inescapable. His habit of appearing to be everywhere and do everything at the medical school became a running joke that evening. So did his nickname, the Silver Fox. The program for the follies included a drawing of DuVal complete with bushy fox tail. DuVal laughed along and plotted his own revenge.

Carol provided him with a suitable costume to execute his plan. She borrowed it from the wardrobe of the local theater company. As the students were backslapping and loosening up with a few drinks at the party that followed the roast, DuVal was transforming himself into just the sort of hippie the patients might find objectionable. He put on old clothes and tucked a wig under an oversized hat. Then he blustered into the room where the party was going on. Keeping his head down, he bumped into people and muttered insults. He pinched bottoms. He made himself obnoxious. No one recognized him until they heard his distinctive voice. The Silver Fox couldn't hide, but he did get a good laugh at his students' expense.

In those early years, the students had classes five days a week and until noon on Saturdays. They often joined the dean and the rest of the faculty to play golf at the 49ers Country Club on Saturday afternoons. In the evenings, DuVal and Carol regularly entertained students at their home with cocktails and congenial conversation. The medical students recognized their dean's skill at getting what he wanted. That's why they called him the Silver Fox. When faculty members first told him about the nickname, he laughed.[69] Obviously, the students had been paying attention.

Charm was a necessary part of DuVal's job. But his application of it was not predatory or cynical. His interest in people and his commitment to the medical school were so genuine that he won supporters easily.

The sense of possibility he could transmit was so real that when people shook his hand, they could almost feel the charge.

• • •

A MARBLE STATUE of Hippocrates that still stands at an entrance to the medical school is a testament to DuVal's success at winning community support.

Years earlier, in 1965, a local man named Nicholas W. Genematas asked DuVal and Harvill to have lunch with him. Before they met, DuVal learned that Genematas was a wealthy man with important ties to the community. This was the sort of person whose support was essential to the growth of the medical school. But DuVal's interest in him was not manufactured. All his life, he'd enjoyed hearing the stories of people who used their unique talents to make their lives special. Genematas had just such a story to tell.[70]

Genematas greeted DuVal and Harvill effusively and ushered them into the restaurant of the Cliff Manor hotel he'd built on North Oracle Road. He'd come a long way, he told them, from his birth in Laconia, Greece, in 1890. His story of working his way up from his first job as a busboy in St. Louis fascinated DuVal. After all, the silver-haired dean of Arizona's first medical school had worked his way through college washing dishes. As Genematas told his story, he brought the conversation around to the most famous of Greek physicians, Hippocrates, whose Hippocratic Oath remained at the heart of medicine (and would shortly be challenged by some of DuVal's students). Genematas asked DuVal if he knew where Hippocrates had practiced medicine. When DuVal said it was on the Greek island of Cos, Genematas was delighted. He told DuVal about a famous statue of Hippocrates in Greece that was sculpted from the pure white marble of Mount Pentilicus. DuVal wondered aloud if the statue was based on Asclepius, the Greek god of healing, and Genematas was even more delighted at the dean's knowledge of Greek art and culture.

It was then that Genematas told them the reason for the meeting. He knew a noted Greek sculptor, Costas Georgacas, who could copy the sculpture of Hippocrates exactly, using the same fine white marble from Pentilicus. Genematas thought that statue should stand in front of Tucson's new medical school as his gift to the community that had welcomed him when asthma forced him to leave the Midwest decades earlier. If he commissioned the work and arranged to have the statue shipped to Tucson at no expense to the school, Genematas asked, would the new dean agree to display it at the college of medicine?[71]

The question stunned DuVal as much as the offer amazed him. Who could dream of not accepting such a gift? This work of art would be a jewel to adorn the medical school in classic style. To have such a gift promised even before the school was open was an act of generosity and confidence that touched DuVal deeply. He accepted with enthusiasm. Genematas made the arrangements, and the two men became friends as the sculpture was being completed in Greece and the medical school was rising in Tucson. When the statue was finished, Genematas had the 12-foot sculpture shipped from Piraeus to San Diego and then transported to Tucson. It arrived shortly before the medical school was formally dedicated on November 17, 1967. Unfortunately, Genematas never saw what his gift looked like at the school. When it arrived in Tucson, he peered at it through the slats of the shipping crate. But Genematas died before it was set in place and dedicated. DuVal made sure the generous man got full credit in the community.

The statue made an impressive statement about the majesty of the school of medicine. It presided over the celebrations and ceremonies that were held outside nearly year-round in Tucson's plentiful sunshine. Even neighborhood kids who took shortcuts through the courtyard on their way to McDonald's knew something important must be going on inside a building that had such a formidable presence stationed out front. DuVal's faculty warned him that the white marble Hippocrates was also a temping target; fraternity row was not far away.

"Those boys are going to get drunk," one doctor told him, "and the eyes of that statute are going to be painted blue and the asshole's going to be red."

DuVal said his medical students would never touch it, and he was mostly right. There were occasional instances when soap was poured into the reflecting pool that had been set up in front of the statue. But the blame generally belonged to other students, not those in the medical school. DuVal felt justified in his belief that his students were as much in awe of this work of art as he was. In some ways, those students were behaving significantly more like children than he would have dared when he was in medical school. But that reflected the times.

For the kind of really childish behavior that threatened the survival of the medical school, one had to look north to the state's elected officials. And, unfortunately, these were the folks who could make real mischief.

• • •

JUST FOUR MONTHS after the medical school enrolled its first students, the Arizona Daily Star warned of "dark days" ahead if the legislature adopted Republican Gov. Jack Williams' "austerity budget."[72] The governor was recommending that no new faculty be hired at the University of Arizona – and that included the medical school, which was already receiving applications for the next class that would be enrolled in the fall. This was a death threat. Who was going to teach the current students their second-year classes if no more teachers could be added to handle next year's incoming class? There were two equally unacceptable options. The students whose arrival had inaugurated the medical school would have to go somewhere else for their second year or the incoming class would have to be severely restricted in size so the doctors on staff could teach both first and second-year students.

It would have been very easy to react with anger to the continued resistance from Phoenix. Instead, the dean heard the message and responded directly to it. First he went to Phoenix to tell lawmakers that the governor's budget would put the school's accreditation at risk. He pointed out that bids were due to go out in two months on construction of the teaching hospital, which, he emphasized, was going to be built without any state general fund money. Hospital construction relied on federal money, state revenue bonds and donations. But why build a hospital if you can't even staff your first two years of basic sciences classes? More to the point, why would the federal government grant money to construct a teaching hospital for a medical school that lost its accreditation the first year it opened? His goal was to make lawmakers see the danger to the investment that had already been made.

But DuVal knew the real answer to the continued discontent of lawmakers was to dispel the notion that he was building a medical school for Tucson. His school needed broad state support as much as it needed water and electricity. If Arizona saw this as Tucson's medical school, public support would fade like the colors of a summer sunset.

DuVal had to make sure it was Arizona's baby. Taxpayers had to feel good about covering the operating costs, and voters would have to let lawmakers know they approved of using revenue bonds to pay a part of the next phase of the medical school. Even if he couldn't convince some of the hard-core opponents in the Legislature, he could sway the public. So he hit the road.

DuVal traveled the state in an old station wagon with Carol, Krutzsch and Dorothy, and Dr. Oscar Thorup and his wife, Barbie. They met with any civic or business organization that would have them. The Silver Fox brought more than sweet talk. He brought numbers. He collected data meticulously between his daily tasks of teaching and administering the new medical school. At night – in a study where a closed door meant "do not enter" – DuVal used that data to build his case.

Sixteen medical schools were being built around the country in early 1968, with contracts out for about nine others. "Never before have so many medical schools been under development simultaneously in the United States," he would tell groups all over the state. Arizona was part of this historic moment, he explained. What's more, Arizona was achieving its goals with demonstrable thrift and efficiency. He had the comparisons to prove it.

With characteristic thoroughness, he included careful caveats about variations in size, style and complexity of the schools being compared. He was not after flash. His argument was built on substance and engineered to hold up under scrutiny. The capital costs of the sixteen schools – excluding those that were only going to offer two-year programs – averaged $44.4 million. The projected cost of the building program in Tucson – including the teaching hospital – was $31 million. The operating costs of the other new programs averaged $106,000 in the first year. Tucson's medical school cost $61,000 in the first year. The average second-year cost of the other programs was $291,000. Tucson's would be $150,000.

The total cost of operating the University of Arizona medical school was about 65 percent of the national average, DuVal explained. The cost of construction was 70 percent of the national average.

"And while we can draw some real satisfaction from knowing our medical school assets now total over $32.5 million, the real lesson may be recognizing the magnitude of the investment that is necessary when we choose to establish new medical schools as a solution to the problem of the shortage of physicians," he concluded.[73]

He had taken the argument a step further. This wasn't just about what a bargain Arizona was getting. This was about the lofty and admirable goal of meeting the nation's need for new doctors. He gave people cool and inescapable logic and topped it off with a cherry of emotional appeal. His listeners were invited to become part of something grander than the feed store or the filling station. This was big, and they could be part of it.

Of course, Phoenix wasn't so easily swayed. Efforts to defund or underfund the college of medicine continued year after year. At one point, the money for the state's first medical school was held hostage unless Pima County legislators went along with a tax reform plan. Yet DuVal's invitation to see the medical school as Arizona's gateway to greatness had enduring appeal.

The medical school grew. In the summer of 1968, the Arizona Daily Star ran a picture of DuVal, Harvill and Star publisher William R. Mathews with shovels and hardhats as ground was broken for the $18.2 million clinical sciences building and 300-bed teaching hospital.[74] That same summer, a proposed federal budget cut threatened the $15 million in federal money DuVal was depending on to pay the bulk of the costs of that building. By then, he was used to offering the kind of glum assessments that reporters love to quote. Without the hospital, he said, "the college would be at a dead end." The federal budget cuts were made elsewhere and the money came to Tucson.[75]

Just as he appealed to the better nature of his students to get them to police themselves, he appealed to others for the sake of the medical school and the community. He usually got what he wanted. His personal warmth and icy intelligence helped him sell the message that what was good for the medical school was good for Arizona – all of Arizona.

That included all of Arizona's young people. This was their medical school, too. DuVal made time to tell them so. In Flagstaff, he told a group of undergraduates about the many different kinds of medicine: "Of course, there's OB-GYN, that's the girls," he said, "and psychiatry – that's the squirrels."[76] He was certainly not a flip or irreverent man, but he wanted these kids to feel that studying medicine involved more than grim guys hunched over microscopes. He wanted to interest the state's youth in the opportunities available now that Arizona had a medical school.

He thought high school was a particularly important time to reach out to potential medical students because his own interest in medicine began around that time. What's more, careers in the medical sciences require that students begin getting grounded in math and science early. Before the concept of "outreach" became commonplace, DuVal was doing it. In rural communities, he would speak to groups of bright-eyed high school students who had been packed into musty auditoriums. They may have been more enthusiastic about getting out of class than hearing some big city doctor, but they listened politely enough. When he was done, the principals would thank DuVal, sometimes with an inexplicable wistfulness in their voices.

• • •

ONE AFTERNOON, as students filed out of the auditorium and back to class, the principal did his gracious best to thank the elegant dean of the medical school. But it was clear there was something wrong. His gratitude was edged with regret and resignation.

"I'm glad they heard you," the principal said. "I want more of them to be interested in health sciences."[77] He paused, looked DuVal in the eye and went on. "But I really don't know if this is going to help. We have a lot of Native American and Mexican-American students here, and you have to understand something. They are bright kids. They were sitting in that audience listening to your every word. But they were thinking: 'He's not talking to me, he's talking to the white kids.'"

DuVal was stunned. It never occurred to him that children would slam the door on their own futures simply because they couldn't believe a white man wanted them to succeed. He spoke at some length with the principal, but then he had to go. He had other engagements, other commitments. That town faded in the rear-view mirror as DuVal continued with a schedule that would keep him up well after his own children had gone to bed.

But he didn't forget.

The reality the principal shared with him represented a weakness in the established order of things, and it was another challenge that many people in those days simply dismissed. DuVal did not. The words kept coming back to him: "He's not talking to me." The faces of those children kept coming back to him, too. He had seen their quiet attentiveness as he spoke, and imagined how they would be inspired to seek him out years later at the medical school. Now he imagined them thinking: "He's not talking to me." He had intended to ignite their imaginations. He spoke about hope and the future and the opportunities awaiting them at the medical school. He was inviting them to step into a world that he found bracing and exciting. It would have been bad enough to think they simply weren't listening. This was worse. They heard him. But they thought he wasn't really talking to them.

The principal's words revealed the existence of a group of young people whose desperation and hopelessness was utterly foreign to DuVal's experience. For him, any obstacle could be overcome with hard work and the application of intelligence. For these children, the world was a place where all the advantages seemed to be in somebody else's favor. For these children, believing they were excluded meant they excluded themselves. All the civil rights laws in the nation couldn't help them if they didn't believe in their own potential. From a moral standpoint, DuVal knew that was just wrong. He would not accept it. From a pragmatic standpoint, he knew there was a great need in minority communities for doctors who could relate culturally to the people they were serving.

In some ways, this was a replay of that rainy evening at the ice cream shack. DuVal was being asked to step out of his comfort zone and get wet. This time, he did.

He made up his mind to convince these kids that he was, indeed, talking to them. He called a friend who was head of a foundation and said he needed money. DuVal used it to set up a project that would reach out to students in high school and get them interested in careers in health sciences. The plan was to identify kids from groups that were under represented in the medical professions and bring them to campus to see the possibilities. DuVal began Project Med-Start in 1969. High school students arrived on campus and were paired with faculty members who could get them fired up about research, biology or other areas. They returned to their schools with the sound of DuVal's strong voice in their heads, telling them that the UA College of Medicine was, indeed, for them, too.

Project Med-Start continues and has become a national model. It offers rural, minority and economically disadvantaged students a five-week course on campus, and lets them know that opportunity is open to all who are willing to work hard. More than 2,000 students have been encouraged to pursue health careers because of the program. It was the result of DuVal's willingness to recognize that a doctor's ability to heal could reach beyond a patient and help the entire community. He saw that his medical school could do more than just train doctors, it could help doctors rethink their relationship with society. DuVal was a champion of diversity before many people were willing to even acknowledge that diversity was a value worth pursuing. The program was so dear to him that his family designated Med-Start as recipient for donations given in his memory after his death.

DuVal believed in diversity in other ways, too. He had long felt that a lifetime in medicine should be about more than hard science. This went back to his own undergraduate days, when he pursued music at the urging of an advisor who appreciated the importance of a well-rounded education. DuVal had been named a Markle Scholar in 1956, which introduced him to the concept of bringing people together in intimate settings to hear leading experts delve deeply into issues of the day. As part of a group of young faculty members chosen from all over the country to be Markle Scholars, DuVal felt the power of those seminars. The topics that were explored by the lecturers were so stimulating that they dominated every cocktail hour and dinner during the long weekends. It was liberating. It lifted the participants above their regular duties and beyond their everyday thoughts. He wanted that experience for his medical students.[78]

He hired Richard Willey, a clinical psychologist, to head a Division of Social Perspectives in Medicine. It was set up to give students just the kind of intensive mental gymnastics DuVal had envisioned. The idea was to get the students away from campus – away from medical studies – and engineer long seminars around a topic that would stimulate them to think past their personal experience. The topic might be how cultural differences can impact the relationship between a doctor and patient. Or it might be about whether a doctor should preserve life at any cost.

These seminars had high ambitions and eventually other pressures on the curriculum prevented them from continuing as DuVal had intended. But the goal remained relevant: free medical students from their studies occasionally and give them the liberty to explore larger questions about life and death, medicine and humankind.

• • •

SUCH QUESTIONS fascinated DuVal on an intellectual level, but he also sensed that finding answers would have practical importance as these young doctors began their professional lives. This was another area where convention and tradition were being confronted with growing dissatisfaction.

Scientific breakthroughs were making medical technologies available before society or its doctors were prepared. The effect was that both were caught unready. Technology created its own imperative and doctors and patients were pulled along. The underlying questions about ethics remained unresolved. In many cases, that left individual doctors in the position of making decisions with little guidance. One solution, DuVal came to believe, would be for communities to get together in some variant of the focus group and hash out issues like euthanasia or the consequences of keeping extremely premature babies alive. But that would take a very long time, if it ever happened. Absent any societal consensus, the physician had to be ready to make his or her own choices. DuVal wanted the physicians he was training to have a strong foundation that went beyond conventional wisdom.

"If there is a common error that you and I make frequently," he told a congregation at The Unitarian Universalist Church of Tucson when asked to deliver a guest sermon,[79] "it is to interpret our progress in civilization by our material advances. We might say, for example, that we have an advanced civilization compared with that of Elizabethan England because we now have the airplane, television and the electronic computer. But may I suggest that this is faulty reasoning? Instead, it is preferable that we judge civilization in terms of what man does to improve himself and his relation to others rather than by what he devises to reduce physical effort or to increase his personal comfort. ... But the key is moderation – remaining in control. Excess always indicates a failure to control. A drunkard is repulsive not because he has imbibed, but because he has voluntarily given away control of himself. The same is true of excess in any form. At its extreme, even the excess of intelligence, without civil instinct, may breed monstrosities. Is not the atom bomb an example of this? Intelligence must be clothed with morals... ."

His sermon to the Congregational Church went on to explore the kind of ideas he thought his medical students should wedge into schedules that were full enough without philosophical detours. His words reveal a man who was not just changing with the times; he was exploring what those changes meant to him and his profession.

"Has our increased intelligence acted as a barrier as well as an aid to our orderly moral evolution? I read recently that one of the characteristics of our day and age has been the appearance of the 'equivocal man.' He is the man who is so intelligent and so well informed that he can't make up his mind. His numbers are increasing. If this is true, will he be like the ass who, when he was placed between two bales of hay is said to have starved to death? I would prefer to think not. On the contrary, I think we should worry more if the ass starved to death because of apathy and indifference, rather than because of intelligent uncertainty. If, indeed, there is an increase in the number of equivocal men, than I would suggest that there is real virtue in this desire to act correctly. It is this personal effort, which is, after all, our salvation. ...

"Our intellectual endeavors, our whole science, will be of no avail if they do not lead man to a better comprehension of himself and of the resources buried in his inner self, which he can use to comprehend the meaning of his life."[80]

DuVal knew that balancing technology with humanity would be a huge challenge for his students. But it was only one of the many non-academic issues that would complicate the physician's duty to keep the sick from "harm and injustice," as the Hippocratic Oath directed. Non-medical issues had begun to insinuate themselves between doctor and patient in ways that Hippocrates could never have imagined. There were stirrings – that have since risen to screams – about the need to improve access to medicine.

Doctors had long enjoyed full autonomy and independence when it came to making decisions about where to practice, which patients to see and what to charge those patients. DuVal thought that privilege was reasonable because the process of becoming a doctor is long and expensive, as his students were well aware. But he also recognized that society had a claim to the doctor's time simply because so many medical schools – including his – were made possible through public funding. This was something students also needed to consider. When he was a young doctor, physicians would donate an afternoon a week to the local charity hospital to treat indigent patients. It represented a collective decision by an independent group of professionals who did not need to be told how to deliver the service for which they had been trained. Such charity was a product of the autonomy DuVal and other physicians accepted as their right.

Challenges to that way of thinking were another aspect of a changing society. DuVal was not willing to dismiss this, either. He explored the issue when he was invited to return to the University of Oklahoma to deliver the commencement address at the college of medicine in 1967. DuVal urged these graduating doctors to consider the implications of the emerging concept that people had a right to receive medical care. That idea, if fully accepted by society, would dramatically impact the autonomy doctors had long enjoyed. If the medical profession was not proactive in addressing the dissatisfaction patients and society at large were expressing, doctors might find a solution imposed on them. DuVal thought doctors should come up with their own answer.

"Do your best to eliminate some of the inconsistencies and contradictions that seem to have plagued my generation of physicians. For example, don't assume that just because you are personally prepared to make your services available to anyone, irrespective of his ability to pay, that this constitutes the basis of a system that will serve to provide health services to any who may need them. We have already tried this route and we found it wanting."[81]

DuVal's evolution in thinking about the correct relationship between physicians and the people they serve continued. In 1969, he addressed the University of Texas graduating class of doctors.[82]

"Having made available the resources which made our extraordinary scientific advances possible, society has now said that it will no longer sit still while the gap between our scientific capability and our social needs continues to widen. ...

"The history of the development of our country has been the history of free enterprise. The chief characteristic of free enterprise is free choice; free choice by the supplier and free choice by the consumer. Thus, when there is a gap in the distribution of a product or service, we have learned that the free market and competition will correct it. Medicine, which has often been described as the strongest of all examples of the free enterprise system, is, ironically, a prime example of a service that obeys none of the basic laws of economics – is not the least bit subject to the phenomenon of the market place. Indeed, the consumer has almost no effect on the supply of physicians, where they will locate, what they will practice, who they will accept as patients, or what the services will cost. And this is the same consumer who, we have now agreed, should have the right of access to competent medical care.

"Then this is the issue. As physicians we believe that we have certain rights of self-determination; rights which many would say should not be tampered with unless we are willing to run the risk of undoing one of the greatest enterprises that has ever been assembled. On the other hand, we live in a society which also has certain rights and which, having provided the resources for our enterprise, has now developed new expectations in the field of health – and, as I have already suggested, its demands on medicine have become increasingly articulate, specific and insistent. The demand is for a solution to the problem of the inequitable distribution of health services in such a way that the rights of all individuals can be respected and accommodated."

DuVal was trying to prepare new doctors for challenges so daunting that they remain largely unresolved four decades later. His words may sound a bit stilted and formal by today's standards. By the end of his life, for example, he had abandoned the singular male pronoun in favor of more gender neutral language. He did not abandon the habit of carefully walking through a problem with stops along the way to consider the complexities. It is worth pausing to see how he led his listeners along with him on that journey years ago. He would joke that his friends and colleagues often said: "DuVal doesn't know what he thinks until he hears himself say it."[83] This acknowledgement of his extemporaneous speaking abilities and the rich, impressive tones of his voice belied the truth of how diligently he sought answers. This is a man who thought deeply about the changes that were quite literally shaking the foundation of his profession and his society. His lack of commitment to the status quo reveals a great deal about him. He held the old values of grace, intellect and education his parents passed on to him. But he used those attributes to bore down on the established social order just as mercilessly as the rudest of the era's student protesters. He just did it with better grammar, grooming and etiquette.

As he pondered the great issues of the day, other questions were simmering in the basic sciences building behind the un-vandalized statue of Hippocrates.

• • •

THE IDENTITY of the medical school needed to be defined in those early years, and that's something that even the Silver Fox hadn't stopped to consider. In retrospect, this situation should have been easy to anticipate. Older schools have the weight of history and tradition to load onto each new faculty member. Newcomers join a known entity and adapt to the particular philosophy and atmosphere. Arizona's new medical school was as open to interpretation as the clear, blue sky over Tucson's mountains. New faculty members weren't so open. Every person DuVal recruited came out of a particular background and orientation. With no established culture to adapt to at the new school, it was natural for each one to try to recreate the atmosphere in which he had been comfortable. Department heads built individual domains. Rather than move toward an aggregate personality that could be expressed by answering the question "Who are we?" as an institution, the medical school faculty looked at each other and asked "Who are you?" The answer was not always one that led to a sense of shared purpose. When the Association of American Medical Colleges named DuVal to head a group made up of the deans of the nation's new medical colleges, he found that the need to evolve an aggregate personality was nearly universal. All the new schools were looking for an identity.

At the UA College of Medicine, each department head was becoming narrowly oriented to the needs of that department. Even the instances when they did work together revealed a lack of cohesion. During faculty meetings, committees of medical school professors would often be set up to deal with particular issues, such as student advancement. Those committees would meet, review the issue and return to report to the entire faculty. It was a common practice designed for efficiency. But instead of accepting the reports that were subsequently presented at full faculty meetings, DuVal's professors would often dissect everything the committee had done in excruciating detail. They were suspicious. They wondered if things had been handled correctly. They didn't trust each other.[84] As a consequence, meetings that began at 7 p.m. routinely dragged on past midnight.

Department heads too often came to DuVal individually for solutions. He was the father figure. White-haired and wise, he made the decisions. If he'd been a man who wanted to rule over an institution, this would have been a good thing. But DuVal was not building an empire. He was trying to establish a college of medicine that would outlast him by many, many decades. That meant it had to develop its own culture, its own system of dealing with the needs of its faculty and students. The faculty needed to begin looking to each other, rather than to the dean, to shape the identity of the new school.

DuVal was not the only one who recognized the need to change things. Faculty members had been stopping by his office and sending him notes expressing their concern about the lack of cohesion. Some of them were quite "passionate"[85] about their discomfort with the situation. A few had even suggested DuVal resign so that his formidable presence would no longer hinder the shift of power from the dean's office to the faculty.[86] DuVal did not sense a "mandate"[87] that he resign, so he told his faculty that wasn't going to happen. But he did take dramatic action. He arranged a faculty retreat in Tubac, a small community south of Tucson with a Western-style resort. It was the same setting where he and his department heads had developed the curriculum for the medical school not so long ago. His goal was to get them away from the school and their individual domains, and challenge them to work things out for themselves. On the first evening, he outlined the problem:

"Each of you comes from a different background; with very few exceptions none of you were together before. For some, this was a first membership on a medical school faculty. Your loyalties were elsewhere; you were a stranger to the desert and to the University of Arizona, just as they were strangers to you. Having arrived, you were eager to adopt your new friends as colleagues, and yet, you did not immediately find the feeling of comfort you had expected. Instead you found elements of competition and uncertainty as you attempted to weave your personal programs, views and aspirations into mutually acceptable patterns with those of your colleagues. Worse, all of this happened so fast – you found it necessary to make important decisions even before you had finished sizing each other up.

"… without an aggregate identity, you are amorphous. And that which is amorphous cannot be represented; representation requires shape, size, mass; in a word dimensions. As a faculty, we don't yet have dimensions. They are coming, of course – they are just not here quite yet. Personally, I don't find this nearly as distressing as a small handful of you apparently do. And no real harm has been done. Passionate argument, after all, is a sign that one cares. It is the alternative to passionate argument that I would find distressing."

He challenged them to develop a set of bearings – today it would be called a mission statement. He wanted them to create their own bylaws and their own structure for operating the college of medicine. "I don't think you have detected it yet," he told them, "but you are at the edge of greatness."[88]

DuVal himself had already delivered greatness to the University of Arizona, but he hadn't detected it yet, either. His College of Medicine had gracefully negotiated the rebellious 60s with its integrity intact, and had launched itself toward a future that recognized the value of diversity and the need for physicians to engage in introspection and outreach.

He'd met challenges to his profession and his school by demanding change from himself and others. He rearranged things that weren't working in the public part of his life. It would be years before he experienced a similar epiphany in his personal life. But true greatness was awaiting him there, too.

• • •

CHAPTER SIX

My early years as a surgeon

Evolution continues in our time, no longer on the physiological or anatomical plane but on the spiritual and moral plane.
"Human Destiny"
Pierre Lecomte du Noüy

After medical school, I learned the skills and judgment necessary to be a surgeon through on-the-job training. I found out rather quickly that things in the real world were not quite the same as they were in the classroom. Experience – trial-and-error – was an irreplaceable teacher. This was particularly true in perfecting the art of medicine, as opposed to mastering its science. I got valuable instruction in the spirit of medicine, as well, as I discovered that the medical code of ethics I had been taught did not necessarily have the same goals as the rules under which society in general operates.

It was also a time of personal challenges. A time of welcoming a son and two daughters to our family, and losing one of those beloved children. Of honing my skills in medicine and surgery and watching our child die because even the best science can do is often not enough. This was a learning process of a different kind. I was used to playing and winning, working and achieving. Nothing had prepared me for kind of utter helplessness a father feels when he cannot help his child.

The lessons were hard and so was the schedule. After receiving my M.D. degree in March of 1946, I accepted an internship in surgery at New York Hospital. During this unusually difficult period, Carol continued to provide our support. I was paid $65 a month, but it barely covered food and my cigarette habit, which was firmly entrenched and utterly unchallenged by the medical establishment. If the dangers of smoking were suspected at the time, no one let on. In fact, in the late 1940s ads boasted of surveys revealing that "More doctors smoke Camels than any other cigarette." That was my brand, as you'll remember, so I was right in the medical mainstream. My duty at the hospital ran continuously for three days and two nights. They provided me with a room where I could sleep if I wasn't needed on the floor or in the ER. I returned home only on the third night. The next day, it was back to the hospital. On more than one occasion, when Carol and I added up our money, we had less than 50 cents.

That was my first internship, and it lasted 15 months. During more than half that time, Carol was pregnant with our first child, David. He was born February 23, 1947 and almost immediately began helping with the family finances. David was an uncommonly attractive child, and Carol took him to a modeling agency where they fell head over heels for him. He did toilet paper ads and a variety of other promotions, making so much that we had to get him a Social Security number. His income so far surpassed mine that I listed myself as my infant son's dependent on that year's tax forms.

While David was enjoying success at modeling, I also reached that pinnacle of fame I'd sought while sitting next to those Chesterfield ads on the subway. It happened one day when I was making rounds as an intern. In those days, wards consisted of four beds loosely separated by curtains that could be drawn to provide limited visual privacy but virtually no noise barrier. One of my patients was a little, old lady with a strong New York Jewish accent. She was reading a magazine when I strode onto the ward, armed with my medical degree, authoritative in my intern's white and carrying a strong sense of my own importance. The furthest thing from my mind was a modeling shoot I had done months earlier for a modern romance magazine. In fact, I didn't even notice my picture on the cover of her magazine. But she did.

She held up her magazine. "That's my doctor," she cried out in a loud voice with an accent so distinctive that I can still hear it. She let the entire ward know. And it wasn't just her word: she had the picture to prove it. As you might guess, word telegraphed far beyond that small ward. Before long it felt like the entire hospital knew.

From that day on, I never modeled again. Nor did I talk about it. My second wife, Ruth, didn't know about my modeling career until she came across an old magazine in a used bookstore and saw my much-younger face smiling up at her.

• • •

TO UNDERSTAND my consternation at being found on the cover of a romance magazine, you should first consider that I was trying to establish credibility as a doctor. Next you need to remember that the people I was working with had impressive reputations. One was Dr. George Papanicolaou, the inventor of the pap smear to detect cervical cancer. Dr. Pap, as we called him, began working in Cornell's Department of Anatomy decades earlier, and he was something of an institution by the time I arrived. He had been studying the menstrual cycle through vaginal smears, and published a paper on that in 1933. During this work, he noticed cancer cells coming from the cervix in some women. By 1939, the value of the vaginal smear as a means of cancer detection began to be seriously recognized. By the time I began my internship, it was a well accepted medical tool. I worked closely with Dr. Pap and greatly enjoyed my association with this famous and formidable man.

We interns were also involved in research to discover what a new antibiotic called penicillin could do. Its ability to kill bacterial infection had long been appreciated, and it had been rushed into production near the end of the war for the sake of our military men. Yet the speed and effectiveness of this, the original miracle drug, was not yet fully understood. We were assigned to uncover its secrets. Our test group was comprised of women who all had gonorrhea. They made ideal subjects because you could culture the cervix every two hours to monitor the progress of penicillin against the infection. We were amazed at how fast evidence of infection disappeared. Penicillin could cure gonorrhea in a matter of hours. In subsequent tests, we found out it worked against all sorts of bacteria. The age of the wonder drugs had begun. Previously devastating ailments were rendered routine. Yet a cautionary note is worth inserting: it was only a few years after penicillin went into widespread commercial production that bacteria began showing resistance to it. Even with today's more extensive arsenal of antibiotics, such resistance remains a problem that gets far too little attention.

As interns, we were also involved in learning how to do blood transfusions. Our methods were somewhat primitive. We began by matching the blood of the donor with the type needed by the patient. We would then draw the blood and pour it into a large, sterile glass container lined with sterilized gauze. From there it was run into the patient.

The grueling schedule of the interns took its toll on me. One day, I was scrubbed and ready to assist surgery. The surgeon and I were sitting on stools over an anesthetized patient. Without warning, I fell asleep and dropped over the surgical field. I woke immediately and did no damage, but the surgeon wanted to know what the hell was going on. He looked into our schedules and raised some concerns. Things didn't change until years later, however, when the negative impact of sleep deprived interns on patient care became impossible to ignore.

In my time as an intern, we were expected to endure a schedule that was purposely designed to push us to our limits. Some might call it hazing. It was certainly tough. There were, however, amenities that made a very difficult job more pleasurable in unexpected ways. One of the bonuses was the celebrities.

Carlos Montoya, arguably the best flamenco guitarist in the world, was in the hospital for several weeks while being treated for an abscessed liver. In the evenings, he would get out his guitar and play. Dr. Jim Lincoln, a fellow intern and my roommate at the hospital, would go with me to Montoya's room whenever possible and enjoy world-class private concerts. Montoya's remarkable talent delivered the kind of tears-in-the-eyes sensation I had experienced listening to Robert Frost not too many years earlier.

When Baron von Rothschild, one of the great bankers of Europe, came to New York to have his prostate operated on, he bought himself a suite on the top floor of our hospital. Because of its fine reputation, many people in lofty positions came to New York Hospital. I found it interesting to care for such people, if only out of curiosity. They clearly lived in a completely different world than the one I knew. Some were as arrogant as they could be. Their wealth called the tunes. Others were just plain pleasant. One of those was Mrs. Harvey Cushing. Her husband was the father of neurosurgery, making him a particular celebrity among young doctors. Even though Dr. Cushing had died by the time his wife came to us, she was well endowed with reflected glory. But she did not milk it. She was a delightful patient.

There were also movie stars. One came to us for surgery to elevate her breasts. After she was anesthetized, my job was to hold her upright so the surgeon could mark exactly where to cut to get the right angle for her uplift. Such celebrity assignments could certainly give the day a little bounce and sparkle.

Another woman provided a very sad, but valuable, memory. I've always loved the music of Edvard Grieg, so I was especially thrilled to find one of my patients had played in the Broadway musical, "Song of Norway," which told the story of his life. She had a very malignant and fast moving brain tumor when she arrived at the hospital, and she was obviously never going to leave alive. Sometimes I would sit beside her bed and sing a song from the musical. She loved that. I believe my singing gave her the comfort she needed to face her death. This brave and elegant lady died in my presence, but not before teaching me that there are things a physician can do to ease a patient's suffering that are not detailed in any medical book.

• • •

NOT ALL THE FAMOUS at New York Hospital were immediately recognizable. The notoriety of two patients who were brought into the emergency room one night was unknown to me. They were bloodied and near death from numerous gunshot wounds when I received them. My first thought was simply this: How do I keep these men alive. My job as a physician was clear and unambiguous. I worked intensely with these two for six weeks – caring for them day and night as they reached and passed various crises. I did my best to repair the damage done to their bodies by the bullets. I used my knowledge to restore them to whatever degree of strength and wholeness their injuries would permit.

When they were well enough to be released, the police took them back to New York's infamous Sing Sing Prison in Ossining. This prison's brutal past made it part of America's mythology. Originally built by prison laborers who slaved to quarry stone and build the tiny cubicles in which they would be housed, Sing Sing had evolved. It was far more modern in the 1940s, reflecting changes in the attitude about the role of prisons. But it was still stark and forbidding. Sing Sing was where the worst of the state's criminals were held. The worst of the worst were executed in an electric chair that had been tested on the site. The men whose bullet-riddled bodies I had done my damnedest to repair were strapped in that chair – each in his turn – and electrocuted after I had made them well enough to travel. I wasn't told of this. I read about it in the newspaper a few months after they left the hospital. To me, they were patients. To the state, they were murderers. I and my colleagues had known they were felons. We hadn't known they had been convicted and sentenced to death before we ever saw them. The gunshot wounds I had so diligently treated were inflicted following an escape attempt. I'd used all of the medical skill I had to save two men so the state could execute them.

The contradiction was stunning, eye-opening and discouraging. I don't question the rightness of providing the care they received in the hospital. Nor would I have treated them any differently if I had known. But the irony is tremendous. I have devoted many hours to pondering the implications of this strange fact: the role of the physician in society and the goals of that society are often not co-terminus. Instead of answers, time has added complications to the questions.

For example, a few years ago, physicians in California refused to participate in executions in which a doctor was expected to administer the lethal dose of a controlled substance to the condemned. Initially, I thought a physician's privileged status created an obligation to cooperate. The law had given doctors – and doctors alone – the right to prescribe controlled substances, including those that were to be used for execution. The doctor had a responsibility to use that privilege to serve the public, and should not shirk that duty. One might not agree with capital punishment, but society had a right to expect cooperation. That was my initial view. But it evolved. My anger at those privileged doctors who refused to respond to society's request was redirected to the lawmakers who put them in an untenable position.

Equally controversial issues arise from both ends of life's continuum – and most of them don't involve bringing criminals to justice. When it comes to abortion, premature babies and end-of-life issues, lawmakers either fail to provide guidance or attempt to establish policies that may well go against a doctor's ethics. If the fundamental role of a physician is to meet the needs of a patient and serve that patient's best interest, then there will be times when a physician has to run afoul of society's rules in all these areas.

In the case of extremely premature babies and terminally ill patients, medical technology has created its own imperative. That's a problem.

We use technology because we can, not because we should. We, as a society, have not taken the time to consider whether – or when – it might be in everybody's best interest not to use the technology. The miracle of keeping a premature baby alive receives almost universal cheers. But it can take a million dollars and several months in the hospital to save a baby that is born at 600 grams. No one particular individual pays the cost of that treatment, we all pay. And we do so at a time when many people in this country – including children – lack basic medical care. The cost of care is not the only consideration. There is the consequence. Those babies often have profound developmental, mental or other problems throughout their lives.

Society's dilemma should be to decide whether to let an infant die even though medical science can save the child. But society has not faced that dilemma. The existence of the technology to save these infants has all but silenced the discussion about the wisdom of using that technology in every case. People have not come together to determine how these decisions should be made from a public policy standpoint.

You might say these are personal, not public decisions, but they too often become public. There are cases where parents and doctor may be in agreement to let a baby with severe congenital problems simply slip away without taking heroic measures. But one nurse can step in and impose her version of morality on the family, calling the police and embroiling the entire situation in a so-called right-to-life controversy.

One of my favorite philosophers, Pierre Lecomte du Noüy, began to address moral questions after a distinguished life as a scientist. His 1947 work, "Human Destiny," is one of the high impact books in my life. I have given copies to several of my grandchildren (and trust they have carefully read and reread them, because, as Lecomte du Noüy pointed out in his preface: "Ideas cannot be assimilated without having been thought over and understood.")

I've "handled" these ideas, as Lecomte du Noüy suggested, for many years. I find that even though the technology in question may change, the basic problem does not. Lecomte du Noüy wrote: "Intelligence alone is dangerous if it is not subjected to the intuitive or rational perception of moral values. It has led, not only to materialism, but to monstrosities. ... the world learned about the atomic bomb ... the public at large was made to realize that a wonderful triumph of science brutally challenged the security of all mankind. And all at once, the so-called civilized countries understood that only a moral coalition could protect them against the threat."

Medical science can be equally brutal when technology takes over personal or family decision-making. But then, so can the laws made to restrain or mandate the use of that technology. There's always the question of whose morals will prevail.

Like birth, the end-of-life is spiked with unresolved questions of morality and medicine. The tragedies that become household words – Terri Schiavo, Karen Ann Quinlan – are the very public extreme. There are many more quiet cases in which family and doctor agree together to pull the plug. I did that with my own father when he was stroked out. By that I mean he was totally paralyzed by his stroke. He was in a vegetative state. Dad's doctor, who had been a classmate of mine at Cornell, told me Dad would never recover. I consulted with my mother and brother and we faced the hard fact: He would be that way until he died. None of us wanted him to linger in such a state. We let him go. It was an agonizing decision, but it was also a simple, dignified act of love. Some would dispute our right to make that decision, but fortunately Dad had a doctor who was focused on serving his patient.

But whether the questions swirl around the beginning or the end of life, one should not imagine that they are new. At the time I was becoming a physician, Lecomte du Noüy wrote, "The rapid development of the material side of civilization had aroused the interest of men and kept them in a kind of breathless expectation of the next day's miracle. Little time was left for the solving of the true problems: the *human* problems." (emphasis in original) Substitute the word "technology" for "the material side of civilization" and you have today's world. The human challenges remain relatively unexamined whether you read about them in a well-worn 1940s treatise or hear about them via iPod on a downloaded National Public Radio discussion.

So let's return to the 1940s with the clear understanding that those long ago days were not necessarily the simpler and less complicated times the merchants of nostalgia would have you believe.

• • •

DAVID WAS A MONTH OLD when I finished my first internship and began my service in the Navy. My first post was at Saint Albans Naval Hospital on Long Island. I spent six months there caring for young men – men about my age – who had been left paraplegic by the war. From there I was sent to the Naval Amphibious Base in Little Creek, Virginia, a huge installation that was the hub of the nation's amphibious forces and underwater demolition teams. Carol, David and I moved into a tiny, one-story block house on the beach near the mouth of Chesapeake Bay. The neighbors called the area "Cinderblock Alley," which captures it pretty well. We bought our first car that year, a 1939 two-door Chevy coupe.

Although I had been trained in surgery, I was made Venereal Disease Control Officer in Virginia, and spent my days overseeing sick call and giving lectures on how to avoid, diagnose and treat venereal disease. It was not particularly satisfying work, but it was the completion of a commitment I made to serve my country in the military in response to the attack in Pearl Harbor.

Near the end of my service, in February, 1949, Carol left David with a neighbor and took the train from Norfolk to New York. On my advice, she had decided not to deliver our second child in Virginia. On her own initiative, she decided to walk around the city during her labor until felt it was time to turn herself in at New York Hospital. Her trusted obstetrician delivered our daughter, Barbara, on February 21, 1949. Now we were a family of four. I was out of uniform and in need of a place to complete my training.

I wanted to return to New York Hospital to finish my surgical internship, but Dr. George J. Heuer, who had been chief of surgery during my first internship, was gone. The surgeon who replaced him wanted to build his own stable of hand-picked, personally trained surgeons. I was a "Heuer man," so he didn't want me. Instead, I took a rotating internship at Roosevelt Hospital. The pay was better and so were the hours.

At Roosevelt, I only had to spend every other night at the hospital. I shared the room to which I was assigned at the hospital with Dr. Erle Peacock Jr., who was later to sue me after I removed him as head of surgery at the University of Arizona medical school. At Roosevelt, Erle and I got along fine. As to the pay: it was higher. But it was below poverty wages if you calculated the hourly rate, which I did. I took my figures down to the hospital administrator and pointed out that I qualified for welfare based on what the hospital was paying me. He agreed, with great embarrassment, that I was right. I didn't go through with applying for government assistance because I wasn't interested in shaming an institution for which I had great respect. I'd made my point. That was enough.

Roosevelt's emergency room popped and snapped. Here I learned the formula that governed whether "jumpers" would live or die. If someone attempted suicide by jumping from the third floor or lower, the jumper's chances of survival were fair. Higher than that and the attempt usually succeeded – but often after a great deal of medical effort was expended in trying to save someone who had already decided his or her life was not worth living. I encountered some of these jumpers literally on the street because my duty included riding the ambulances to emergency scenes. I rode into Harlem and the Puerto Rican district of Manhattan many times, and it was an extraordinary experience. I delivered babies there in theaters, apartments and hotel rooms.

Roosevelt got a full spectrum of patients. From those whose poverty was hopeless enough to make them suicidal, to those whose talent made them seem more than merely human. On several occasions dancers from George Balanchine's New York City Ballet troupe were brought into Roosevelt's ER. I told Carol how impressed I was with their superb physical condition, and she urged me to go to the ballet with her. I was swacked. That's the word I would have used then – and did use for the next 50-odd years until it was pointed out to me that it is not a word one could find in any dictionary. I then eliminated it from my vocabulary. What it meant in relation to the ballet was that I was wowed, smacked upside the head, to see something so well done and so appealing to the senses. There was sound, there was drama, there was expressive movement, there was color, light. I felt that any person who had so many outlets for expression must be free of all stress and tension. Of course, the more I got to know about these wonderful artists – both through performances and in the ER – the more I realized my naïveté. Ballet is a highly competitive and demanding field that takes a toll physically and emotionally.

Yet the art those dancers produce has held my interest to this day. I was so impressed that I applied for a position as staff physician for the troupe. My name was second from the top when we left New York. If I'd been called, this might be an entirely different story.

The path I chose took me to a surgical residency at Veterans Hospital in the Bronx. I began in July, 1950, under the mentorship of the greatest surgeon of his day, Dr. Allen O. Whipple. I hero-worshipped Dr. Whipple because of his standing in the world, his accomplishments and his quiet dignity. His reputation was sterling. Even though there was always a big and respectful distance between us, Dr. Whipple was part of every decision in my professional life from the time I met him until he died. His picture still hangs in my study.

Dr. Whipple earned much of his fame long before he came to VA Hospital. In fact, he had retired after decades as the head of surgery at Columbia University's Presbyterian Medical Center before he arrived at VA Hospital to establish a surgical training program there based on his Columbia model. Dr. Whipple was known for his work on the pancreas. He devised an operation for removing malignant pancreatic tumors that is still known as the Whipple procedure. His impressive accomplishments and the respect he enjoyed in the world of medicine were not obvious in his modest demeanor.

I published my first three papers in peer-reviewed journals during my four years of residency. The first was on the surgical techniques necessary for replacing the jaw with acrylic plastic. The second was a review of about 400 cases of cancer of the tongue and floor of the mouth. The third was very closely connected with Dr. Whipple, and reported the technique of caudal pancreaticojejunostomy to treat chronic pancreatitis with pancreatic ductal obstruction. I envisioned this procedure to treat the chronic inflammation of the pancreas by draining the duct that runs through that organ. I asked Dr. Whipple's permission to try it, which he granted. He was subsequently most impressed at how well it worked. Patients who had suffered from the painful and debilitating condition would awaken after surgery and exclaim that the only pain they felt was from the surgery, the other pain was gone. Dr. Whipple said I should present my paper on the procedure to the New York Academy of Medicine, and he used his influence to get me on the program. I wanted him to put his name on the paper as co-author, but he declined. It was my idea, he said, I should get credit. Dr. Whipple did go with me to New York and introduced me, which was a proud moment. The operation was called the DuVal procedure and was used for years until somebody came along and improved on the principle I had established.

• • •

OUR FAMILY was living in an apartment in Ridgefield, New Jersey, when I began my residency. The commute was dreadful.

The 1939 Chevy had further deteriorated from the used condition in which we bought it. The front fender had a habit of flopping loose, so I drilled a hole through the body of the car and wired it on with a coat hanger. The guard at the hospital parking lot looked at it one day and said, "Doc, don't you have any pride?"

I did. It was money I lacked. With two children, the expenses were impossible. I sought a loan from an attorney named Ernest Cuneo. He was married to my mother's cousin, which gave me a passing acquaintance. My association with him was cemented when I was at Roosevelt Hospital and he brought his maid into the ER with acute appendicitis. I took her upstairs and did the operation – successfully, of course – and Cuneo and I became friends. He had a brilliant mind and an impressive list of clients. He was a confidant to New York City Mayor Fiorello Laguardia, and wrote a memoir entitled "Life with Fiorello." I talked to him about my financial situation during my residency and asked if he would be willing to give me a loan, at whatever interest rate he wanted to set, and I would pay him back when I began practicing. He agreed and began sending us monthly checks. I was still paying him back in the 1960s when I became dean of the medical school in Arizona.

We'd never had our own home, and Carol was getting tired of rented rooms, with or without roaches. One weekend, she went out and found a house to buy for $25 down. It was a bargain because the developer of the Ridgewood, New Jersey, neighborhood had gone broke before the place was finished. Our front yards were mud pits and all the neighbors had to come together to rake up debris, put up retaining walls, plant grass and add other amenities. The tasks brought us close the way people who share a common disaster often bond as a result. We held neighborhood lobster parties and spent a lot of time together socially. The two-story house was nice enough, so maybe "disaster" is too strong a word. But we did live in a sea of mud when we first arrived.

Before we moved, Pete Harrison and his wife, Joanne, moved into the neighborhood, bringing a bit of Montclair back into our lives. Another friendship developed during the Ridgewood years that would also endure throughout our lives. After Richard Stewart "Scotty" Jenkins and his wife, Dot, joined the contingent of those getting their start in that close-knit community, our families found we had a lot in common. Before long, the Jenkins and their children joined our summer treks to Maine, with Dot sometimes accompanying Carol and the kids for the long drive Down East. Scotty and I would join them weeks later. Scotty died in 1981, but both Carol and I have remained close to Dot, as well as to Pete and Joanne. Good friendships grew from those muddy beginnings in Ridgewood – where Dot once again makes her home.

It may give you some sense of the place to hear the story of Pete and Joanne's son's arm injury. I was in the shower one day when Joanne rushed into our house carrying her son, whose arm was gushing blood. I emerged, towel around my waist, and pronounced the injury superficial before returning to the shower. The access we had to each other's homes, the trust and the sense of interconnectedness reveal a lot about the atmosphere. Pete says my reaction was an example of how reliable my calm counsel could be. The wound was, after all, entirely superficial.

What Pete recognized as my admirable calm was not always an attractive attribute. In fact, in relation to our second daughter, it may have appeared to be a lack of deep feeling. It wasn't.

• • •

OUR THIRD CHILD was born when I was half-way through my residency. Her name was Nancy, and she was a gorgeous infant. She was also doomed. Nancy was born with spina bifida of a very serious nature. Her feet were deformed, she developed hydrocephalus, or fluid in the brain, and was mentally retarded. Despite surgery and scrupulous, loving care from Carol, the little girl had to be institutionalized. Carol and I got advice from doctors on the best facilities, and we picked one within reasonable driving distance. It was clean, the staff was competent and had experience caring for children like Nancy. She was a little more than a year old when we took her there. She died in her second year.

This was the most significant kind of sorrow because it involved the death of a child. But I got over it much more easily than Carol did. For her, it was extremely traumatic. I grieved. But I let it go. I think it is a characteristic of mine to put something that is unpleasant out of mind. I'm very quick to cover up and bury the past; I don't live on yesterdays. I didn't consciously turn to my professional life to get rid of the memory, but I did not delay work to go through the grieving process, either. I went back to the hospital as soon as it was expedient to do so. It was the natural thing for me to do.

Only recently did I connect my feelings about the death of Nancy and the death of my father. They deserve to be together in my thoughts. In both cases, I was being selfish in my reaction. I don't like unpleasant memories, so I sweep them away as quickly as possible. When my father died, no one really suffered as a result of my decision to turn away from the pain. The way we handled Nancy still troubles Carol. I know that. When Nancy died, the difference between Carol's reaction and mine was significant, and it made things very difficult. But our marriage and our family survived. More than that, it thrived.

As I neared the end of my residency, Carol was pregnant again. Her desire for another child overcame her fear that she might give birth to another baby with profound birth defects. Her pregnancy represented a courageous and hopeful decision for our family. Professionally, I was looking to the future as well, and hoping for a little wisdom to leaven in with the courage.

• • •

ONE OF THE SURGEONS I worked with was Dr. Russell H. "Houghty" Hooker. He had a very fine, up-scale practice in Mount Kisco, New York. He and his partner extended a very warm and enthusiastic invitation to me to join their group. It was a tempting hook, and their bait was the promise that by the end of my second year with them I would be paid $200,000 annually. That's the equivalent of about $1.5 million today. An impressive sum for somebody with a pregnant wife, two kids, a mounting debt to a family friend and a car held together by a coat hanger.

At the same time, Dr. Whipple was advising me to go in a completely different – and much less lucrative – direction. He told me I had a lot to contribute in academic medicine, and he urged me to try that first. If I didn't like it, he said, I could always go into private practice. Going into academia after being in private practice was much more difficult, if not impossible, he cautioned. He gave me the names of three top-flight surgeons with whom to interview for positions that would lead me on an academic path. He wanted me to interview with them all and select the one I liked best.

Two roads, as Robert Frost might have said. But it didn't really take me long to realize which one I wanted to take. Unlike the poet, I have no wistfulness about what might have been. To me, money is a means to an end, not an end in itself. I have never regretted my decision to follow Dr. Whipple's advice. Rather than join a lucrative practice and treat patients, I chose to do work that would make a difference in my field and shape the next generation of doctors. To paraphrase my father's nemesis, Franklin Delano Roosevelt, happiness doesn't come from the possession of money, it comes from the joy of achievement. And while I'm throwing quotes around, I toss in one more by Lecomte du Noüy:

"We all have our role to play individually. But we only play it well on condition of always trying to do better, of overreaching ourselves. It is this effort which constitutes our personal participation in evolution, our duty. ... Unless we develop our personality we will have left no trace in the true, human evolution. We will have played the part of one of the paving stones in the road, when we might have been a milestone. We will not have worked for the advent of a superior conscience."

• • •

CHAPTER SEVEN

The dean goes away

I t was Spring of 1971. The teaching hospital was nearly complete
and the first class of doctors was graduating. They were
independent thinkers who gave every indication that they'd been
paying attention when DuVal urged them to move beyond their elders.
The students who studied medicine in the building behind the stone
statue of Hippocrates had voted – with no faculty member present
– to substitute the Declaration of Geneva for the Hippocratic Oath.[89]
It was a moment to savor.

But the dean was a bit distracted. Nobody could miss it. Even in
the news coverage of the graduation ceremony, DuVal was identified
for something other than the work he'd been doing at the College of
Medicine. He was a nominee for a job in the Nixon administration,
the paper announced. It was a garnish of prestige to him and the
school he founded. Or so the paper and the community thought. Few
knew that the offer came as DuVal was helping his faculty wrestle
with its identity crisis.

Shortly after he and the faculty returned from their retreat in Tubac,
DuVal was called to Washington, D.C., and offered the position of
Assistant Secretary of Health at what was then called the Department
of Health, Education and Welfare. It was not the first time this particular
position had been offered to him; he'd been asked to take the position
twice in 1969. Nor was this the first time someone had attempted to lure
him away from Tucson. His file of job offers – along with copies of his
polite refusals – was growing thicker by the month.[90]

But the timing and nature of this offer was particularly intriguing. It was to be an 18-month assignment, which meant DuVal would not be resigning, as some of his faculty had suggested he should. But he would be going away. His absence would force the faculty to come together and begin acting like the kind of collective decision-making body DuVal wanted them to be. That was exactly the task DuVal had set for them. Some of his professors told him it would be impossible for the faculty to move beyond its dependence on him as long as he remained there. He found those arguments more convincing than the concerns of faculty members who said the school was not yet stable enough for him to leave.

What's more, unlike any of the other job offers, this one was tempting because of the man who would be his boss, Elliot L. Richardson. He saw in Richardson a man of enormous intellect who was committed to being the best kind of good public servant. Richardson would hold four Cabinet positions during his long career, more than any other person in U.S. history, and become a national hero by defying a disgraced president. Something of that remarkable future was evident to DuVal. Richardson impressed him as a person who understood the need for a well functioning bureaucracy to support the government. He respected the system. He expected it to work well on behalf of the people it served. He would ultimately resign his office as attorney general in the Nixon administration rather than follow the president's order to fire the special prosecutor who was investigating the Watergate scandal. When DuVal met him, Richardson was in the first of his Cabinet positions, and years away from that historic event. Richardson's gravitas was evident to the dean of Arizona's first medical school. As secretary of the Department of Health, Education and Welfare, Richardson handled a budget that was bigger than all but six of the world's nations and balanced duties of enormous complexity. HEW had already touched DuVal's life by making the money available to begin the University of Arizona medical school, but that was only a small measure of its tremendous clout.

As head of the health division of HEW, DuVal would be an administration insider at the heart of government. He could make things happen. He would be in a national leadership role as the changes he'd talked about to those graduating classes of medical school students began to play out in the field of medicine. His boss would be the guy who answered directly to the president. His boss would be a man that DuVal found captivating. "He was soft-spoken, exquisitely intellectual, and with a great sense of perspective mixed with common sense," DuVal recalled.

• • •

ADD URBANE and handsome to the description and you could have been talking about DuVal himself. If DuVal recognized his similarity to the man he so admired, he never said so. He did say he thought Richardson was possibly the smartest man he ever met. That was a big part of the appeal. DuVal, who had been engaged in teaching young doctors, felt he could learn a great deal from this man. Richardson could teach him about the process of government, the use of power and the practice of politics, which, Richardson told him, was not about compromise, but about the art of reconciling competing claims. Richardson would be without peer as a mentor and guide through the highest levels of U.S. government, DuVal thought.

Nevertheless, DuVal did not jump at the job. When they met in Washington, he told Richardson that he was honored to be asked, but that he was not inclined to leave his position as dean of the medical school. He merely promised to give the offer serious consideration. Then he returned to Tucson.

DuVal was being coy. Leaving the medical school at that time looked like less of a problem than an opportunity for the school to begin to mature. But there were other considerations. Carol and the children would have to remain in Tucson if he moved to Washington. The pay Richardson was offering was not adequate to support a family in that expensive city because the DuVals would also have to maintain their home in Tucson, where he would return in 18-month's time. What's more, DuVal was still repaying the money he'd borrowed during his medical training. Carol was initially cool to the idea of her husband accepting a job so far from home. The children weren't asked; this was a decision that would be made by Mother and Dad.

Richardson was relentless in trying to sway that decision his way, and he had a veritable army of assistants to help with the effort.

Much of the drama of Richardson's campaign to win DuVal would be lost in this age of cell phones and Blackberries. Those devices do not instantly single someone out of a crowd. They don't provide the opportunity to return to the crowd after being publicly summoned and report on a conversation with a high-level member of the Executive Branch. Richardson used the technology of his day to great advantage. The drama began shortly after DuVal returned from Washington. He drove to the Tucson airport for a flight to Las Vegas, where he would deliver a speech at the annual meeting of the Southwestern Surgical Congress. Before he got on the plane, he heard his name called over the public address system. When he responded to the page, Richardson was on the phone, urging DuVal to accept the job. DuVal was cordial, he said he'd consider it. When he arrived in Las Vegas, he once again heard himself being paged in the airport. When he reached the courtesy phone, the man on the line identified himself as a high-ranking officer in HEW. This man, too, urged DuVal to take the position. When DuVal checked into his hotel, there was another call waiting for him from another high-level member of HEW. Of course, DuVal didn't stop to announce to the bellboy that he was getting calls from Washington. But the calls didn't stop. At the convention, it became a topic of conversation because he was summoned for a series of calls that took him away from meetings and meals. He would return to his companions to explain that someone else with an impressive title had just called about the job Richardson wanted him to take. He'd never met most of the people who were calling, but they all said his resume revealed him to be the perfect person for the job. It was easy to see that this was a campaign orchestrated by Richardson. It was also easy to be flattered. And persuaded.

DuVal accepted the job, effective July 1, 1971. He would have to pass an FBI background check and receive Senate confirmation. But a month before he was scheduled to begin, DuVal got a call from the White House asking him to join the president for a speech to the annual meeting of the American Medical Association. It was a bit of a surprise, but even a novice bureaucrat knows that when the White House calls, it's time to clear your calendar. But if he was looking forward to getting to know the leader of the free world on this AMA junket, he was disappointed.

A driver met DuVal's plane from Tucson at Washington National Airport and ushered him to a limo for the ride to Andrews Air Force Base. Richardson met him there, and they boarded Air Force One together. Nixon arrived a few minutes later and retired to his private quarters without saying a word. When they landed in New Jersey, DuVal was directed to a small van that became part of the motorcade led by the president's car. Riding with him were Richardson, Nixon's top domestic affairs advisor John Ehrlichman and chief of staff H.R. "Bob" Haldeman. DuVal found them wonderfully interesting people, which made the revelations two years later of their involvement in the Watergate scandal all the more fascinating.

When the motorcade arrived at the site of the convention in Atlantic City, DuVal was left to wait in a room with Mrs. Nixon. Their pleasant conversation that day and at subsequent meetings left a strange impression on DuVal. He thought Mrs. Nixon, a heavy smoker, was a devoted wife, who seemed a bit cowed in her position as First Lady. Such a title could have been uplifting, but it didn't seem to have that effect on the dutiful Mrs. Nixon.

• • •

AS FOR THE PRESIDENT himself, DuVal said the description of Nixon that is attributed to Arizona's Sen. Barry Goldwater was dead on: Nixon seemed like a man who never played poker with the boys. The president was uptight, uncomfortable. He could be social and engaging, but DuVal thought it took a lot of effort on the president's part. In the dozen or so times Nixon and DuVal interacted, the president was always cordial. He was also The President, and he made sure those around him remembered that. Nixon's lack of personal charm was not the sole reason DuVal voted against his re-election, even while serving in his administration. But the vote itself says a lot about Nixon's inability to inspire confidence in the good doctor from Arizona.

Nixon did not speak to DuVal before the AMA event. DuVal was summoned from the room where he was waiting with Mrs. Nixon and directed to sit on the platform. His chair was strategically placed a little behind and to the right of the podium where the president would speak. DuVal was highly visible. When Nixon made his entrance after being lavishly introduced, the president made a point of stopping to touch DuVal on the shoulder. After the president finished a speech that DuVal found "entirely forgettable," the events of their arrival were reversed. The motorcade returned to the airport, Air Force One returned to Andrews – with the president closeted in his quarters – the limo took DuVal back to Washington National and he flew to Tucson. Nixon never once spoke to him on that trip, but DuVal understood that as the new head doctor at HEW, his presence was calculated to make points with the members of the AMA, an organization with which he had a solid reputation.

On the trip back, DuVal got a rude reminder of what life was like without all the pomp and uniformed chauffeurs. He had a middle seat at the back of the plane, surrounded by young children who seemed to be vomiting for the entire journey to Denver. While changing planes there, DuVal was delighted to see himself on the television sets around the airport as news footage of Nixon's trip to the convention played on the news. His first impulse was to yell out to his fellow travelers, "Hey, that's me up there!" But the enduring scent of the dismal plane trip he'd just finished tempered that. He remained quiet, found his next flight and hoped for calmer seat mates.

DuVal returned to Washington a month later to begin the tour of the Capitol that would precede his confirmation hearings. The first stop was at Sen. Barry Goldwater's office. DuVal knew Goldwater casually because of his position at the medical school. On one occasion, Goldwater had called to tell DuVal that he was going to be voting against a government spending bill that included money for the medical school. The senator told DuVal that as a conservative, he felt it essential that he vote against the expenditure. But Goldwater wanted the dean to know that he'd been assured the bill had enough votes to pass without his support. DuVal appreciated the phone call, even as he wondered about the integrity of the politics behind it.

As an Arizonan who was the nominee for the position of Assistant Secretary of Health, DuVal benefited from Goldwater's position and his graciousness. The senator welcomed him warmly to his office and the two chatted at length. Goldwater told him how the process of confirmation would work and took him around the Capitol to meet key members of the committee that would vote on his appointment. Sen. Edward Kennedy, who was chair of the committee, was also gracious and cordial. He assured DuVal that, based on what he knew of the Arizona doctor, there would be no problems at the hearing. He was correct. DuVal was subsequently approved unanimously by the committee and endorsed for his new job by the full Senate.

Carol came to Washington to help her husband find a place to live and to help him get comfortable in it. Expenses were an issue, and so was transportation. She found him a small townhouse near the HEW building. It was a predominantly African-American neighborhood, and it provided DuVal with a rich learning experience.

"I often think back to situations in which I found myself at the cleaners, shoemakers or some other establishment of that type, not only being asked to wait my turn, but when it was possible to do so, salespersons would always take a Black customer first and leave me to last," DuVal said. "Ironically, this did not make me as angry as it might have. Instead, it taught me what it was like to wear another person's shoes in a segregated environment. I have never forgotten that lesson."

DuVal's temporary departure from Tucson for a high-powered job in DC was a source of local pride. An editorial in the Tucson Citizen[91] was headlined "Good luck, Monte." It said, "Tucson and the UA have been fortunate in having a man of Dr. DuVal's character and ability to develop the college of medicine from scratch." Over at the Arizona Daily Star, the editorial headlined "DuVal Leave Justified," said, "It would be unfortunate if Dr. DuVal were to leave the University of Arizona to accept a permanent post elsewhere; but if he can perform a greatly needed national service he should be allowed to do so on leave." The paper clearly wanted him back when the job in Washington was done because "Arizona needs the long-term services of this noted physician and administrator."[92] In Phoenix, an Arizona Republic editorial said "Arizona's loss will be the nation's gain." It pointed out that the job in DC was "a tough and frequently frustrating one" that had "defeated several predecessors."[93]

Medical journals were also opining on DuVal's new job. The June 1971 issue of Arizona Medicine said he "must bring order from the controversy in the present problems at HEW."[94]

In the national journal Medical World News of June 4, 1971, DuVal was described as a man of "almost theatrical good looks" who was taking a job that was seen as "one of the hottest potatoes in government."

"If anybody can pull together the uncoordinated health efforts in the H in HEW, Monte DuVal is the guy to do it," Dr. William G. Anlyan, vice president for health affairs at Duke University told the journal. "He's everything aboveboard. He has the charisma to weave his way through some of the stickier wickets he'll have to face."[95]

• • •

THE WICKETS were about power. The job of the health division of HEW at that time was to oversee such agencies as the National Institutes of Health, the Centers for Disease Control, the Food and Drug Administration and the Health Services and Mental Health Administration. The heads of these agencies had large staffs and powerful, interested constituencies from the food and drug industries, universities, medical schools, research institutions and state and local governments. These agency heads were in the habit of bypassing the assistant secretary of health and going directly to the secretary of HEW.

Richardson told DuVal that he wanted him to reorganize things so these agency heads reported directly to the assistant secretary instead of the secretary. As assistant secretary, DuVal would then carry their concerns up the chain of command if he felt the need. Richardson was upgrading DuVal's job and instituting a pecking order. Those who wound up with less access than they formerly enjoyed would quite naturally squawk.

Before he left Washington, DuVal would accomplish the goal Richardson set for him. He would also have a hand in achieving things that were more far-reaching and significant than an administrative reorganization.

One of those accomplishments had to do with the reauthorization of the 1963 Health Professions Assistance Act, which had provided the funding for Arizona's first medical school. Disagreements between Rep. Paul G. Rogers, chair of the House Health Committee, and Sen. Kennedy, chair of the Senate counterpart, had paralyzed the reauthorization. Deans from medical schools across the nation contacted DuVal when his appointment was confirmed with a simple message: "It's up to you, Buster."[96] The funding in that bill was essential, and the Association of American Medical Colleges kept the pressure on DuVal to get things moving.

Although he had met both Rogers and Kennedy, he didn't know either man well as he launched one of his first efforts as assistant secretary of health. He called both and set up meetings to try to figure out what the problem was and how to resolve it. In DuVal's mind, the concern was over which "extras" should be included in the bill. Kennedy had a list of issues he wanted addressed, including the geographic mal-distribution of physicians, the imbalance between specialists and family practitioners, the growing dependency on foreign medical graduates and the quality of care at state institutions. The senator wanted the bill to address those things. Congressman Rogers didn't think they should be included in the bill. That was the impasse.

DuVal went to Kennedy and told him that the issues he'd raised were utterly reasonable and deserved a great deal of attention.

"It's not so much that they don't belong in any bill," he told Kennedy, "it's that they don't belong in this bill. By holding up this bill, you are holding the medical schools hostage for decisions that don't lie within their jurisdiction. They can't influence what happens after the student has left. They can't influence the student's mind in terms of choosing whether or not he wants to be a surgeon or a pediatrician or a family doctor. Similarly, medical schools can't control whether foreign medical graduates come to this country."[97]

DuVal had the satisfaction of seeing the differences resolved, and the wisdom to understand that he wasn't the sole reason those disagreements were overcome. But the bill he'd intervened to save did pass. The medical school dean from Arizona thought that set a good tone. The feeling of satisfaction was counterbalanced by the odd and arcane ways of Washington.

Shortly after he arrived, DuVal got a call from his brother thanking him for the thoughtful and insightful response to the letter he'd sent. DuVal was befuddled. He hadn't received a letter from his brother and he certainly hadn't sent a response. In fact, he had been feeling somewhat alarmed by the fact that he received very little mail in his important new position. His brother read to him from the letter that carried the signature of the assistant secretary of health. DuVal couldn't help appreciating the elegant tone, but he certainly didn't recognize the words. The next morning he called the Executive Secretariat, the office that handled the paperwork for the department, and asked for an explanation. He was told that the letter from brother Bill had been received and responded to along with all the other letters that were routinely processed through the office on his behalf. DuVal thought that if he was supposed to be in charge, he should get the mail. So he asked to receive all incoming mail. Later that day, it began arriving in his office in huge canvas sacks that began to pile up. Just opening all that mail would have been an impossible task, let alone answering it. DuVal called the Executive Secretariat and reversed his order. He also called his brother to tell him to send the next letter to his townhouse or risk getting another response from some anonymous person.

DuVal took his work ethic with him to Washington. He would arrive in his office on the fourth floor of what was then called the North Building (because it was across the street from the South Building) at 6 am. He would return to his townhouse at 11 p.m. But it wasn't all grinding work. He took his sense of humor with him, too.

The office adjacent to his was occupied by the Surgeon General, a man with whom DuVal did not get along especially well. After the staff offices had closed and most everyone else had cleared out, he and DuVal were often left alone working late in their respective offices. To annoy him, DuVal would light a cigar, lie on the floor and blow the smoke under an unused door that connected their offices. It gave him a great deal of pleasure because even though the Surgeon General had to know where the smoke was coming from, he never said a word.

"He wouldn't give me the satisfaction," DuVal said.

His sense of humor also came in handy when he had to testify before Congress. According to protocol, the administration provided the first witness when bills were being heard. When the subject was health, DuVal was the one giving testimony. He and Rogers became good friends and would often share a drink the night before his testimony. Rogers would sometimes warn DuVal that he was going to have to rip into him with questions that made the congressman's opposition to the president's position clear. DuVal appreciated both the warning and the good-natured assurance that there was nothing personal in this political show. Even when the harsh questions came from elsewhere, DuVal was usually ready.

On September 2, 1971, the Tucson Citizen recounted an interesting exchange between DuVal and Sen. Warren Magnuson, chair of the HEW appropriations subcommittee. DuVal was attempting to answer the senator's questions about the administration's proposed budget cuts to regional medical programs when Magnuson cut him off.

"I know all your arguments," the senator snapped. He then demanded to know what was being done "to cut down all that duplication" in the administration's health agencies. DuVal, who'd been on the job only a few months, responded that he had a man in charge of looking into that.

"He's got a hard job," Magnuson said, "every time I go down there you've changed the names of the agencies. You must have the biggest staff of sign painters in town."

DuVal replied, "Well, the administration believes in full employment, Mr. Chairman."[98]

Tucson Citizen writer Charles Turbyville, who recorded the exchange, suggested in his article: "DuVal will no doubt continue to acquit himself well at congressional hearings and behind the scenes as well. It's highly doubtful that his winning ways will result in any legislative victories for his administration. An election year approaches and there is rising public discontent with the country's health care system... "[99]

The assessment was overly pessimistic. During his tenure in Washington DuVal not only helped finesse reauthorization of the Health Professions Assistance Act, he also mediated between House and Senate to help win approval of the National Cancer Act. The pen President Nixon used to sign the bill is displayed at the Arizona Cancer Center in Tucson.

Another lifesaving initiative that he not only authored but pushed through Congress was the Emergency Medical Service Act. As a member of the White House Advisory Committee on Technology, DuVal saw the potential advantages to trauma patients from the advances being made in long-distance communication. He reasoned that this technology might be used to tighten up and integrate all of the individual elements involved in responding to car accidents. For example, linking the initial call that an accident occurred with the emergency room would alert doctors that patients would be arriving. Linking the first responders with the emergency room let the ER doctors know the type of injuries they should prepare to treat. The concept is so accepted these days that it is hard to imagine it was ever considered innovative. But DuVal and his staff spent many hours discussing the best way to achieve the coordination we now take for granted. He presented a plan to the president. Nixon endorsed the idea and told DuVal to write a bill, which the administration supported and the Congress passed.

The Women's, Infants' and Children's program (WIC) also owes a debt to DuVal's efforts. It grew out of a White House desire to expend additional money on a health program. The question was whether the money should be spent on children or on out-of-hospital drugs for Medicare-eligible seniors. The recommended funding increase would not cover both.

"Richardson bounced this one to me and, after appropriate

consultation with many of my staff and agency experts, I responded with the recommendation that it would be better to spend the money on pregnant women and their newborn infants," DuVal said.[100]

The recommendation was forwarded to the White House and massaged by the Domestic Council. What emerged was the WIC program, which was established in the Department of Agriculture to focus on nutrition. DuVal would later wonder if he'd made the right decision as he watched the escalating cost of drugs for seniors become a huge national problem in succeeding decades. But the success of WIC in improving children's health is an achievement that can't be dimmed simply because subsequent administrations failed to address the needs of elders.

DuVal's years in the emergency room gave him the inspiration to push an initiative of his own. In New York City hospitals, he'd seen the results of a violent culture in which guns were plentiful and easy to get. After patching together so many bodies that had been ripped apart by bullets, he reasoned that preventing those wounds would be better – and cheaper for society – than treating them. He had no problem with guns as historic relics. They didn't bother him at all when they were mounted over the mantle. Nor would he quarrel with the interpretation of the Second Amendment that made gun ownership an individual right that enjoyed almost sacred status. He disagreed with that interpretation, but he wasn't inclined to quarrel with it. He thought he had a better way.

He called in the legal counsel of the FDA and asked if he could use product safety laws to regulate the sale of ammunition. Amid the sound of jaws dropping, DuVal insisted that he was, indeed, serious. He asked the lawyers to get back to him ASAP. The answer was unequivocal: he had no authority in the area. Any issue involving guns or ammunition was under the jurisdiction of the Bureau of Alcohol, Tobacco and Firearms.

Another issue where DuVal's recommendations ended up in the "voices crying in the wilderness" file dealt with illegal drug use. Nixon initiated the War on Drugs by declaring drug abuse to be "public enemy number one in the United States." To Nixon's credit, this was the one time in the still running War on Drugs when more federal money went to treatment of drug abuse than to law enforcement. Nevertheless, DuVal suggested waging the drug war in an entirely different way. Based on an extensive conversation he'd had with

England's Minister of Health Sir George Godber, DuVal urged the administration to look at the model then in use there. By essentially legalizing drugs and setting up clinics to supply the needs of addicts, England had virtually abolished the supply side of the problem by taking the profit out of drug dealing. DuVal talked to Richardson about this logical approach, and Richardson promised to discuss it with the president. Obviously, nothing came of it.

• • •

BUT DUVAL WASN'T done kicking sacred cows. Not yet. A bill before Congress dealt with the tar and nicotine content of cigarettes. The aim was to require cigarette makers to produce a cigarette with tar levels low enough to be in the public's health interest and high enough to prevent the emergence of a black market in tobacco. DuVal saw the bill as intrinsically flawed. The only level of tar-producing tobacco that was acceptable from a public health standpoint was zero, but the level of tar needed to avert a black market would have to be significantly higher than that.

The administration had taken a position opposing the bill as punitive and constraining on the tobacco industry. Yet DuVal saw an opportunity to do something positive for public health with this vehicle. The man responsible for developing the administration's position on this bill was Paul O'Neill (the same man who to was became chairman of ALCOA and later Secretary of the Treasury in 2001). DuVal called him with an idea. He wanted to use the testimony he would give for the administration on this bill to point out the benefits to the public health of requiring reduced levels of tar and nicotine in cigarettes. O'Neill said he would consider DuVal's suggestion. On the day he was scheduled to give testimony, DuVal was still waiting to be told the administration's position. He was to appear before Congress at 10 a.m., but the morning wore on without a word. At 9:30, he was told the administration would oppose the bill. However, DuVal was given permission to bring up his ideas about the potential benefits of a low-tar cigarette during the question and answer session that always followed testimony. He did so, and felt pretty good about it.

Not long afterward, he got an invitation to lunch.

When he arrived, he found executives from the nation's top cigarette manufacturers waiting with stern faces. They began by taking him to task for espousing a position that strongly suggested there were dangers in cigarettes, and, what was probably worse, that cigarette manufacturers had the ability to reduce those dangers. There were a few things he needed to understand, they said. One of them was this: What was good for the tobacco industry was good for the USA. DuVal's testimony had not been good for the tobacco industry. They wanted him to tone it down. DuVal was not cowed. He told them that he had taken a position based on what he saw as the merits of the argument, and he was willing to defend that position even in the present company. He did so, and felt pretty good about it.

A few months later at a retirement party for Sen. Lister Hill, two tobacco executives took DuVal aside and told him they had been giving his suggestion a great deal of thought. A "light" cigarette was in the works, and they wanted DuVal to take a moment to revel in the fact that he'd had something to do with the decision to try this. He felt pretty good about that, too.

A smoker of unfiltered Lucky Strikes at the time, DuVal nevertheless saw the potential for a reduced tar cigarette to decrease the amount of lung disease in the nation. To have played even a small role in encouraging the tobacco industry to move in this direction made him feel very good, indeed. His elation deflated years later, though, as the truth about "light" cigarettes began to emerge. Because of reduced tar and nicotine levels, smokers inhaled more deeply and lit up more frequently. Any health benefit was negated. Such "oops" moments were part of a learning curve. They did not discourage DuVal from expressing his views and standing up for what he believed was right.

• • •

HE HAD AN OPPORTUNITY to do just that again in the early summer of 1972 when The New York Times published an article exposing the federal government's scandalous Tuskegee experiment. The details, which are now well known, were a shocking revelation at the time. The Centers for Disease Control had begun an experiment in the 1930s that involved hundreds of Black men with active syphilis who lived in and around Tuskegee, Alabama. Their disease was left untreated. They were simply monitored while another group was given the so-called "magic bullet" treatment of alternating weekly injections of bismuth and mercury. The experiment had been ongoing through all the intervening decades that had brought better treatment for the disease.

DuVal's reaction was utter and complete horror that such a cruel experiment on human subjects had even begun. He ordered it shut down immediately and was met with surprising opposition from the people who were overseeing the experiment.[101]

They wanted him to understand that every patient – even those whose syphilis went untreated – had received regular medical treatment for every other illness or medical problem. When penicillin became available in the 1940s and was shown to be effective against syphilis, the decision not to give it to the experimental group was justified for two reasons. The first was entirely monstrous: giving them penicillin would make the study useless. DuVal found some merit in the second reason: because the subjects had been infected with syphilis for such a long time, there was a risk of serious side effects if they were given penicillin. Called the Herxheimer reaction, this sometimes fatal phenomenon was the result of bacteria dying off in such large numbers that they gave off more toxins than the body could handle. It did offer some justification for not treating the population of men who had been infected for decades. The penicillin would have rapidly killed off large numbers of syphilis bacteria, and put the patients at great risk.

Nevertheless, DuVal stuck to his decision on moral grounds. There could be no justification for continuing an experiment that harkened back to days when some people were considered less human than others. DuVal also named an advisory commission to recommend compensation for those who suffered. The shameful experiment caused many men to die from a disease that was treatable and resulted in wives and babies being unwittingly infected. Partly as a result of that commission's work, the survivors and their families received $10 million in compensation in the mid-1970s.[102] In 1997, President Bill Clinton invited DuVal back to the White House to participate in a ceremony honoring the few living survivors of the experiment. DuVal recognized it as a slightly cynical ploy by Clinton to shore up his legacy by demonstrating his commitment to minority groups. But DuVal went, and he was moved to tears by what he saw. His hometown paper, The Arizona Republic, reported that DuVal's eyes misted over as Clinton delivered a long-overdue apology.

"We made the only kind of amends we could make at this rather late date," DuVal told reporter Adrianne Flynn.[103]

While in Washington, DuVal's lessons in the multi-faceted world of politics included international experiences, as well. As the U.S. representative to the 1972 World Health Organization meeting in Geneva, Switzerland, he first got a taste of the careful protocol that lubricates such events. His staff and the staff of the minister of health from the USSR had to work out details such as where their respective cocktail parties would be held, which delegation would have the first one and who would be invited. As host of the U.S. reception, DuVal enjoyed himself immensely and he had every reason to believe his soviet counterpart was equally pleased with the social aspects of the meeting.

Undercurrents of tension swirled both around the petition of East Germany and China for admission to the World Health Organization, and the resolution that proposed censuring Israel for its treatment of displaced persons. But such controversies were common in that Cold War atmosphere. It was a ringing phone in a dark hotel room that pushed this event past protocol into diplomacy. The call that awakened DuVal was a courtesy heads-up from the State Department. Nixon was about to announce the mining of Viet Nam's Haiphong Harbor, he was told, and the White House wanted DuVal to know that before the meetings got underway in the morning. DuVal was to do everything in his power to prevent this from becoming an issue during the opening of the Plenary Session of the WHO.

In the silence of that darkened hotel room after DuVal hung up the phone, there was no promise of peaceful sleep. There was not even the hope of a fitful sleep. After considerable tossing and turning, DuVal got up and went down for a very early breakfast. He felt utterly alone. He was the head of the U.S. delegation, so there was no one to turn to for support or direction. He was expected to handle a situation of monumental international consequence simply by avoiding the subject. As he hunched over his plate of ham and eggs in the empty restaurant, he felt a tap on his shoulder. It was Nicholas Venedectov, the Soviet deputy minister of health. In English that he'd honed during three years in post-graduate study in the U.S., he asked simply, "What the hell did you do that for?"

There was no doubt what he meant. Venedectov also had the look of man who couldn't get back to sleep after receiving a high-level phone call.

"I had nothing to do with the decision," DuVal responded. "I was just told to try to avoid the topic."[104]

Venedectov had been given the same instructions, and the two men agreed that neither would raise the subject. The bond of silence grew into a friendship. A year or two later, Vanedectov represented the USSR while DuVal represented the U.S. at a ten-day meeting in Oxford, England, that was designed to discuss the strengths and weaknesses of health care systems around the industrialized world. Most evenings, he and DuVal would club crawl through the underground pubs of Oxford, drinking beer and offering the kind of blunt assessments of their respective systems of government that they would never dare to voice during the official meetings.

In 1972, DuVal's lessons in international relations continued when he headed the U.S. delegation at the Western Hemisphere Ministers of Health in Santiago, Chile. While he was at one of the numerous meetings, he was handed an official-looking envelope. Inside, he found a brief note from Chilean President Salvador Allende inviting him to lunch at noon the next day. DuVal accepted, of course, and had the rest of the day to think about this odd and unexpected request.

In the language of diplomats, one would say that relations between the United States and Chile deteriorated after Allende was elected in 1970. He was the first Marxist democratically chosen to lead a nation in the western hemisphere, and he raised U.S. ire when he nationalized the copper mines shortly after taking office. In the language of those late-night pub crawls, one would say the U.S. loathed Allende. The process of nationalizing the largely U.S.-owned copper industry had been going on for years through negotiation and compensation, but Allende saw this as kowtowing to the U.S. When he took office, he rejected further compensation and immediately claimed the industry, ignoring the protests of the U.S. State Department. His policies fueled soaring inflation and food shortages, which led to violent protests by both his supporters and his opponents. The CIA supported the Chilean military leaders who opposed Allende. When the president of Chile invited DuVal to lunch, Allende was only a year away from being violently overthrown by Gen. Augusto Pinochet.

• • •

THE CORDIAL and private luncheon at the palace was attended only by Allende, his wife and DuVal. Allende, a physician, may have seen DuVal as a natural ally because of their shared profession. DuVal was overwhelmed by the graciousness of the welcome, but he was also aware that he was being groomed. There was no other way to explain this extraordinary meeting. Allende wanted DuVal to take a message back to the U.S. government. He acknowledged that Chile did not know how to run the copper mines. He wanted help. He wanted the Americans back. DuVal was asked to tell Washington that the Americans would be welcomed back to Chile to share their knowledge with this communist government. DuVal agreed to carry the message. He reported the entire incident to the State Department on his return and was told "thank you and goodbye."

A year later, Allende was dead and the U.S. was establishing relations with Pinochet. DuVal had no idea whether the U.S. had a role in the coup, and he didn't take the time to look into it.[105] He didn't think about it much at all, except to note that Chile had one of the oldest democracies in the hemisphere, and Allende represented the one aberration in which the people of Chile picked a communist. But they did pick him, he noted.

Hobnobbing with famous politicians, diplomats and foreign leaders was an education, but the person who made the biggest impression on DuVal during his tenure in Washington was the man whose personality had attracted him in the first place: Richardson. The two men shared private lunches and became good friends. He regarded Richardson with the same reverence he had reserved for Dr. Whipple years earlier. With Whipple, however, the respect had a great deal to do with the man's standing in the world. DuVal was in awe of Whipple because of his reputation long before they met. With Richardson, the sense of hero-worship grew from meeting the man himself, watching the way he handled situations, seeing how he used his intelligence to get things done.

Richardson used two phrases that amused DuVal. One was "Where one stands depends on where one sits." DuVal heard him use it over and over to good effect. On one occasion, a senator proposed a military medical school. Richardson asked DuVal's opinion, and the medical school dean said he was opposed. He reason was simple: "I don't think the government should be in the business of granting degrees." Richardson went along and the administration opposed the idea. At the start of Nixon's second term, Richardson was named Secretary of Defense and he asked DuVal to move with him to the

Defense Department. DuVal wrote him a letter saying he would never feel comfortable in Defense and neither would Richardson. As an aside, DuVal noted that now that Richardson was going to be head of Defense, he could make sure the military didn't open any medical schools. Richardson sent back a note in beautiful calligraphy that simply said: "Where one stands depends on where one sits."

The other expression of Richardson's that amused DuVal was "It beats the private practice of law." After seeing one of Richardson's very good ideas rejected by the president in favor of a plan that looked very much inferior, DuVal asked Richardson if such things didn't leave him discouraged or disappointed. He said, "No. It beats the private practice of law."

After DuVal left Washington, he called Richardson at home to ask it what he'd heard about the bombing of Cambodia was true. Richardson said it was.

"Elliot, should we really be doing this," DuVal asked.

Richardson's response told him clearly that the bombing had not been the secretary's idea. "Monte," he said, "it beats the private practice of law."

Left there, the phrase might have come to represent the sound of a man accepting something he should have fought against. But the phrase was not left there.

As the Watergate scandal threatened to drown Nixon, the president was fighting release of the tapes he had made secretly of conversations in the White House. The Senate committee investigating the break-in of the Democratic Party's national headquarters and the subsequent cover-up of White House involvement wanted to hear those tapes. Special Prosecutor Archibald Cox, who was also investigating the president's involvement, wanted the tapes released. Nixon offered to provide a summary of the tapes, but Cox refused. He wanted the tapes. Nixon ordered Richardson, who was then Attorney General, to fire Cox. But Cox had been appointed by Richardson with Richardson's promise that he would be allowed to do his job without interference. Richardson refused the president's order to fire Cox, and resigned in October of 1973.

By that time, DuVal was back in Tucson. When he heard the news, he called Richardson at home. "Elliot liked martinis and it was perfectly obvious that he'd had a few that disastrous day," DuVal recalled. "We talked for 15 minutes on the phone and I said, 'we, out here in the boonies, think you are a giant for standing up and taking a position on principle and acting on it and sacrificing your career.' … I made other nice words. I also said, 'I am reminded that on some occasions in the past you have used the expression 'it beats the private practice of law.' Elliot's response was again a pause. I remember it quite vividly. Then he said, 'there are times when principle has to come first.'"

After he hung up the phone, DuVal cried.[106]

• • •

CHAPTER EIGHT

My political education in Oklahoma

Back where I come from, we have universities, seats of great
learning, where men go to become great thinkers. And when they
come out, they think deep thoughts and with no more brains than
you have. But they have one thing you haven't got: a diploma.
　　　　　　　　　　　　　　　　　　　"The Wizard of Oz"
　　　　　　　　　　　　　　　　　　　　　　L. Frank Baum

I had arrived on the other side of academia. In addition to a diploma, I had a medical degree, years of clinical experience and was certified by the American Board of Surgery. I knew the secrets of the human body. I could open it up, perform the kind of controlled violence that is surgery, repair damage that might not even be visible from the outside, and restore that body to proper functionality. Though most surgeons might not like the association, these were the vaguely occult mysteries that my horoscope associated with medicine. But I was more than just a fully recognized practitioner of this arcane specialty called surgery. I was a teacher. I was ready to train others to be the medicine men and women of their age. You could say this was my calling. This is the role I chose for myself when I turned down the offer to join a highly lucrative private practice. I've never regretted the choice.

My job now was to provide students with knowledge about state-of-the-art medical techniques and procedures, and equip them with the flexibility to embrace the new methods and new knowledge that would come rushing at them throughout their careers. I had to help usher them into the society of those to whom people entrust their lives. I also wanted to keep them humble enough to remember that science can't explain everything. They needed to learn the difference between health and wellness, and that's a concept that many learned and long-practicing physicians have trouble grasping.

There are people, for example, who may present the picture of perfect "health" when you look at their X-rays and the results of their tests. Yet their complaints remain. They are sour, unhappy and restlessly searching for some diagnosis to tell them "what's wrong." They are not healthy in the sense that they have not found harmony between body, mind and environment. There are also people – physicist Stephen Hawking is a good example – who have gross and profound physical disabilities. Name a physical challenge, and they have intimate knowledge of it. They may need all sorts of medical intervention to sustain them. Yet they are healthier in many senses of the word than the malcontent whose tests all come back negative. The person with the physical challenges has an outlook that is bright, cheerful and optimistic. That person is contributing and enjoying life.

These are contradictions medicine does not embrace, but they are among the things students need to learn as they become physicians. They may be able to cure disease. That is accomplished by identifying the pathogen and eliminating it, to the extent possible. Health may result. But wellness is not the primary goal. The goal is to get rid of the pathology. This does not automatically take the patient from a state of unwellness to wellness. Too many people, both physicians and patients, don't understand that. The average person often looks to the doctor to perform some magic that will make him or her all better. Training doctors means giving them skills that can sometimes achieve that goal. But training physicians must also mean making sure those young doctors remember they are just a man or woman behind the curtain. They are not great and powerful wizards of wellness.

• • •

TEACHING WAS the work for which Dr. Whipple thought I would be well suited. I believe he was right. I relished the challenges and the interactions with bright young people. I also was moving rapidly toward situations that would allow me to reach beyond hospitals and exert my influence in politics, the arts and other community matters.

It was during these years that my hair turned white. I could attribute it to the deep thoughts and intense pressure, but genetics is probably a more honest explanation. Both my father and brother grayed prematurely. My hair did not turn gray, actually. It went silver. And rather than age me, it gave me gravity and an air of experience that my years alone might not have communicated. I rather liked it.

I began my academic years almost simultaneously with the birth of our son, Fred, on May 24, 1954. It was an uncommonly hopeful year. The first successful kidney transplant was done that year, and school children were being inoculated with Dr. Jonas Salk's polio vaccine. The Supreme Court called race-based segregation of schools unconstitutional, closing the door on an egregious practice. After years of his reckless bullying, the American people finally began seeing Sen. Joe McCarthy for what he was. The public knew the answer to the rhetorical question asked of him: "At long last, have you left no sense of decency?'

Fred and I both had our work cut out for us. For Fred, that task was mastery of all the sensory wonders of his ever expanding world. We too often take for granted the amazing journey of discovery babies begin at birth.

I was mastering my own new world.

I had taken a post with Dr. Clarence Dennis, one of the three men Dr. Whipple had recommended to me. A distinguished cardiovascular surgeon, Dennis was chief of service at State University of New York College of Medicine at Kings County Hospital. I joined the faculty to teach surgery, oversee residents and treat patients.

Like Bellevue, Kings County was a universe unto itself. One of four or five remaining big county hospitals in the nation, it had an astonishing 3,000 beds. The emergency room, which was one-quarter mile from X-ray, was equipped with 120 beds. Patients were cared for in open wards of 16 to 20 beds to a large room.

Getting to work was a long and dismal commute. Carol, with a new baby and two other children, had the task of driving me to the Erie Railroad Station at 5 a.m. I took the train to Hoboken, got a ferry to lower Manhattan and caught the subway to Brooklyn. It took one-and-a-half hours each way. When we could endure it no longer, we bought a house in Garden City on Long Island. I retrieved part of my day from commuters' limbo. Carol lost daily contact with the friends we'd made in Ridgewood.

Most notable in Kings County were the patients. Often they'd bring in some guy from the docks and say he got all banged up when a crate of bananas fell on him. It wasn't until I saw Marlon Brando in "On the Waterfront" that I began to realize the significance of these "accidents."

And then there was Willie Sutton. Yes, the famous felon who is widely credited with saying "because that's where the money is" when asked why he robbed banks. Just as some now insist Marie Antoinette never recommended a diet of cake for the peasants, some say Sutton never stated the obvious about bank robbery. It doesn't matter to me one way or the other, except that I prefer precision and accuracy to falsehoods that gain credibility simply through repetition. When I first saw Sutton, he wasn't saying anything quotable. He did, however, live up to his reputation as an escape artist. He arrived with a bullet in his chest, which I took care of. He did not wait for the rest of his treatment plan. The last time I saw him, he was flat on his back with a tube running out of his chest. He managed to pull out the tube and walk out of the hospital. He went on to rob other banks. I may have helped to eliminate the problem that landed him in the hospital, but nothing I could have done would ever have made him "well" in the larger sense of the word.

I can't say I spent a lot of time pondering such mysteries. I was humming along in rhythm with the same dynamic metropolis I had known since childhood. The hospital was a microcosm of the city, and the city was the center of the known universe. That famous Saul Steinberg New Yorker magazine cover illustration called "View of the World from 9th Avenue," depicts only wasteland beyond the Hudson River. It was done years after we left New York, but it is an accurate reflection of how New Yorkers see themselves. New York was the entire civilized world. In the summer of 1956, when I was approached about a position at the University of Oklahoma, I had to go home and look up the state in our encyclopedia. I found it to be smack in the middle of the United States. Dr. John Schilling asked me to picture myself there. He had been recruited from the Department of Surgery at the University of Rochester in upstate New York to be the first full-time chief of the surgical service at the University of Oklahoma's school of medicine. He wanted me to be his right-hand man, overseeing residency training, student education and department finances.

• • •

IT WAS A LITTLE BIT like being asked to leave Oz for a move to Kansas, which isn't that much different from Oklahoma to a New Yorker. We believed that the glittering, full-color world of New York City was where people from Oklahoma dreamed of moving to escape their dreary existence. We lived lives orchestrated with the flair of a Rodgers and Hammerstein musical. They existed in black and white. Nevertheless, I found the idea of going west to be appealing. The job sounded terrific.

Throughout my career, I have been offered many jobs that carried high prestige and suitably lofty salaries. I have only taken jobs that I thought would be interesting and challenging, without regard to the salary. Donald Rumsfeld asked me to join him in the number two position when he was running pharmaceutical-maker G.D. Searle & Co., for example. I didn't like the man and the job didn't look very interesting, so I turned it down. The offer in Oklahoma City preceded that one by decades, but I did like the man who made the offer and the job promised to be an enriching opportunity.

It did not disappoint.

The move was wonderful for the kids. David and Barbara excelled in top-notch schools in Oklahoma City, and so did Fred once he was old enough to begin kindergarten. Carol and I made friendships that have endured a lifetime. We became involved with the local symphony and theater in a community where one person could actually make a difference. We did this all while enjoying the biggest house we'd ever had. Carol found us a roomy four-story right behind the governor's mansion.

It was through the hospital that I became acquainted with the man who would move into that mansion in 1959. A patient named J. Leland Gourley came through the ER one evening complaining of pain in his right hand, which he blamed on too many handshakes. It was an occupational hazard, he said. He was campaign manager for James Howard Edmondson, a young Democratic candidate for governor. Gourley and I hit it off immediately and became terrific friends. When Edmondson took office, we became friends as well as neighbors. Our son David and his boy were always together.

Edmondson asked me to serve on a statewide commission on higher education that he was establishing to look into all the universities and their Boards of Regents. I met with that group regularly for several years, producing a report of recommendations for the governor.

It's worth noting here that I was a Republican at the time, following Dad's politics comfortably and without much thought or doubt. But my friendship with Edmondson, who went on to become a Democratic Senator from Oklahoma, was easy and mutually respectful. Those were days before the kind of razor-edge partisanship that defines politics today.

Back then, a Democratic governor did not hesitate to take advice from a Republican physician. Our families shared many barbeques and, at my request, the governor wrote the rules for serving liquor in the house the medical school faculty had converted into a staff lounge. That was a time when Oklahoma was officially a "dry" state where alcohol could not be legally sold. This meant that the suitcases of every businessman contained a few bottles of booze on the return leg of every out-of-state business trip. Those who ran out of booze during a party could call a bootlegger for in-town delivery, but you had to take two bottles of rye for every bottle of Scotch because Scotch was much harder to get.

Edmondson ran his campaign with a promise to crack down on such doings and enforce the ban on alcohol sales. This won him a lot of support in that Bible Belt community. He was as good as his word. When he won office, he shut down the black market in liquor and began seizing bottles from the luggage of returning business travelers. Out-of-state conventions were cancelled. Parties lost their zest. Once they were forced to live under the constraints of the law, people of Oklahoma turned out in droves to change the law. They repealed the state ban on alcohol. Edmondson's attempt to dry up the state revealed the hypocrisy of the prohibition. Many years later I would call Arizona's Gov. Janet Napolitano with a suggestion that she try a similar tactic on the problem of illegal immigration. I felt that if people truly felt the consequences of eliminating immigrant labor, they would recognize the hypocrisy of that prohibition, too. She turned me down.

• • •

POLITICS IS A MESSY business. My political lessons in Oklahoma City included a primer on why the best man doesn't always win. When the chancellor of the state's higher education system resigned, I easily persuaded Gov. Edmondson that the perfect man for the job was Glenn Dumke. He was then president of San Francisco State College and had impressed me greatly when I'd met him during commission hearings. The Oklahoma Legislature, however, preferred a man named E.T. Dunlap, who was president of a small local college in eastern Oklahoma and maintained a keen interest in local politics. The backdrop to this – or the predictably ugly head of politics, if you will – was that Gov. Edmondson was trying to get a small sales tax increase through the Legislature. One night he called me to let me know that the position of chancellor had become a bargaining chip. He caved and gave them Dunlap in exchange for winning the tax increase. I appreciated his phone call, and told him that I entirely understood how these things worked. In reality, I was just learning about the unintended consequences of getting involved.

In New York City, the actions of one person don't seem to have much real impact. But in Oklahoma City, we could make waves. Big ones. I became very involved in local politics, which may have been part of my growing sense of duty. I began repaying my debt to Ernest Cuneo during these years, but that wasn't enough. I felt a tremendous amount of indebtedness that went far beyond him and the money he loaned our family. I had been privileged with an education, a wonderful family and an opportunity to do my work in a public sector position. I owed the public. It never would have occurred to me to dishonor either the obligation to Cuneo or to the society that had given me so much. That sense of obligation has been a driving force in my life.

It played out in several ways in Oklahoma.

At that time, the restaurants and other public spaces were still segregated in Oklahoma City. That could not be allowed to continue. The head of our Department of Psychiatry was Dr. L. Jolyon West. We called him Jolly. He organized a march through downtown Oklahoma City in late May of 1961 to demand that people of color be allowed to eat at any restaurant of their choosing. To elevate the profile of the event, Jolly called his long-time friend and tennis buddy, Charlton Heston to lead the march. Heston did, carrying a placard with large lettering that said: "All men are created equal. – Jefferson." Those of us who knew Heston as a successful movie star were impressed that he would undertake something that was so controversial at the time. Indeed, what looks like a no-brainer – that the color of a person's skin is no reason to deny that person's liberty – was not widely accepted in those days. Many people who held positions of power and respect were openly supportive of segregation, and that odious position generally did not hurt them either professionally or socially. So even though I have great personal objections to Heston's subsequent public performances as ultraconservative head of the National Rifle Association, I felt great admiration for what he did that day. I was able to tell him that myself a few years later when he and his wife Lydia invited Carol and me to join him at his home for dinner. Jolly, who had moved to head the Department of Psychiatry at UCLA, was also there with his wife, Kay.

It wasn't just the policy on integration that needed changing in the early 1960s in Oklahoma City. Local government also needed updating. The mayor and council were part-time, low-paid positions. I was among a small group that decided to elevate the caliber of these elected positions and the quality of the officials who ran for those offices. The election was a year out when we began our systematic approach. Four members of our group each took on a district and sought to find the best candidate for council to represent the needs of that district. I got the assignment of looking for a mayoral candidate. Because we knew that running our candidates for office would take money, my task also included fundraising. I approached a handful of downtown business people, mostly bankers and industrialists, and asked them to make substantial contributions. The first and most generous was Dean McGee, president of Kerr-McGee Oil Company.

We were not trying to help these powerful people buy themselves a city government, and we took steps to make sure that was not the impression or the result. For one thing, the contributors did not even know who the candidates were when they donated money. Our group, called the Association for Responsible Government, sought contributions before we identified our slate of candidates. As the name suggests, we identified our goal as being good government that was intelligent enough to serve a growing city. It was on that basis I made my pitch for funds. The association placed the contributions in a bank account while we identified candidates. When the campaign started, all the candidates' expenses were paid directly from the account. We made sure that no candidate could trace the origin of the money, and no donor could follow his contribution to a particular candidate. We got superb coverage from our local newspaper and on Election Day, our slate won by a substantial majority. The man who became mayor, Dr. Jack Wilkes, was president of Oklahoma City University when I convinced him to try politics. He took office in 1963.

Also among our friends were Oklahoma Symphony Orchestra conductor Guy Fraser Harrison and his wife Ceil. In addition to seeing them socially on a regular basis, we also helped with fundraising for the orchestra. For one of those events we were able to persuade comedian Danny Kaye to appear in a two-hour routine with the orchestra as his backup. He was, of course, superb. The packed house he attracted did a great deal of good for the symphony's bottom line. However, what happened after the show was even more interesting to me personally.

We were invited to a reception for Kaye after the event. In the course of meeting and greeting, chatting and mingling, I found myself alone with the comedian. I expressed my appreciation for what he had done for our symphony orchestra, to which he offered what was probably the same sort of generic acknowledgement he'd been providing all evening. Then I went on to say what enormous respect I had for his particular talents and the way he had chosen to use them to entertain so many people.

He looked at me with great sadness in his eyes and said, "I greatly appreciate your comments. My career has shown me that I am able to make children everywhere laugh in what appears to be great joy. But the exception is my own children. I've never been able to make them laugh."

I was totally lost. How do you reply to such a personal revelation from such a public man? Why would he say such a thing to a complete stranger? I said the only thing I could think of, with a physician's hope to make him feel better.

"Your business, at which you are uncommonly successful, is to make children and adults laugh," I said. "At home, your business is being a father and I suspect that is the way your children wish to see you, rather than as a clown."

"I don't think I have ever thought of it that way, thank you," he said.

I felt deeply rewarded by his response.

• • •

I WAS LESS introspective about my own efforts as a father. I was –
and remain – enormously proud of my children. But as I began teaching
and taking on more and more responsibilities, my dedication to my
work became almost an obsession. I couldn't let go. Even on vacation.
It was a long trip from Oklahoma, but each summer, our family
would return to vacation at the Nubble in Maine. Generally, Carol
went out a few weeks early with the children and I joined them later.
I relaxed a bit more and enjoyed the company of my children more
during these vacations than I usually took the time to do. But I did not
stop working just because I was not at the hospital.

Around the Nubble, anglers caught bottom feeders they called
Dogfish. I knew from my studies that these fish had two separate organs
to perform the function that a single organ, the pancreas, performs in
humans. The way in which the human pancreas successfully performs
two separate and discrete functions had fascinated me since my days
with Dr. Whipple. I thought perhaps I could learn something about
the human organ by seeing how the fish's separate organs functioned.
What, for instance, would happen if you tied the pancreatic duct and
kept the pancreatic fluid from getting to the digestive tract? It should
not impact the insulin production in the fish, because that function
was being performed by another organ. I rigged up a special operating
board that enabled me to keep the fish's head and gills submerged
while the rest of the body was out of the water and accessible. I would
tie the pancreatic duct or perform some other modification, sew the
fish back up and put it back in the water on a long leash to monitor.
They did quite well through the operation, but you cannot keep a
fish like that alive on a leash for long. They are meant to swim free. I
ended up abandoning the experiments.

This was a manifestation of my workaholism. Yet Barbara has
fond memories of my fish operations because the kids in the area
were fascinated and would gather 'round for an impromptu anatomy
lesson. As a teacher, I was happy to oblige. In one case, the fish was
pregnant and the babies came spilling out. Barbara caught them in
a bucket and ran to release them in the water. She always showed
an inclination to help others. Her instinct with the baby fish was
characteristic of the course she would follow later in life.

I never shared these experiments with Dr. Whipple, because nothing
really valuable came from them. But I did keep in touch with my
respected mentor and was honored when he accepted my invitation

to serve as visiting professor in Oklahoma City. I wanted my students to have a taste of his competence, modesty, integrity and capacity for caring, which served as a model for me all my professional life. Our students and faculty were suitably thrilled to have this accomplished man share his knowledge, if only for the brief time he was there. Not long after he visited us, he died quietly in his home.

During our years in Oklahoma, we made a point to share family dinners together and discuss the serious things that were going in the world. These were "heady" discussions that were aimed at getting the kids thinking beyond their backyard. Fred says that might be where he got his interest in politics. He showed his inclinations early, although he has since changed party affiliation. During the campaign of Republican Henry Louis Bellmon for governor, eight-year-old Fred made campaign posters for him out of shirt cardboards. Bellmon was so impressed that when he took office in 1963, he invited Fred to the Governor's Ball. Carol and I attended as our son's guests.

Carol and I also had a remarkable experience as a result of a trip we took to Mexico with my boss, Dr. Shilling and his wife, Lucy. While I was at a meeting about surgical procedures, Carol went on a bus tour that had been arranged for spouses. She sat next to a woman who was a pediatrician from what was then called the Soviet Union, a nation with which the United States was at Cold War. Although there was a distinct language barrier, this woman doctor and Carol hit it off quite well. Two years later, a group of physicians from the Soviet Union stopped in Oklahoma City during a tour of the United States. We thought they might enjoy visiting a private home, so Carol and I invited them to dinner. When the group arrived, we were surprised that the first person through the door was the pediatrician Carol had gotten to know in Mexico.

This delightful coincidence set the tone for a wonderful evening of conversation about the difference between our countries, although there were limits. I was talking about freedom and choice when the leader of the Communist group asked that I go no further. Nevertheless, he and I opened a long-distance discussion by mail after the group returned to the Soviet Union.

Our home was a great place for entertaining and we took full advantage of that. Carol frequently had neighbors and friends in to share coffee on a charming stone patio under the second-story window. During one of those gatherings, Fred opened the upstairs window and tumbled out, landing on his head near the group. He was rushed to the emergency room of my hospital, while I was in surgery, about halfway through a Whipple procedure.

A little context it important here to understand how this family emergency played out. The operation I was performing to remove cancer from the head of the pancreas usually takes four or five hours, and does not generally have good results because of the nature of the underlying disease. I began with particular optimism about this patient's chances, however, because I felt I could remove all of the tumor. When one of the emergency room officers came to tell me that my son was in the ER, the stress was incredible. As a father and husband, of course I wanted to be with my son and wife. As a surgeon, I knew that the patient's needs were better served by me than anyone else available at the time. I decided to remain and complete the operation. I trusted that the doctors in the ER were entirely up to the challenge of serving Fred's needs.

That night, I was beside my son in the intensive care unit. He recovered completely, with no adverse effects. What's more, my patient beat the odds and became one of a very unusual group of five-year cures. His case was later written up in surgical literature as a success story.

• • •

THE TRADITIONAL DEFINITION of success as the achievement of a desire or aspiration can certainly be applied to a patient who regains health. The surgeon also enjoys that achievement. But defining success can be a remarkably relative and elusive task. I have a hard time, for example, applying it to a "successful" actor like Charlton Heston, who stood up for humanity with us in Oklahoma City but made one of his last public appearances with a gun raised above his head vowing that only death would wrench it from his hands. At what did he succeed with that gesture? Certainly nothing that could remotely be associated with the betterment of humanity. For the actor, Danny Kaye, one wonders if he felt success as a father was more elusive than success as a comic. These days, the public gobbles up gossip about the private troubles of celebrities. But what can anyone ever know of how the "successful" define success? In my own case, my success as a surgeon and a teacher provided great personal satisfaction. But my success at an endeavor I'd undertaken for the sake of the medical school proved a little too effective for the powers who presided over the Oklahoma university system. In the course of my work, I had been assigned to find a way to promote the interests of the medical school in the Oklahoma Legislature. I went about it in the most pragmatic and sensible manner I could devise. Rather than engage in a lot of idealistic talk about the value of a medical school, I let the politicians know it was in their selfish and political best interest to be good to us. It was a three-pronged approach.

First, I took a look at patient records, not by name or nature of the complaint, but by postal code. I identified which parts of the state were sending us patients. Then I built charts that compared the number of patients we served from each district with the number of votes by which the office holder from that district had won the election. I could go into almost any lawmaker's office and show him that the number of people we'd taken care of from that district exceeded the number of votes by which he had won office. Lawmakers learned that the hospital represented an enormously powerful constituency. This technique was especially effective when combined with a service I began providing to our lawmakers.

I set up a very small group of physicians that took care of lawmakers. We had enough diversity to provide any type of care necessary. Some of the requests were routine things that a rural lawmaker might need during sessions far away from home at the Capitol. Others were somewhat extraordinary, such as the lawmaker who'd sustained scratches on his back from a visit to a prostitute. We fixed him up and gave him a good excuse to take home to the wife. There were also those social diseases that lawmakers didn't particularly want to discuss with the family doc. Needless to say, for the routine and – particularly – the extraordinary services, lawmakers were extremely grateful to our doctors.

The third prong was to create a group of physicians who were willing to lobby lawmakers. They made sure the legislature knew the implications of the data we collected about the hospital's constituency. They also made sure lawmakers knew that our doctors were ready to help them out with any medical problem – in complete confidence.

Through these three strategies, the college of medicine established itself as vitally important to lawmakers. That was my goal, and it succeeded. Lawmakers knew we represented a large and important constituency, we had provided personal – and perhaps marriage-saving – services to lawmakers, and we weren't shy about using our political clout. Our productive and close relationship with lawmakers made us stand out in Oklahoma's system of higher education, which included more than a dozen public colleges and universities. That system of higher education was represented by a super board of regents that had considerable political clout of its own. To the regents, the college of medicine was one small part of the whole complex of higher education that they represented. They saw us in that context as they began preparing a massive bond measure.

At my urging, representatives from the college of medicine went to the board and made a case to include the cost of a new teaching hospital in the bond. We had an excellent argument. Our hospital was a 19th century antique. It could barely meet the needs of students and patients. It would badly fail to meet their needs in the very near future. But new hospitals are expensive. The board turned us down. Board members felt the cost of the hospital would sink the entire bond measure. They weren't willing to take a chance. As representatives of the whole university system, they made the practical choice. If I'd been in their position, I probably would have made the same decision. They were being good stewards of the entire system, and I've always felt that the needs of an institution are more important than individual needs. I didn't blame them then – or later – for deciding to sacrifice a new hospital for the sake of winning an election.

But I wasn't representing the entire system, and that gave me a different perspective. I was being a good steward of the college of medicine. It was in the best interests of the medical school for me to use the political good will we'd established at the legislature on behalf of a new hospital. So I did. We went to lawmakers and asked them to add a separate bond issue to the ballot for construction of a new teaching hospital. It would pass or fail on its own merits. What's more, voters could reject it without rejecting the larger, system-wide bond question. That's the way I saw it.

It wasn't hard to find people to support a new hospital. I gathered a small group to work on a campaign of public education. I also got in the car and visited Rotary Clubs and other civic organizations in communities around the state. Our campaign spoke directly about the consequences of failing to upgrade a hospital where many people in the state had received health care, and many more might someday arrive in search of care.

When the votes were counted, the hospital won. The larger bond measure for the university system did not. Voters rejected that one.

This was success. I had orchestrated it. But it cost me. There was a great deal of resentment directed sharply at me from the board. If my measure hadn't been on the ballot, theirs would have had a better chance. That's the way they saw it. They lost because I acted against their expressed wishes.

Up until this time, I had a field of opportunities to contemplate in Oklahoma. I was popular at the college of medicine, in the legislature and among all those civic groups I'd been visiting. I was so popular with business leaders that they took me up on my idea of creating a medical center complex around the new teaching hospital. The complex eventually included the Presbyterian hospital and the Dean McGee Eye Center. As architectural plans were being developed, I urged the designers to accommodate a substantial dip in ground level on the eastern end of the proposed site of the new hospital. They labeled the area "DuVal's Ditch" on their plans and the name stuck. The name also applied to my standing with the board. I was not held in high esteem. Up until this time, I was getting signals that I should think about seeking the position of dean of the medical school or even the presidency of the university. But after the election, the regents made it clear that they wanted no part of me in either job. What's more, E.T. Dunlap, the fellow who got the job as chancellor despite my efforts on behalf of another candidate, also held me in low regard. I felt that he, too, would be ready to block my advancement. I'd ripped my knickers on that bond issue and foreclosed any real opportunities to move up.

Yet those Oklahoma years were more about gain than loss. Our family grew strong together there, with wonderful educational opportunities and fine friendships. Carol and I learned the joys of becoming involved in community arts organizations. I gained experience in courting small-town civic groups and state legislatures that would be extremely valuable in Arizona. We also added that most quintessentially American of elements to our family tableau: a dog.

• • •

HER NAME WAS BETSY. When I first saw her, she was in the kennel where dogs were kept prior to being subjected to surgical research at the hospital. I have very strong feelings about using animals in research, and subsequently took actions that resulted in the use of fewer of them at the University of Arizona. I do believe their use is necessary in some cases, however, and I think it is acceptable if it is humanely done. Whenever an animal is used for experimentation, it must be treated with great respect for the fact that it is a sentient creature. I feel very protective about animals and care deeply about them. Yet there are times, such as with new pharmaceuticals, when it is essential that tests be done on something that is alive.

Betsy, however, was an animal I could not bear to see used and sacrificed. She was a short-haired mixed breed with a strong dash of Rhodesian ridgeback and German shepherd. She had a very appealing manner, even behind the bars of a cage. One day, I took her out of the kennel, put her in my car and drove her home. She adopted our family and we welcomed her into it without hesitation or reservation. She took a particular fondness to Fred. When he was old enough for school, Betsy would walk with him to the bus stop and wait until he got on the bus. With an exquisite sense of timing, she would walk up to the bus stop and be ready to greet him when he returned home. She was truly a member of the family.

Late one afternoon, Carol called to say she thought Betsy was pregnant. Not long afterward, we took her along on a trip to visit friends in Kansas City. That night she gave birth to 10 puppies in their garage. Nine survived and eventually found homes with friends of our family. The next time Carol called me at work with news of Betsy, it was to tell me she thought the dog was in heat. I immediately went home, brought Betsy back to the lab and spayed her. That terminated her reproductive years, but she remained a part of our family throughout our time in Oklahoma

When we moved to Tucson, she came along for the adventure of a lifetime.

• • •

CHAPTER NINE

Controversy, courtrooms and a fast car

The return from Washington was more heartache than homecoming. It didn't help that DuVal had been warned. He never imagined it would hurt so much, and in so many ways. Tucson was his home. The desert his element. The community his personal cheering section. That's the way things always had been. The political games lawmakers played with funding for the medical school were about a long-standing rivalry between Phoenix and Tucson. They weren't about DuVal. He had to deal with the challenges this rivalry presented, but he never felt like he was the target of any animosity from adversaries. They weren't putty in his hands – but they were malleable. Well liked and well treated, DuVal was so much the silver-haired golden boy that some suggested he consider running for the U.S. senate, an idea he rejected for several reasons – not the least of which was the simple fact that he loved what he was doing. He only went to Washington with the understanding that he'd be returning to Tucson – and the UA College of Medicine – when his assignment was done.

He had turned down presidencies of four universities to stay in Tucson. When Harvill retired in 1971, DuVal received a petition asking him to apply for that job. The petition had the signatures of so many UA faculty members that he liked to joke it could be coiled like a roll of toilet paper. He tucked it away and treasured it. There also was a lot of pressure to take the job at Michigan State at Lansing. The presidency of the College of Maryland, not far from the Capitol, looked briefly appealing. But DuVal thought there was some truth in the old joke that the job of college president was equal parts babysitting the undergraduates, finding sex for the athletes, arranging parking for the faculty and providing sports for the alumni. It looked too broad and too shallow. When his friend, former Gov. Sam Goddard, nominated him as president of Harvard, he took it as a tremendous complement. But he didn't pursue it.

He knew that university presidents did far more meaningful work than fundraising and back-slapping. He also knew the challenge and satisfaction – not to mention success – that raising money for a worthy cause could provide. He'd persuaded people to support financial needs of the hospital in Oklahoma City, the UA medical school and hospital, as well as assorted charities and arts endeavors. It had been professionally necessary and, in the case of charities and the arts, part of his civic duty. But university president? He knew that job wouldn't be as soul satisfying as building something. It could never be as rewarding as seeing a medical school – his medical school – rise on the desert.

So after eighteen months in Washington, DuVal was ready to go home to Arizona. He missed puttering around the yard of the family's El Encanto home, where cactus ruled the front yard and such arid-land staples as oleander provided a softer look in the back. During his stay in Washington, he'd often return on weekends eager to tackle a to-do list of home and yard chores. Barbara's future husband, Bill Fenster, tried to make points by performing some of the odd jobs while DuVal was away. While he appreciated it, DuVal was also disappointed when he arrived to find that he'd missed an opportunity to play gardener and handyman. His heart was in his desert home.

His heart was also about to break, both poetically and physically.

For a man educated in the classics it was only appropriate that DuVal would plant the seeds of his own misery. Like the hero of a Greek tragedy, his hubris got him in trouble. He thought he could handle any obstacle. And why not? He always had. He thought he could handle any person. Again, why should he doubt abilities that had not failed him yet? His reasonable approach, his cool logic, his commanding presence, his engaging manner had always seen him through. His powers of persuasion were legendary, even at the notoriously tightfisted Arizona Legislature. When Carol spoke before a legislative committee in favor of funding for the arts, one lawmaker told her to ask her husband if she needed money because "he gets it all." DuVal was used to getting his way.

So he ignored the advice of friends and hired a man he'd once shared a room with during his training at Roosevelt Hospital. He considered Dr. Erle E. Peacock Jr. a friend as well as a highly capable surgeon and teacher. But when he picked Peacock to be the first head of the department of surgery, "my friends told me it was a mistake," DuVal said.[107]

Peacock's qualifications were impeccable, but some saw him as too focused on his goals for the department of surgery to be a team player. DuVal, whose vision of the medical school included a great deal of team playing, dismissed the concerns. He was confident of his ability to resolve any conflicts in his own favor. "I thought, 'we've both got big egos, but I'll win,'" DuVal explained.[108]

He also believed Peacock would help the new medical school build a first-class surgery program. "He was very talented, he brought a lot to the table," DuVal said. He also brought a style that DuVal found counterproductive.

The periodical Medical World News wrote in its March 22, 1974, issue that "Peacock made a strong first impression … when he joined the staff at the University of Arizona's fledgling medical school in Tucson. The quality of surgery in Tucson was less than inspired, he informed a staff meeting at a well-established local hospital. But it would improve, he assured his listeners, under the influence of the new medical school's surgery department – which he was then in the process of organizing." The article noted that Peacock was well-known for work on surgery of the hand and control of scarring, but "with that speech he began acquiring a different reputation – one for outspokenness and controversy."[109]

DuVal's goal from the day he began planning the medical school in that makeshift office was to involve, not alienate, local doctors. He felt cooperative relationships were in the best interest of the medical school as an institution. During the early years, such relationships were essential for pragmatic, as well as philosophical reasons. The medical school would have to rely on local hospitals to place interns and residents until the teaching hospital was able to handle them all. Even after the teaching hospital was ready, DuVal did not want his medical school to play the role of Lone Ranger. There was more to be gained from overcoming the town-and-gown phenomenon, which too often left local doctors feeling resentful and medical school professors feeling isolated. It was counterproductive for the head of surgery to appear to be diminishing the quality of the local surgeons. DuVal wanted polite, gracious and cordial relations between his faculty and community doctors.

Shortly after he hired Peacock, DuVal was called into Harvill's office. The university president informed DuVal in his careful and studied manner that he had encountered "considerable opposition"[110] from local physicians to the idea of Peacock heading the surgery department. DuVal told Harvill not to worry. He could handle this.

He was wrong.

While DuVal was away in Washington, he received a congenial and chatty letter from Peacock outlining his efforts on behalf of the department of surgery. Peacock had ideas that he wanted to share. He was informing his boss about an effort that was well underway. DuVal sensed that Peacock was quite proud of what he was doing, and he expected the dean to be proud, too. After all, Peacock was devoting his considerable skill to creating the best department of surgery in the country. How could the dean not be thrilled? DuVal, however, found the things Peacock was doing to be alarming and potentially damaging to the school of medicine.

Peacock's idea was to transfer patients to the university hospital from a residency program that long had been operating out of local hospitals. DuVal believed the move would eviscerate that program, deny patients to local hospitals and set UA's teaching hospital apart from the community. While some might argue that the existing residency program would be obsolete because of the medical school teaching hospital, DuVal did not feel that way. What's more, he wanted the medical school to take advantage of the resources in the community. Yet Peacock was negotiating with Pima County and taking other steps to accomplish his ambitious agenda.[111]

DuVal expressed his concerns by return mail on April 4, 1972:

"I am not able to make a judgment as to the ultimate significance of your references – especially when I am at this distance from Arizona – but I have communicated my concern to Jack Layton [serving as acting dean] who is examining it from a closer vantage point. If the evidence shows that you have taken these actions unilaterally, and without appropriate consultation with the Office of the Dean, in the mistaken view that what is good for the Department of Surgery is good for the College of Medicine, I would have no choice but to conclude that this was a serious breach and overextension of your responsibilities as a Department Head and, at the least, I would have to indicate to you that you had lost my confidence.

"Perhaps this is as good a time as any to repeat something I know that I have told you before. You have done a remarkably fine and stimulating thing for the developing College of Medicine of Arizona by the manner in which you have represented surgery. Unfortunately, the same skills and techniques with which you have vested this effort are also capable of destroying it. One of the hallmarks of great institutions is that its whole is always greater than the sum of its several parts. Within such an institution, anyone who puts the satisfaction of the needs of one of the parts ahead of the concern of the whole is infinitely more apt to damage the whole than he is to improve the part. I hope that the evidence will not show that this risk is currently being run by the Department of Surgery."[112]

DuVal saw the institution that he and others had worked so diligently to build as being far more important than the aspirations of any one person or department, no matter how high-profile that department. No matter, even, that the department was surgery, DuVal's own specialty. As a fellow surgeon, DuVal understood what he called "the nature of the surgical personality," which he described as outgoing, pleasant, strong-minded and aggressive.

"You can almost tell when you meet the freshman class who the surgeons are going to be. You can identify them," he said. "Nurses will say they'd rather work on the surgical service than any place else because those guys are just nifty. But they are also controlling. When they become department heads, they want to run roughshod over everybody else."[113]

DuVal knew local hospitals had a stake in the existing residency program. They might be willing to see a gradual lessening of its size and importance, but they would not take kindly to watching someone try to systematically dismantle it. One local hospital informed DuVal that if the surgical residents were shifted away from its program, the hospital would close its doors to the medical school's pediatrics residents. That would represent a significant loss because the head of pediatrics, Vince Fulginiti, was establishing what DuVal thought was a wonderfully successful program by reaching out and involving the community and its doctors.

As he prepared to return to Tucson, DuVal felt a little like he was planning a cookout while watching dark clouds gather. He was hoping the storm would not break until he was able to exercise his remarkable powers of persuasion on Peacock. But the rumble of distant thunder was unmistakable. In early 1973, he got a letter from Jack Layton telling him: "You're coming home soon, and I have to tell you, you are going to face one nasty problem."[114]

The Silver Fox flew home and tried the silver-tongue approach. He told Peacock that he admired what he was trying to do for the department of surgery. "If you were at Harvard and had many, many years experience, you could do this," DuVal recalled saying. "But I can't hurt all the other departments in the medical school just to make a strong department of surgery."

DuVal felt Peacock was not persuaded. So DuVal removed him as head of the department of surgery in the fall of 1973. These internal personnel matters were traditionally handled in private. No one had to know the reasons. No one benefits from airing the family laundry. But this time it wasn't that easy. Peacock remained on staff as a professor and a cadre of supporters coalesced around him. Even after an acting department head was named, his supporters treated Peacock as though he were in charge. Peacock sued the Board of Regents and the university. He sued DuVal. He told his story to the press and won public sympathy.

Local newspapers had gushed about DuVal's remarkable accomplishments when he left for Washington. Now they clucked. They raised questions about whether he had assaulted the time-honored traditions of academic freedom by removing Peacock. They weren't happy that the state might get stuck paying a settlement in a personnel matter. DuVal's air of personal authority and command had been lavishly praised when he was raising money to erect the medical school, but now these attributes were portrayed as high-handed and imperial.

Both Peacock and DuVal were powerful leaders and both attracted a committed following within the medical school and the community. It became a bitter fight. There were allegations – denied by Peacock – of threats against the medical school.[115] There were allegations that DuVal was a tyrant. The campus paper was particularly hard on DuVal.

"The institution got a bloody nose and I got a bloody nose," DuVal would say decades later. "It was the public's perception that things were not good at the medical school. That is a terrible blow when you've worked so hard to get something off the ground."[116]

Tucson was very much a college town in those days. A great many people depended on the campus either directly or indirectly for their livelihood. Now that the medical school was no longer a novelty, it was expected to live up to extremely high standards for the sake of attracting even more jobs and prestige to the community. The local newspapers had done a lot of "gee-whiz" stories about the medical school. That wasn't news anymore. But a dispute over a fired head of surgery was juicy stuff. The press played it up big. The day's news was the topic of discussion over dinner at the DuVal residence night after night. It consumed the family. The atmosphere got so unpleasant on campus that university security installed a special button out of sight under DuVal's desk so he could summon help if someone came into his office that he couldn't handle.[117] UA President John P. Schaefer testified in court about anonymous telephone death threats against DuVal and Douglas Lindsey, acting head of surgery.[118] Schaefer did not link the calls to Peacock or his followers, but talked about the potential for violence in the volatile atmosphere on campus.

The university's lawyers told DuVal not to worry about being named personally in Peacock's lawsuit. But how could something like that not pray on his mind? He had only recently paid off the money he'd borrowed when he was in medical school. His children were not yet finished with higher education. Was this to be the end of all he had built? Of course, the rational man – the scientist – knew that the lawyers were right. But the man who remembered the story about how his father had spent a lifetime repaying a debt of honor could not help wonder how this would end. How would this effect his reputation?

• • •

NOT SO LONG AGO, DuVal had challenged his staff to come together and evolve a unified institutional identity that would transcend his role as all-knowing patriarch. Now factions were split along personal and ideological lines, his authority as founding dean was being publicly questioned and his actions were the subject of legal proceedings.

During one phase of the court battles, DuVal did something he later characterized as a truly noble gesture. It involved Dr. Harvill, a man for whom DuVal had an enduring respect and admiration.

Harvill had retired as university president, but he was called to testify during Peacock's lawsuit. DuVal believed that one of the key issues in the case was whether there had been a history of problems with Peacock. DuVal had prepared a memo detailing information he'd provided to Harvill about such problems.[119] He planned to talk about that memo when it was his turn to testify. In fact, DuVal was looking forward to publicly answering those who said his decision to fire Peacock had been unfounded and unexpected. DuVal listened as Harvill, his old boss, testified.

The attorney asked: "Did, to the best of your recollection, through your end of term in 1971, did anyone express to you any dissatisfaction with the behavior or performance of Dr. Erle Peacock?"

Harvill answered: "No. I don't remember any."[120]

DuVal was stunned. When the court went into recess after Harvill stepped down, DuVal had some soul searching to do – and he had to do it quickly. DuVal weighed his desire to defend his actions as head of the medical school against the loyalty he felt for the man who had given him the chance to build that medical school. He had to choose. If he testified as he'd planned – if his statement became part of the official record – it would provide strong evidence that he had not acted rashly when he fired Peacock. It would help vindicate his professional performance, which had been widely criticized and second-guessed. But his testimony would utterly contradict Harvill.

"I couldn't make it appear Harvill had lied on the stand," DuVal said.[121]

Perhaps more to the point, he couldn't make it appear that a man he greatly admired had forgotten something of such importance to the university. DuVal pulled his lawyer aside and said he wouldn't contradict Harvill on the stand. He wanted to withhold the memo. DuVal would not do anything to hurt Harvill.

For DuVal, withholding his testimony was exactly the right thing to do at that moment. It fit his very personal definition of nobility – a concept he would continue refining for the rest of his life. The crux of it would always remain the same: nobility was doing precisely what needed to be done, regardless of the personal costs, at precisely the right moment. It meant acting without reluctance, regret or the expectation of gratitude. DuVal gave up his chance to be "right" in court for the sake of the man who had trusted him to create a college of medicine. It was a selfless act by a person who had a very well developed sense of self. For the rest of his life, DuVal remained very proud of his decision to protect Harvill, a scholar who had given him the chance to make history. Shortly before his death, DuVal cited that incident as the most concrete example he could remember of doing something that he would characterize as truly noble.[122]

When it happened, though, it was a simple matter of quietly protecting the reputation of someone he deeply respected. Harvill never knew about the dilemma his testimony created for DuVal or the decision his dean made on his behalf.

On August 23, 1974, the headline in The Arizona Republic said it all: "Fired Surgeon wins $470,000."[123] The judge had dismissed some counts and reduced the original $11 million claim to $4 million before the jury began deliberations on whether Peacock's constitutional and civil rights had been denied when he was removed as department head and subsequently fired. The jury sided with Peacock for a reduced judgment. Ironically, the story about the verdict ran next to another story explaining that a UA faculty committee on academic privilege and tenure had held two hearings into the Peacock firing and voted to support the way DuVal and the administration handled the matter.[124]

The following month, after hearing the university's motion for a mistrial, the judge ordered a new trial.[125] DuVal got the news when he returned from a 10-day meeting in England. After a sleepless cross-Atlantic flight, he was devastated to learn that the courtroom drama would have to play out again. DuVal knew what he needed most was a nap. But he was restive. Instead of sleeping off the effects of a long flight and the unsettling news, he went in the backyard to trim some very tall oleander bushes. It was 91 degrees that Sunday, September 29, 1974. The sun had weakened from its summer ferocity, but DuVal was also weaker than usual. Perched on a step ladder and reaching for a branch with his pruning shears, he felt a sharp pain in his chest. DuVal, the man, thought he'd better get off the ladder as quickly as possible. DuVal, the doctor, reasoned that his coronary arteries had shut down from fatigue and stress. DuVal, the scientist, observed with amazement that a heart attack could hurt so much.

• • •

HE COLLAPSED on the ground, unable to call out, unable to get up. He threw the pruning shears through the back window – the window into the study where he'd spent so many nights preparing to face the latest challenge to the funding of the medical school or puzzling out the shape of an effective curriculum. There was a crash, of course. That was the idea; he wanted to summon Carol. He needed help. But Carol didn't hear the window break because she was under the hair drier. In a cold sweat, DuVal lay in his beloved backyard thinking that if someone didn't find him soon, the shockingly blue sky through that untrimmed oleander branch would be the last thing he'd ever see.

Of course, Carol did come out in time, and the ambulance arrived to take him to the hospital. As if to remind him of what his work had meant to his community, the ambulance was staffed with paramedics who were there, in part, because of DuVal's own efforts. He had used his influence and powers of persuasion to encourage the necessary changes in the law so that trained paramedics could deliver emergency care at the scene. It was part of a growing national awareness of the shortcomings of the old "scoop and run" model in which ambulance drivers merely loaded patients into the back for a fast ride to the hospital. Today's model, with trained paramedics who provide emergency care before the patient even arrives at the emergency room, was not immediately accepted by Arizona in the mid-1970s. Private ambulance companies and some medical professionals were opposed to so radical a change. DuVal helped to break down that opposition and get the law revised. His efforts gave paramedics a chance to save lives. In an appropriate twist of fate, DuVal became the first patient treated by the first team of paramedics in Tucson.

DuVal arrived at the hospital where his old friend Sandy Rosenthal had also been admitted for a heart attack. While he recuperated in the hospital, DuVal's daughter, Barbara, gave birth to his first grandchild on October 11. They greeted each other, the baby in a nurse's arms and DuVal in a wheelchair at the door of Barbara's room.

He would tell his doctors that his coronary had been brought on by stress, but they pooh-poohed the idea. It was another case where DuVal was way ahead of the curve. Later, he'd be proven right about the correlation between stress and heart attacks.

After two weeks in the hospital, DuVal was sent home, where he received visits from his old boss Elliot Richardson and from U.S.S.R. Minister of Health Boris V. Petrovsky, the latter causing a minor collective gasp. A communist? As a friend? The two had met when DuVal, as assistant secretary of health, took Petrovsky on a tour of

Fort Detrick, a former Army super-secret germ warfare laboratory that had been turned into a civilian-run cancer research facility. Nixon had declared in 1969 that the United States would cease production of chemical weapons. DuVal suggested the president invite Petrovsky to tour the reconstituted facility the first day it was opened to the public, and Nixon embraced the plan. The president called this a move "from swords to plowshares" and recognized the public relations advantages of taking the Soviet minister on a tour. DuVal met Petrovsky at the airport with pomp and limousines, showed him through Fort Detrick and the two hit it off nicely. When the Soviet minister later returned to the United States on other diplomatic business, he heard about DuVal's massive coronary and decided to detour through Tucson to wish his friend well. This was another reminder to DuVal that the good things he had done in his life were not going to be eclipsed by the current controversy at the medical school. As for Richardson – his visit was the real treat. Pictures of him with DuVal outside the family's home – even with DuVal dressed in a robe – reminded the community of the stature of their medical school's founding dean. Richardson was regarded as a national hero by many for his courageous refusal to fire Archibald Cox during Nixon's attempt to stonewall investigations into Watergate.

Less than three months after the heart attack, DuVal was back in his office. The department of surgery was still in turmoil. Asked how he managed to get through days in which the medical school continued to be buffeted by controversy, DuVal would say, "How do porcupines make love? Very carefully."[126]

A year later, the controversy continued. A member of the state Legislature's House Appropriations Committee was calling for the resignation of both DuVal and Schaefer with a threat to cut off funding for their salaries if they remained.[127] State Rep. Tony West cited disputes arising from the Peacock firing as one of his reasons for wanting DuVal and Schaefer out. In the news coverage, DuVal was not referred to as "founding dean." Instead, he was identified as a man who had been "instrumental in setting up the medical school in the late '60s." It was sort of like saying Michelangelo was instrumental in decorating the Sistine Chapel. It hurt like hell.

Not all the press coverage was critical of DuVal, however. A few months earlier, on June 27, 1975, an editorial in The Arizona Republic put the blame on Peacock:

"Even though the U.S. Supreme Court this week upheld the University of Arizona's method of removing Dr. Erle E. Peacock Jr. as head of surgery, the trauma is far from over for Arizona's only medical school.

"Dr. Peacock may or may not try to revive a damage suit against the school (his first effort was declared a mistrial). He has an incredible $14 million libel suit pending against the UofA's vice president for health services [DuVal]. And he and a hard-core group of supporters have given no hint of ending agitation against their employers and the taxpayers. ...

"It is perhaps something of a perverse tribute to Dr. Peacock that he ... has been able to keep the medical school in such turmoil. Since Spring of last year, the school has been in court defending itself, fighting off organized sniping attacks from Peacock supporters and trying to serve more than 120,000 in and out-patient admissions to the school's medical clinics.

"When the school suspended Dr. Peacock as head of surgery, the administration judgment was that he was disruptive, arrogant, hostile, insulting and rude – those are the words used in the school statement. With that judgment at hand, there seemed to be little logical question of the school's right to decide how to run its business.

"But Dr. Peacock went to court claiming he didn't have a fair hearing, among other things. It was this claim that was knocked down by the nation's high court this week, in effect agreeing with the university's handling of the dispute.

"It's time that the university medical school got back to its chief business – training young new medical specialists and caring for the tens of thousands of patients who come to its clinics.

"Dr. Peacock has been an impediment to those goals. His small group of agitating followers – some organized under the banner of Surgical Educators' Defense Fund – wants to keep the pot boiling.

"At some point, the university and the Board of Regents are going to have to put an end to this nonsense. If Dr. Peacock doesn't like his $58,725 salary, and his followers don't like the university having the right to run the medical school its way, then they should be told of the clear alternative available.

"Find another place that lets a faculty member instead of the university president run the show."[128]

The controversy also attracted the attention of one of the nation's premier newspapers, Los Angeles Times. The paper sent a reporter, who wrote a very long front page story headlined: "Feud tears at heart of medical school." The April 23, 1976, account is a glimpse into a very uptight world.

"There is something of a siege mentality about Peacock and the surgery residents and interns who support him," reporter Michael Seiler wrote. "Witness the bulletin board on his outer office where tacked up is a section of Joseph Heller's Catch-22:

'Without realizing how it had come about, the combat men in the squadron discovered themselves dominated by the administrators appointed to serve them. They were bullied, insulted, harassed and shoved about all day long by one after another. When they voiced objection, the chief administrator replied that people who were loyal would not mind signing all the loyalty oaths they had to …' "

Seiler called Peacock "an angry man." Peacock told the reporter that "I knew this was a bad university … so I came here thoroughly prepared for this sort of thing to happen on a much lesser scale."

The reporter quoted Peacock as saying he was not planning to leave: "I came out here to build a great department of surgery and a great medical school, and start a renaissance in medical education that I believe is desperately needed. There's no way in the world I can turn my back on it because unprincipled men perform acts of tyranny."

In his turn, DuVal told the big city reporter, "If nothing else, it will end by erosion. There were 28 faculty in the surgery department; now it's 18 and three more are leaving soon. Peacock is going to be down to six supporters in the department. He won't be a spiritual leader then anymore. In the meantime, we've started the process to dismiss him as tenured professor. The end is in sight, no matter what."[129]

What DuVal referred to as the "goldfish bowl phenomenon" kept an uncomfortable focus on the medical school, yet the good things that continued did get some recognition. On January 29, 1976, an editorial in the Arizona Daily Star noted that investigations showed research grants were growing and so were the number of applicants for the medical school, indicating "there is still a respect for the work being done" there. The college "has been weakened, but has not yet been damaged irreparably," the paper said. "Yet there are strong indications that if the two-and-a-half year dispute goes much further there will be extensive harm to the College of Medicine, the university's training hospital and the University of Arizona," the editorial said. Noting that there were still three legal cases outstanding, the paper said it was time for "extraordinary measures" to prevent permanent damage to the school. DuVal's hometown paper, which had joined hands with him to raise money for the medical school, urged both him and Peacock to resign.[130]

Neither took the paper's advice.

Decades later, DuVal still acknowledged Peacock's brilliance as a surgeon and a teacher, but he summed up the whole thing this way: "The single biggest mistake I made in starting this medical school was bringing Peacock here."[131]

• • •

YET EVEN AS the controversy played out, DuVal's expertise was sought by an impressive list of state and national committees, commissions and advisory groups. He went through his days without being all that porcupine-careful, either. The local newspapers might have been raking him over the coals, but DuVal one-upped them when it came to maintaining a dignified profile. He became a TV star.

Shortly after he returned from Washington, the Arizona Medical Association approached him with an idea. The group was planning a call-in program about medical topics on the CBS affiliate in Phoenix. DuVal was asked to be the host. He agreed, despite the four-hour round trip to Phoenix and back that would be necessary to make each 30-minute segment. It was an enjoyable diversion and it allowed him to help educate the public about medicine, serving both his love of teaching and his conviction that well informed people make better patients.

During the height of the controversy at the department of surgery, Carol urged DuVal to do something for himself. She said it was time for him to get a car like the one a friend owned. He'd expressed his admiration many times, so she knew how much he liked it. It didn't take much convincing to get DuVal to drop into the dealership and have a look. When he came home, he told Carol he'd just ordered an ice-blue Datsun 280Z – just like the model in the brochure they'd shown him. She immediately recognized a problem. She went down to the dealer.

"Change the order," she told them. "He doesn't want blue. He wants hunter green." And she was right about the color. DuVal had to agree that what he'd really wanted was a classic hunter green roadster.[132]

Carol had been right about the car itself, too. It provided a great deal of diversion. DuVal used a back road, U.S. 89, instead of Interstate 10 on his trips to and from Phoenix. The road had less traffic and he could really open up that car. 100 mph. 110 mph. He got to Phoenix in record time to host the half-hour "Medical Opinion" program. The show became quite popular during its five-year run, even earning a regular blurb in TV Guide that told viewers the topic that would be discussed that week.

DuVal remained active in the local community, too.

An opportunity to make a difference in the arts in Tucson presented itself in a way that only a truly creative person could see. In the late 1970s, the Legislature ordered an out-of-state owner to divest itself of a number of dog racing tracks being operated in Arizona. Dog racing and arts? Yes. DuVal saw a potential source of money for Tucson's arts community. What if a group of community members pooled some money, bought a dog track and ran it for the benefit of local performing and fine arts groups? It could create a steady and growing source of revenue. DuVal thought he was on to something. He called his friend, Tucson attorney Marvin Cohen, and they drove down to the track at Amado to see how things were done. The managers were delighted with the interest from two leading citizens. They showed them the books, they fed them and they told them what dogs to bet on during dinner. The dogs the managers recommended always won, and DuVal left with more than $200 in $2 bills.

The next day, DuVal took his Z car to have the tires checked.

The mechanic put it up on the lift and popped off the wheels while DuVal waited. The guy joined DuVal in a tiny room with uncomfortable chairs and the dueling smells of new tires and old coffee.

"How fast are you driving that car, Doc?" the mechanic asked.

DuVal demurred. "Why do you ask?"

"Because the inner tubes are all fused to the tire," the mechanic said, "they musta gotten pretty hot."

DuVal had the tires changed and paid with his $2 bills.

"Oh," said his mechanic, "I see you've been to the track."[133]

That story didn't make the newspaper, but one about the dog-track dollars for the arts plan did. The way it was played made it look like the good citizens of Tucson wanted to capitalize in the weakness of poor betting folks to finance their gala arts events. The plan fizzled, and it wasn't the only one.

DuVal was named chair of the Arizona State Committee on Medicaid when he returned to Arizona. The group had worked long and hard on a plan to bring federal Medicaid dollars to Arizona. That plan also fizzled. For many more years, DuVal would be deeply involved in several more efforts to bring Arizona into the federal Medicaid plan. Nothing was fully embraced by the state. Finally, Gov. Bruce Babbitt asked DuVal to put together a plan on his own. "Babbitt was very good about it," DuVal recalled, "he said, 'I don't give a damn about committees, just take a look at it and tell me what we can do.'"[134]

• • •

AT THE TIME, Arizona was the only state not participating in Medicaid. A frontier mentality, an iron sense of independence and an aversion to federal programs meant Arizona was losing out on the federal matching money and struggling to meet the needs of low-income patients. DuVal knew a successful plan would have to overcome the resistance that had doomed earlier efforts. It would have to be market based. DuVal knew just the approach. A Stanford professor named Alain Enthoven had designed a health-care plan as a consultant to the Carter administration. It provided universal health insurance based on managed competition in the private sector. It sounded like just the sort of thing Arizona might buy.

DuVal invited Enthoven to Arizona and they sat down with some of the political leaders to discuss the idea. DuVal was excited about the possibilities as they all shook hands and parted company. But later he got a call saying the consensus was that the plan was too complicated for Arizona. A disappointed DuVal had to try again to design something his state would buy.

Using Enthoven's plan as a template, DuVal tailored something specifically for Arizona. It was 1982 before the state finally adopted the plan, but it has since become a model of efficiency that has been adopted in more than a dozen other states. Known as the Arizona

Health Care Cost Containment System (AHCCCS), it brought quality health care to many people and won praise from patients, hospitals and doctors. Services are provided through managed care organizations that contract with the state in a competitive bidding process. Instead of a fee-for-service payment scheme, the plan uses a capitation model. Providers get a set rate each month to provide care, and they assume the financial risk for costs that exceed that rate. Patients can choose from several different plans, which creates checks and balances that would have made the framers of the Constitution proud. This was one of the features DuVal found most appealing. In order to retain a sufficient number of patients to survive, provider networks have to keep quality high. In order to be profitable under capitation, provider networks have to be efficient.

The plan that evolved from DuVal's model was praised in congressional testimony by Arizona Gov. Janet Napolitano on July 13, 2006. She said, AHCCCS "provides a robust, cost effective model for other states as they and the federal government seek alternative models that can sustain the Medicaid program. Expanding the Arizona model to new populations could cut Medicaid spending without eliminating services, limiting enrollment or increasing cost sharing for the poor."

DuVal kept track of the progress of AHCCCS and became a leading force for expanding it to more and more people throughout his life. But at the time he turned it over to Babbitt, he had other things on his mind. DuVal had left the state by the time Arizona adopted AHCCCS.

Despite the fun car, the TV show and the deep roots in the community, DuVal was exhausted from the controversy at the medical school. His family felt it, too. Carol told him he needed a change. All the problems he was facing at the medical school were problems he had created, she said. He needed something different. He needed other problems to solve.

"You need to get out of this environment," she told him.

DuVal agreed, "I've played out my string here."[135]

But one doesn't have to read between the lines to see the depth of his emotion as he left the medical school in 1979. He wrote a poem in that study where he had worked so many late nights. He read it at his farewell dinner and filed it away carefully with his important papers.

I came alone in '64
A medical school to build
The fight with Phoenix had gone before
But the critics had not been stilled.

So I traveled the state
With a message to sell
And the people were great—
Maricopa as well.

The campaign indeed prospered
Matching money came through
So John, Phil and Oscar
joined up as a crew.

Paul Johnson and Don
With David and Jack
Nailed the curriculum down
On the retreat at Tubac.

Sixty-seven was busy
Days of leisure were past
Our building was finished
Just in time for the class.

Then Vince and Don Christian
Took D.M. by surprise
While Lou, Ben and Alan
Made the VA come alive.

Paul Capp and Rube Bressler
Who were stolen from Duke
Helped prove that our desert
School was no fluke.

Dan Capps from Seattle
With others as well
Joined forces in battle
To house the unwell.

Our research grants expanded
Alumni classes were three
When Peacock disbanded
T.H.M.E.P.

The reaction was awful—
But the faculty's might,
When combined with Neal's lawful
Positions, proved right.

With a past that seems stressful
What's ahead you'll endure
For our school's been successful
And its future's secure.

Fifteen years is too tough
For one person to stay
So "enough is enough"
Is my rule for the day.

But if parting's sweet sorrow
Is grist for your mill
Be assured that tomorrow
I'll be backing you still.

For my thoughts and my heart
Will remain with you fast
Because of the part
That you've played in my past.

• • •

CHAPTER TEN

My lessons in medicine from non-doctors

Traditional religion tells us that we must conform to God's idea of humanity to become fully human. Instead, we must see human beings as liberty incarnate.

"A History of God"
Karen Armstrong

As a consequence of my position at the medical school, I was invited to all sorts of things, and, if they interested me and I thought my participation would help the community or the school, I would participate. I met Mo Udall at one such event.

We had both been invited to the dedication of a stunning mosaic by Ted DeGrazia, who was a Tucson icon himself, and someone else I was privileged to know. Ted was a marvelous artist renowned in Arizona both for his work and his fascinating approach to life. He was part of the community and he took an interest in it. Ted designed a wonderful card and gave the medical school the rights to market it and keep all of the profits. It was the kind of warm and personal gesture of support that the school received from so many of the people of Tucson. But I would have gone to the dedication even if DeGrazia hadn't done that. I loved the free and graceful way his work depicted the desert and its Mexican and Indian heritage.

What's more, it was an opportunity to meet Udall, a man I respected on reputation alone. When I saw him face to face, I found he had an easy manner that was immediately engaging. We hit it off from the start. I'm a firm believer in chemistry, and we had it. As a consequence, we subsequently did a lot of things together beyond the recurring invitations to dedicate this or commemorate that. As a member of Congress from Southern Arizona, he was used to these obligatory appearances. As the founding dean of Arizona's only medical school, I was, too. When our paths crossed during such events, it was always a pleasure. But to my true delight, our friendship extended beyond the grip-and-grin moments.

When we first arrived in Tucson, Carol and I took an interest in a local theater group headed by a man named Sandy Rosenthal. He put on plays in the basement of a rundown hotel or any other place he could find cheap space to rent. Drama classes lured local talent. It was called the Arizona Civic Theater. We would sit around the dining room table with Rosenthal and plan for its growth. We set up a board of directors and I was president. This meant I could perform on stage during intermission. But my role was always the same. I was the guy who asked for money. Sandy paid me back for all of this, of course. He used his artistic sense to help me select the colors for the hospital corridors.

Now Udall had an apartment at the Tucson House, and that's how he became part of our theater world. As the theater became professional and began to bring in actors, we needed a place where the out-of-town talent could stay for the weeks of rehearsals and performances. As Tucson's premier high-rise residence at the time, Tucson House was the natural choice. It was elegant and close to downtown. It also had rooms suitable for classy parties and cast celebrations. Rosenthal, his wife Ruth, head of the UA's drama department Peter Maroney, attorney Marvin Cohen, civic leader Cele Peterson, Leo Rich, and, of course, Carol and I were among those who did our best to entertain the visiting actors and actresses. Parenthetically, I've always thought they should have named that theater downtown after Carol, not Leo, because she did so much. She held ACT together, doing just about every job they had except artistic director, which was Sandy's job. At any rate, so many well known people of Tucson were part of building the theater that it would be impossible to list them all.

Mo was one of our supporters and he loved to join our Tucson House parties when he was in town. Even when he was running for president, he'd break away from the Secret Service and come down to join us. He could have a good time with the best of them, singing with the piano and sharing his legendary wit. We made a lot of good memories. During his run for president, Mo tapped my son Fred to organize his youth campaign, and that brought us into contact with some frequency. Udall would have been a much better president than Jimmy Carter. He might even have served two terms and kept Reagan out of the White House. I remain amused by Mo's assessment: "For those of you who don't understand Reaganomics, it's based on the principle that the rich and the poor will get the same amount of ice. In Reaganomics, however, the poor get all of theirs in winter." It was during Reagan's administration that I began to be disenchanted with the more extreme ideas of the far right conservatives. I'd been raised a Republican, but I was an Elliot Richardson-Nelson Rockefeller Republican. As the party moved farther right, I became an Independent. I've never been a Democrat, though I have voted for some Democrats and I certainly would have voted for Mo Udall. Enthusiastically.

• • •

I ADMIRED MO tremendously. His sense of humor was keen and the reputation he captured with the title of his book, "Too Funny to be President," was well deserved. I treasure my copy of the book that he signed and handed to me after a thoroughly warm embrace.

When Udall began to develop the first symptoms of Parkinson's Disease, he paid me the compliment of seeking my advice with respect to where to go and whom to see for medical help. Whether or not the help I tried to give him slowed the progress of his disease I do not know. During his last few years, he deteriorated tragically. When he ultimately had his disastrous fall down the stairs, he broke several bones and it aggravated the Parkinson's to the extent that he ended up in the hospital in Washington, D.C.

When my work took me to Washington, I would stop in to see him. It was difficult to communicate with him due to the clinical destruction of his ability to speak, but I felt better knowing I had paid my respects. I only hoped that my visits, along with those of others, meant something to him. One day when I arrived at the hospital, I found Mo curled up in a wheelchair in the corridor, unresponsive and unarousable. He looked a little like a sleeping baby, although there was none of the peace and sense of promise one sees in an infant. Tears came to my eyes. It broke my heart. I knew I would not see him again. But there was something else causing my deep sorrow that day. The striking contrast between the extraordinary, dignified and magnificent human being whom I'd called friend and the pathetic, undignified figure that lay before me was tragic. This big, tall, wonderful person was simply melting away. I am a physician. I have seen the effects of debilitating disease. But this was different. This was a man I had laughed with at parties. A man who had carried life like a shining jewel, and had done so much good for Arizona and the nation as a member of Congress. Seeing him in that state changed my life and made me ask myself hard questions about the responsibility a physician has to such a patient. Those questions stimulated me to spend many years working on end-of-life issues.

There were other friends whose medical experiences made me question the role of the physician. Two in particular come to mind. In both cases, I was asked to offer my advice on diagnoses that they had received and courses of treatment that had been recommended to them. I was not the physician in either case. I was functioning in the role of a friend who had knowledge of medicine. They sought me out – separately and with no knowledge of each other – and asked me to tell as much as I could about ailments such as they suffered. I was happy to help, though sorry about the need that drove them to ask for my help.

One was not a public man so I won't reveal his name. He had an aneurysm in the arch of the aorta. His surgeon wanted to operate. My friend asked me what I could tell him about the problem and the surgical solution that was being proposed. I told him that if not treated, the aneurism would surely rupture and he would bleed to death very rapidly. It would be a horrible death, but it would be over quickly – too quickly for much hope of intervention once it happened. I also told him that the problem would most likely respond to surgery before a rupture occurred. Following successful surgery, he could live a long life. He thanked me, and he chose not to have the surgery. To him, surgery meant doing violence to the body and he didn't want any part of it. Everything I had outlined happened just as I said it would. Within a year, he was dead.

I've often thought about how he put his personal principle, his beliefs, ahead of professional advice about his health. It was a perfectly proper decision. I do miss his friendship, and I am sorry about his decision for that reason.

The other friend was writer Norman Cousins, who was editor of Saturday Review for many years. After a remarkably accomplished career in other areas, he began working on the effect of humor on illness. He was entirely correct, of course, about the impact of attitude on health. Cousins called me for lunch one day when he was in Tucson. During the course of the meal he told me his doctor had recommended a coronary bypass.

"Can we talk about this," he said.

"Of course," I responded.

"Is it risky?"

I said yes, but in competent hands the operation has a good success rate. I told him about my own heart operation, which had been a complete success.

"Is there discomfort?" he wanted to know.

"Of course," I said. "They slice your chest open and you will have a great deal of discomfort for a few days. But my feeling is that you could have a very good result."

This was a man of extraordinary intelligence and accomplishment. He was also a believer in biochemistry of human emotions as a means of fighting disease. He would say that "ten minutes of genuine belly laughter had an anesthetic effect and would give me at least two hours of pain-free sleep." He declined the heart surgery.

To him, also, surgery was an assault on the body and he did not want any part of it. He did ultimately die of heart failure.

These were very different medical problems faced by very different men. But both were treatable conditions that would surely be fatal if not treated. In both cases, these men thanked me for sharing my knowledge and refused treatment that had been prescribed by their personal physicians. I did not question their decisions. I was not my place to judge their actions, although others in my profession did.

I've always felt the best thing a physician can do is to tell the patient what you've determined is going on with his or her health, give that person the information on possible treatment alternatives and let the individual decide the course of action that should be undertaken. I can remember times when I have laid down scenarios about the unpleasant result of choice "B" in such a way that it certainly made the person look at choice "A" in a far more favorable way. I admit to trying to sway the decision. But when a patient – or friend – makes a decision, that is unchallengeable. If somebody trusts me to give them advice, I will offer it based on what I've been taught and learned as a physician. But it is not my business what someone does with that advice.

I have colleagues who fault my thinking on this, but I continue to defend a person's ability to define his or her relationship to the world. That is the heart of liberty, and it must extend to one's determination of how to leave the world, as well.

There are two other men who acted on personal principle with entirely different results, but whose decisions were also based on something far beyond their immediate welfare.

One, of course, is Elliot Richardson. This was a man whose intelligence impressed me from the moment I met him. But his personal integrity went beyond simply being captivating. It was satisfying to see a man who so valued public service that he would sacrifice his own high standing in government in order to avoid dishonoring that service. You know the story, of course. I was lucky enough to have left the Nixon Administration before the dam broke on Watergate. But Richardson was Attorney General in the fall of 1973 when Nixon began to really hear the walls cracking. The president called on Richardson to fire special prosecutor Archibald Cox. Richardson refused. By resigning in protest rather than following this unacceptable order, Richardson kept his honor as the administration lost credibility.

The final man in this group of four was Dr. C. Everett Koop. His friends and colleagues called him "Chick." I'm sure you can figure out why. Chick graduated from Dartmouth a few years before I did. But I didn't know him until after we both finished medical school and took up careers as surgeons. Chick distinguished himself primarily as the architect of techniques for separating conjoined twins. He and I became friends through our joint membership in the American Surgical Association. When Ronald Reagan became president in 1981, he needed someone he could appoint as U.S. Surgeon General. Because of his personal philosophy, the president wanted a very conservative candidate. Reagan's search team turned up Chick Koop, a very religious and pro-life conservative. He was so conservative, in fact, that when he came before the Senate for his confirmation, his appointment was held up for 18 months before he was allowed to assume his office. Both the president and Congress thought they knew Chick – by reputation alone – well enough to predict how he would handle the job. They were both wrong.

Midway through the 1980s, we began to see the early signs of a worldwide epidemic of AIDS. It was quickly apparent that this disease was spread among drug users by dirty needles and by homosexual relations. Obviously, the key to preventing AIDS was public education. As Surgeon General, Dr. Koop prepared pamphlets with very explicit instructions on how to avoid AIDS. These instructions included descriptions of homosexual relations and warnings about the importance of using condoms. By necessity, these instructions were very descriptive. They had to be. Chick distributed this information widely throughout the United States.

About the time the pamphlets hit the news, I was in Washington for a meeting of former assistant secretaries of health. We were brought together to serve as an advisory committee for Dr. Otis Bowen, the new Secretary for Health and Human Services. Chick was there, too. During the course of the afternoon, he was called to the White House. When he returned, he told us that some members of the president's staff were decidedly upset over the brochures and pamphlets. They demanded he justify his actions. Chick told us that he had responded by noting that, as Surgeon General of the entire United States, he felt obliged to speak for all citizens. He would not leave out certain groups. He would not discriminate against homosexuals or equate their disease with a judgment from God, as many in the religiously conservative community continue to do to this day.

As a principle of public health, his logic certainly cannot be faulted. But I think the approach also has universal application. You might say that it addresses the issue of disenfranchisement, serving as a reminder that in a representative government those who represent the various districts and states around the nation should remember that they represent all the residents of those districts and states and not just special interest groups or single parties. This is a lesson all public officials would do well to ponder.

For my part, I have often thought about the way these four men made choices based on personal principles. They exercised their liberty and it made them more fully human in the best sense of that word. To be able to make a contribution or do something that's beyond your own self interest can be a great source of satisfaction.

Richardson and Koop acted in a greater public interest when they overrode the desires of the man who appointed them. Those men both happened to be the president of the United States, but they were still men, and it is worth considering that in context.

• • •

OUR NATIONAL COMMITMENT to "life, liberty and the pursuit of happiness" is a prescription for individual strength rather than being oriented to the strength of our society. But Richardson and Koop acted in the interest of the society. They were honoring another typically American ideal. The one that says no one is above the law. They did not confuse the man who held the office of president with the higher ideals he was supposed to represent. In Koop's case in particular, he did not confuse his personal religious beliefs with his duty to serve all the people. My two friends who declined medical treatment acted in a more personal realm. But their decisions were also founded on principle. They did not want to subject their bodies to violence, even the controlled assault inflicted by a skilled surgeon. Some might ask if those decisions should be weighed against the impact they had on their families. I don't think we are allowed to make such a judgment on behalf of someone else's decision. The decision represents personal choice, and it deserves respect.

I have often been asked how I feel about abortion. I don't favor root canal surgery, but there are times when it is necessary. I feel the same way about abortion. Where the justification derives from a medical reason, the decision should be made solely on that basis. If the decision has a moral base, I do not believe that men should be making moral decisions for women. I believe further that the reasoning of an adult woman should take precedence over that of a non-person.

I've wrestled with this because during my life I have been strongly anti-abortion and then strongly pro-choice. I don't think anybody is "pro-abortion." The attempt to use this description shows how much of this argument depends on how you label the different sides. I don't like the slogan "right to life," because life is not a right. Life is something that was given to me. I am alive because my parents decided they wanted to have a child. Another set of parents might have decided not to have the child. Thus, the one who gets born as a consequence of conception is privileged. Such children were born because of their parents' decisions. That may sound a bit afield, but so does the concept of a "right to life." How do you explain that concept when the person who calls himself or herself a "right-to-lifer" is perfectly comfortable going out on the weekends to hunt? The commandment "Thou shalt not kill" does not restrict itself to humans.

Once you begin to think about this, it has all sorts of applications. Say you go out to your garden to dig up a carrot. That carrot had a life. Did it have a right to life? Did you violate that right?

If it is a matter of eating food to keep yourself alive, you make that decision and you win the contest over the life of the carrot. You have been given the ability to reason and make that decision. This is what makes us human. Our choices help define our moral sense in ways that are way beyond my complete understanding. But I do recognize that there is a segment of society that believes the source of evil is choice. This reasoning goes like this: if you were, indeed, created in the image of God, then you are perfect except for those times when you make choices that lead you away from that perfection. Evil comes from the fact that you asserted your choice. I don't buy this. I think the heart of liberty is the right to make the choices that shape your life. You get to solve for yourself the mystery of life. I cling to that. I think this ability to define your existence is absolutely essential. It is what makes nobility possible.

People could make eloquent arguments that any of these men I described did the wrong thing. One could say that Richardson and Koop, for example, had an obligation to serve the person who put them in office. I would disagree. But I recognize that we are moving into areas where emotion and belief systems are perhaps stronger than reason. Puzzling my way through these concepts is a lifelong pursuit. I have a strong need to find answers that satisfy me.

My grandfather and my brother were Presbyterian ministers. I was brought up a Presbyterian and baptized in that church. As the years went by, I attended other churches on occasion. The only one that appealed to me was the Unitarian Church. When I attended that church (and once gave a sermon), I was stimulated intellectually, but not spiritually. I do not attend church now. By this description, I am neither Christian, Jew nor Muslim, but I do not feel left out or excluded from what life's experiences offer. And while I respect, at a high level, those of my colleagues and friends who draw personal strength from their sectarian choices, my beliefs are my own. I would be uncomfortable trying to share theirs.

In the realm of religion, the subject of homosexuality sometimes becomes needlessly divisive. I believe our world has been enriched by the contributions and creativity of myriad homosexuals throughout history. Their contributions to art, poetry, music, literature and science are outstanding. Where the Bible says "Come to me all ye children," I read an invitation that is inclusive, not exclusionary or discriminatory. Similarly, if marriage is a union between two persons who are deeply committed in love, willing to share their lives and support each other, I can make no distinction between homosexuals and heterosexuals.

• • •

I'VE COME TO THESE conclusions after a great deal of self-examination. In that respect, I suppose I am different from a great many people. Some are perfectly happy to go through life and accept what they've been told. They've gone to the same church since they were six years old, and they have never questioned the doctrine they were taught. They don't go beyond that. They don't have to ask why. I find that fascinating because it is so different from my approach. I have to ask myself why. I demand of myself a greater explanation and I will pursue it, even knowing at the beginning that when I am through it will only be an explanation that I needed and I sought, and that it has no relevance to anybody else. I'm not going to go out and sell my views. But I'm happy to share them. Everyone who knows me, knows that.

I don't believe in life after death, but I do believe that no one ever disappears completely if he or she strives to do good and expects no reward except the joy of having contributed to the progress of the species. Our intellectual endeavors will have served no purpose if they do not lead people to a better understanding of themselves – of the meaning of their lives.

The polyp that blindly fights for life at the bottom of the sea has no idea that it is laying the foundations of a coral atoll that will one day swarm with higher forms of life. Humans know. Each has the ability to understand that he or she is the predecessor of a finer and more perfect human species. Each should be proud of the tremendous responsibility and promise this represents. The privilege to participate in what Pierre LeCompte du Noüy called our collective moral evolution is what gives us a glimpse of greatness.

But in this society, where capitalism has produced a staggering array of choices for even so simple a purchase as a loaf of bread, it is easy to lose sight of these grander challenges and opportunities. I have to respect those people who find a way to rise above the petty choices that are all around us and make choices about the larger issues that reflect their carefully thought-out principles.

The four men whose decisions I've outlined here did that.

And Mo Udall? He was bigger than life with accomplishments that reflect the best of what the species is capable of achieving. He raced against a deadline imposed upon him by disease, and he won a great deal along the way. His death represented the loss of a great politician and a great human being. My friend. The way disease claimed his body is a reminder that medical science can only do so much. The slow ebbing of his strength and vitality before death raises real questions about how well medicine serves the terminally ill. I cannot yet answer those questions, but I will insist that energy – that creative force – be put into framing the right questions and finding answers. It is one of the challenges of our continued moral evolution.

• • •

On June 22, 1971, Dr. Merlin K. DuVal was appointed Assistant Secretary of Health, Education and Welfare by President Richard Nixon, reporting to Elliot Richardson (right), Secretary of HEW.

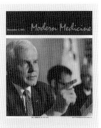

During his service as Assistant Secretary of Health, Monte appeared on the cover of Modern Medicine magazine.

Elliot Richardson visited Monte shortly after his heart attack in 1974.

A 1973 family photo: standing — David, Fred; seated — Carol, Allyson, Trisha, Barbara Fenster, Bill Fenster, Adam Fenster and Monte.

Monte & Carol, 1980

Monte with grandchildren: Case, Adam and Tiffany Fenster and Stephanie DuVal, 1994

President of the National Center
for Health Education, 1979-
1983, San Francisco

Vice President for Medical
Affairs, Good Samaritan
Hospital, 1988-1990, Phoenix

Monte was especially proud to receive an honorary Doctor of Science
Degree from Dartmouth in 1972. Pictured: Dudley Wainwright Orr,
Arthur Loeb Mayer, Monte, Walter Cronkite Jr., Hannah Arendt,
Dartmouth President John Kemeny and Chinua Achebe.

November 15, 1991,
Dartmouth also honored Monte
with The Presidential Medal
of Outstanding Leadership
and Achievement. Pictured
with Ruth and a Dartmouth
volunteer.

With President Bill Clinton
and Vice President Al Gore in
Washington, DC, following the
May 16, 1997, Ceremony of
Apology for the Tuskegee syphilis
experiment. As Assistant Secretary
of Health, Monte halted the
controversial project in 1972.

The University of Arizona College of Medicine
Reunion
November 10, 2006

Row 1: (l-r) Founding faculty members John Palmer, Founding Dean Monte DuVal, Philip Krutzsch, William Sibley, Jay Angevine, Robert Anderson, Bill Dantzler

Row 2: Dean Neal Vanselow, Bill Buchsbaum, Bill Denny, Bob Gore, Doug Stuart, Todd Overton, Class of '71, Chris Mathews, Schuyler Lininger, Friend of the College, Dean Keith Joiner

A trail ride in southern Arizona, 1992

Vacationing in Egypt in the 1960s

David's photo of Monte relaxing on the California Coast, 2002

A family vacation in Croatia, September, 2006

Monte's 75th birthday in Puerto Penasco, Mexico

Seattle, September, 2003

Croatia, September, 2006

Monte and Ruth

Caribbean Cruise, 1985

Greece, 1994

California, 2004

Monte's 84th birthday, October, 2006

Monte and brother Bill, 1998

Bill and Nancy DuVal, 2003

Four generations: Barbara Fenster, Adam and Keyo Fenster with Monte, 2004

Four generations: Monte, David, Allyson Klipa and Aleksandar Klipa

The family celebrated Monte's 75th birthday, October, 1997, in Puerto
Penasco, Mexico. Back row: Fred, Nancy, Case Fenster, Adam Fenster,
Bill, Galyn Savage, Tiffany Fenster, Barbara Fenster. Center row: Carol
and Jack Whiteman, Allyson, Stephanie, David. Front row: Ruth and
Monte, Bill Fenster

Family vacation in Alaska, 2005. Back Row: Bill Fenster, Monte, David, Terry Hanson, Fred. Front row: Barb Fenster, Carol Whiteman, Ruth, Galyn Savage, Jennifer.

Vacation in Croatia, 2006. Monte, Galyn Savage, David, Ruth, Fred, Jennifer, Terry Hanson, Bill Fenster, Carol Whiteman, Barbara Fenster.

David's family

Galyn and David

Colbert and Stephanie Henning

Allyson and David Klipa with
Aleksandar and Adriana

Barbara's family

Bill, Case and Barbara Fenster

Tiffany and Scott Burrell with
Monet and Marley

Shannon and Adam Fenster with
Lunden and Keyo

Fred's family

Fred, Will, Jennifer and Monte

Carol and Jack Whiteman, late 1980s.

Monte and Ruth in Merida, Yucatan, Mexico, 2005

Photo by Jeb Zirato, original painting by J. L. Symondes Greeson, 1979
Portrait hanging in the DuVal Auditorium, University Medical Center, Tucson

Faingold   Denver - Hilton

The foundations of family relationships

This is where "Monte" begins to take over from the hard-driving Dr. DuVal. At this point, the surgeon, founding dean of the medical school and high-level government official begins to look at his life in an entirely different way. He decides to change.

His children say his transformation began with the heart attack and subsequent triple-bypass surgery. After looking deeply into his own mortality, they say, Monte became a gentler man. No less persuasive, no less intellectual, no less aware of his power to shape his world by facing the challenges and opportunities of life, but more accessible and more attentive. He still had a hard time sitting through even an hour of television, but he was becoming far less restless when talking to members of his family. He began to be interested in them as people.

It is not that he didn't care earlier in his career. He just didn't make the time to show he cared. Nor did he make a conscious decision to sublimate his personal relationship with his family to his professional obligations. He just didn't think about it. Unlike the conventions of society and education that he recognized as ripe for change during the protests of the 1960s, he didn't recognize the need to rebel against the convention that said a man's job should come first.

During the days when he was building the medical school, he took great pride in the accomplishments of Carol and the children. It was a given that they would do well. He expected it, he took it for granted and he was happy to tell his colleagues about it. But except for dinner, the family spent little time together. These meals were much like those he had shared with his brother and parents. Monte was the head of the family. He would join them at the table and engage them in provocative conversations about the big issues of the day. It was his way of helping them hone their thinking skills. But those dinners were far too short.[136] When the meal was over, he immediately retired to his den, shut the door and began tackling his professional challenges. His family remained hungry for more of his time. If his wife or one of his children knocked on the door and disturbed him with something they had forgotten to mention during dinner, he looked up from his work. He politely addressed the subject. But he would also look at his watch. The message was unmistakable. They were intruding on his time, distracting him from his work.[137]

Monte modeled the kind of work ethic it takes to do great things in the world and create the monumental institutions. His children grew to adulthood in a city where their father had nearly rock star status. They had countless advantages. But they did not grow up with memories of warm and sentimental times with Dad. They did not have his attention.

They never complained to him. They never brought up the cost of his workaholism. Carol would later say that her husband's detachment from his family mirrored the relationship many of his colleagues had with their families. But unlike the protesters who opened Monte's eyes to the need for change in the student-teacher relationship, nobody pointed out what was missing in his home. He thought it was perfect. He never asked for a second opinion.

Monte had to take a ride in an ambulance to see things differently. He had to become the patient to understand what was missing in the doctor's life of professional commitments, tight schedules and absolute obligations. "I began to realize that I was not really living," he said. He did the things that his position and his profession demanded, and he did them compulsively.

"I was not well," he said.[138]

• • •

TWO WEEKS AFTER the heart attack, his first grandchild was born. Monte was still convalescing in the hospital when Barbara delivered her son, Adam. Monte was in a wheelchair, keenly aware of his own mortality, when he saw the child, the next generation of his line, for the first time. New life and near death intersected in the hospital he built. That was nothing new. But this time it was his near death and the life of his new grandchild. The man who was always in a hurry was forced to slow down enough to really take a look at how his daughter had grown into her own life and become a mother. He saw in the baby a profound and humbling promise of a future that would extend far beyond his own life.

He saw Fred differently, too, from his angle of repose in a hospital bed. His youngest son, who rushed home from college after the heart attack, was the one most like him in that habit of over-achieving. Fred was always in a hurry. Always doing more. Now that Monte had taken stock of the price of that lifestyle, he wanted to warn his son. He told Fred that it was wonderful to have built great buildings and founded a medical college, but there was something equally great that he had not achieved. He had not taken the time to build his family relationships. If he was given another chance, he told his son, he would live a different life. It was not an apology. Monte did not regret his life's choices. It was a cautionary tale and a confession. He subsequently sent Fred a letter urging him not to follow too closely the example set by a father whose public life had been his primary concern.[139]

David, his oldest son, said Monte's moment of awakening came after his triple bypass, Oct. 25, 1976. David was there when they brought Monte out of surgery. Monte's body had been chilled, and it was oddly green. David held his hand while he came through the deep fog of anesthesia into consciousness. When he awoke, Monte seemed very much the same man he had always been. Three days after the surgery, he walked down the main hall of the medical center with a smile on his face. The pain was excruciating, but Monte wanted as many surgeons as possible to see him up and moving. He wanted them to see that the controversy with Peacock had not beaten him.[140]

Yet David sensed he was not the same man. Monte had become more relaxed about his own feelings. He was less judgmental and more curious about the people in his life who were important to him. Although Monte had always seen himself as an extrovert, David thought that had been his mask. After facing death, the mask fell away. Monte was more willing to share his real feelings with others. The result was an openness to deeper relationships.

Monte also recognized a difference in himself after his heart was pieced back together. He began gradually awakening to the fact that he had been living an unhealthy life. His work had nearly killed him. It had left him a near stranger to his family. Yet it was not bringing him the satisfaction he'd felt in the early years. Despite all the breakneck meetings, red-eye flights to seminars and the undeniable success of the medical school, he was not experiencing that old exhilaration and excitement. He was bored.[141] What's more, after sixteen years at the University of Arizona, Monte didn't think he had anything more to give the institution he'd created.[142]

As winter's darkness closed in on 1978, Monte accepted an invitation to meet with J. Alexander McMahon and Walter J. McNerney, who were members of the board of the National Center for Health Education, and, respectively, presidents of the American Hospital Association and Blue Cross/Blue Shield. They wanted him to work with them, and Monte knew it. Both were good friends, so Monte also knew the brief meeting at an airport hotel in Phoenix would be pleasant whether it yielded anything more substantial or not. What's more, Monte had something of a proprietary interest in the center. It had evolved from a Nixon administration initiative he'd overseen during his years as assistant secretary of health. As a member of the President's Committee on Health Education, Monte had endorsed the idea that a private-sector organization should be created to help Americans understand their ability to influence their own health. The National Center for Health Education was the result of that recommendation. It was three years old when McMahon and McNerney met with Monte. It needed a president.

Monte did not accept immediately. The job would involve fundraising and administration, which were not particularly interesting to him. What's more, the job would also require him to leave the desert and move to San Francisco. Carol urged him to go, but she was not willing to go with him. A play she had been writing, "Katsina," was nearing completion and she was eager to spend as much time as possible polishing it and conducting readings that would provide her with critical feedback. What's more, her work with Arizona Theater Company consumed more and more of her time now that the children were on their own. She was committed to the play and the theater company, and she didn't want to leave.

• • •

SO JUST AS MONTE was beginning to realize the need to become closer to his family, he left home. He accepted the job on March 19, 1979, and drove his Z car to San Francisco. He left the medical school, where his goal had been to teach young men and woman about healing sickness, to head up a not-for-profit center where the goal was to teach people how to assure their own wellness. He did it at a time when he was thinking a lot about his own health, both physical and emotional.

Monte arrived at a very interesting time in the city's history. A few months before he got there, a former city supervisor named Dan White shot San Francisco Mayor George Moscone and Supervisor Harvey Milk. White had voted against San Francisco's historic gay rights ordinance. Milk was openly homosexual and Moscone was a supporter of gay-rights. Thousands of demonstrators marched in protest when White was convicted of manslaughter, not murder, after a trial in which his lawyer employed what came to be called the "Twinkie defense," suggesting that junk food left White with a "diminished capacity" at the time of the killings.[143] The chants of "civil rights or civil war" reverberated from San Francisco's gay community after the verdict. They were followed by the White Night Riots, in which San Francisco police raided nightclubs in the predominantly gay Castro District.

This was the backdrop as Monte began his new life. He gained an interesting perspective because his first home in San Francisco was a rented room in the home of a gay man who lived near Nob Hill.

Monte walked down the hill to work each morning and back up afterward. When it rained, he took the street car. The cat's feet of fog replaced the desert sunshine as a regular companion. The laid back ways of California replaced what Californians called the old-folks ways of Arizona. Later, he moved into a small condo west of Ghirardelli Square. But he still walked to work. The Z car stayed parked most of the time.

Monte had never been a man to celebrate time off. But in his new office, the calendar had smiley faces drawn on all the holidays. He wasn't used to getting a late start, either. But that was something else that set him apart in his new job. In this environment, Monte was usually the first to arrive in the morning. Instead of being greeted by efficient and admiring support staff who wouldn't dream of making the dean get his own coffee, Monte made his own coffee – but not before he turned on the lights and fired up the copy machine in the empty office. He may have been the president, but he wasn't the king.

Nor was he the celebrity here that he'd been in Tucson. But that didn't mean he lacked powerful friends. Shortly after he began his new job, he dropped in on Casper Weinberger, who had been in the Nixon administration when Monte was in Washington. Weinberger would soon become Ronald Reagan's secretary of defense, but Cap, as Monte called him, was then senior vice president of the Bechtel Corp. The headquarters were a few blocks from Monte's office. As the two high-powered executives shared a cup of coffee, Weinberger said that he, too, performed many of the early morning tasks at his office. It was a new take on executive duties.

In his role as health educator, Monte was exploring new approaches to other established ideas, as well. He accepted many invitations to speak at conventions and seminars, and began delivering a lecture called "Health: Is there a role for medicine?" The topic infuriated the medical establishment because doctors thought of themselves as the gurus of health. How could there not be a role for medicine? Medicine was everything, the whole thing. Monte was questioning the foundation on which those beliefs were built. As he learned more about the connection between mind and body, he looked deeply into his own profession and invited his fellow men and women of medicine to see what he found. There was more to health than the absence of illness. There was more to wellness than what a physician can deliver.

Monte knew people make decisions in their own best interests. His job was to find ways to show them the connection between their lifestyle choices and their self-interest in maintaining wellness. He'd made that approach work with the medical students who hated the dress code. Once he handed control over to them, they had to determine for themselves if their need for self-expression through clothing was worth undermining their authority as medical professionals. Armed with information about the stakes and the consequences, they came up with their own set of limitations. They served their own best interests. But behavior and consequence were very closely connected in that case. The challenge was to convince people that making tough choices today for the sake of a more healthy tomorrow was worth the sacrifice. Deferred gratification can be a hard sell.

He'd seen this work in another realm, also back in Tucson, when he'd been approached by one of his department heads. The man said his teenage daughter had recently started smoking. Nothing the father said about the health dangers got through to her. She liked the habit. She liked the way it made her feel. He asked Monte to talk to her. Monte protested. Why would she listen to him if she didn't listen to her own father? Nevertheless, he agreed to give it some thought. A few weeks later, Monte and Carol were at the colleague's home for dinner. The daughter, heading out for an evening with friends, circled the table to pay her respects to the guests before leaving. As she said goodbye to Monte, he stopped her and looked deeply into her face.

"Judy," he said solemnly, "I see you are a smoker."

After a quick and accusatory glance at her father, she said, "How do you know that?"

"No one had to tell me, Judy," Monte explained. "I can see it in your face. Smokers have a peculiar pattern of wrinkles and I can see them already beginning around your mouth and eyes."[144]

Her look of astonishment was no doubt of great pleasure to her parents. A few days later, Monte shared their delight. Her father called to say the girl had quit smoking. The incident demonstrated what Monte long suspected: telling young people about the life hazards of something like smoking is, to them, a non-relevant intellectual exercise. The way to reach them is through their value system.

Now he had to find a way to do that on a much larger scale. The National Center for Health Education was dedicated to finding ways to educate K-12 children about how their decisions impacted their future and their health. The task also involved convincing American businesses of the value of providing programs that promoted health to their workers. The idea was ahead of its time. That was part of what made it attractive to Monte. It was also marbled with the kind of ethical dilemmas he loved to puzzle through.

• • •

A NARROW LINE runs between educating someone to make intelligent, well-considered decisions and advocating for the decision itself. One had to balance education and prevention with mandating life choices. It was a challenge. Monte could not imagine, for example, the government telling people they must exercise each day or lose their Social Security benefits.[145] Yet such a mandate would represent a logical progression from cause to effect and decision to consequence.

These things were on his mind when University of Arizona President John Schaefer invited Monte to deliver the commencement address to the class of 1979, just a few months after he left the university.

"Three immutable postulates attach to a commencement address," he told the graduates. "The first is that, after it is over, no one should be asked who the speaker was since no one will remember. Second, the speaker's subject is seldom of any significance. And third, neither the first nor the second is of any importance. These are among the reasons that I have decided to talk to you today about the automobile seat belt."

It was an unexpected and off-beat subject. But Monte told his audience that it went to the heart of what it means to be an American. Seat belts were a concrete example of the increasing awareness of the health consequences of one's choices. Use them, and your risk of injury in a car accident was greatly reduced. On the other hand, taking risks was not always a bad thing. Surgery, for example, shows that "important benefits can come from taking well-thought-out, calculated risks," he said. What's more, "your right to take a risk, for the purpose of achieving some end that you consider desirable, is about as American as apple pie. If someone, somewhere, wants to deny you the right to take that risk, it suggests that someone places a different value on things than you do and, more importantly, that that value judgment is more important than yours is. This worries me."

But it wasn't the only perspective he wanted them to consider.

"In a time of limited resources, one man's freedom may be another's constraint. If you choose to smoke, I lose my choice of breathing clean air – because there isn't room for both. If you choose to build a tall building immediately west of my home, I lose my treasured view of the sunset – because there isn't enough space for both. If you choose not to wear a seat belt, and have an accident, I may have to give up my fishing trip to Guaymas in order to pay your medical bills.

"Does all of that add up to a message? I think it does. Our society is unique in this world. It is based on the premise that each of you should be provided with every reasonable opportunity to use whatever strengths, energies and talents you choose to mobilize toward the enrichment of the quality of your individual lives; that the key to success of this philosophy is your capacity to retain – for yourselves

– the right to make your own choices... The alternative – turning over your choices to someone else – is, in my own view, a much less attractive alternative."[146]

It was the fifteenth time Monte had attended a commencement at the University of Arizona, but the first time he'd been the speaker. His call for young people to make the right choices or face a loss of choice fit neatly with his new profession as a health educator. But like that job itself, Monte's warning was ahead of its time. Businesses were not entirely convinced in the early 1980s that it was in their best interest to provide health education to employees. They have since embraced the idea. Smoking cessation classes, flu shot clinics, stress reduction programs and domestic violence awareness campaigns are a familiar part of the workplace. Schools were also reluctant to embrace programs that taught students the negative effects of certain choices. It hadn't been that long ago, after all, that stern warning messages seemed to have the effect of encouraging, not discouraging, drug use by students. In later decades, schools, too, became promoters of healthy choices. But they did not always do so by choice. Recent laws against selling junk food on school campuses are the kind of mandates Monte warned might result from the failure to act on information about the prevention of illness and the promotion of good health.

In addition to the problem of determining who decides how to act on information about health, Monte understood that even the best choices sometimes can not overcome the odds. "Now that I am in the business of health promotion," he told an audience in Salt Lake City, "I am sensitive to the fact that I had the misfortune not to have correctly chosen my parents. I adored them both, but they carried lousy genes. As testimony to this, I've already had one coronary and a triple coronary bypass. This made me begin to think about health. Parenthetically, when I underwent the surgery for this problem, the executive committee of the medical staff, after learning that I was in the hospital, sent me a telegram stating that they had passed a resolution hoping that I would recover quickly. The vote had been five to four."[147]

Monte layered humor into his speeches, but the joke reflects his thoughts about his own wellness. The public and the private man were becoming more unified, less guarded. In a speech given to 400 people at the fifth anniversary seminar of Intermountain Health Care, Inc. on April 11, 1980, he expressed ideas that were as personal as they were professional.

"Health is not the absence of disease, but, like charity, hope, faith or courage, is an attitude. Health is something that is yours. You do not have a right to it except as you take care of it. You cannot assign it to someone else. This concept, that health is a personal commodity, is going to begin capturing the imagination of the American people."[148]

Monte discussed the nature of the difference between medicine and health education in another speech later that year before the Society for Prospective Medicine meeting on health promotion:

"We might say that medicine is essentially a passive art. The physician does not go to the patient; rather, the patient brings his complaint to the physician who, in turn, responds. Furthermore, the physician's entire training and orientation is to sickness and pathology; to their detection and their elimination … health is a positive commodity, a value to be pursued and incorporated as part of the conscious human experience before it is lost."[149]

In both speeches, Monte reached a point where he told his audience the logical next step would be to offer them a few words of sage advice. Does society have a right to mandate healthy choices? What role do physician, politician and private citizen play? Who should pay the cost of unhealthy choices? Monte did not provide the answers. He offered a story instead. It was the same story to both audiences.

He told them about two men who were leading a mule through rugged territory. One man was old. The other was young. As they walked along, they met someone who said it was silly for the old man to walk while the burro was obviously strong enough to carry him. The men thought about the wisdom of this, and the old man got up on the burro. As they continued their journey, they met another stranger. He said it was silly for one of them to walk when the burro was obviously strong enough to carry them both. They thought about the wisdom of this, and the young man got up on the burro behind the old man. As they continued their journey, they met another stranger. This person said it was wrong for these healthy men to burden the animal just for their own comfort. They thought about the wisdom of this, and hopped off the burro at once. The old man went into the woods, cut down a tree and together the men stripped it of its branches to create a pole. Then they tied the burro's ankles, fore and aft, threaded the pole through and, with one man on either end, raised the pole to their shoulders and carried the burro, swinging upside down, between them. They reached a raging river that was spanned by a rickety foot bridge, and started across. But the burden of the three of them together was too much. The bridge gave way. The two men and the burro went crashing into the water. The men, who did not have their ankles bound, were able to make it to shore; but the burro, having been tied at the feet, drowned. The moral of the story, Monte told them, was that if you listen to everyone's advice you may lose your ass.[150]

Monte did not give advice lightly. He preferred to make his listeners think things through on their own.

He did not make promises lightly, either. He acted on the promise he'd made to Fred that day at the hospital. He moved decisively toward his family, step by careful step. One Thanksgiving he flew to Phoenix and he and Fred spent the holiday varnishing bookcases for the apartment where Fred would live during law school at Arizona State University. Fred, whose accomplishments in high school failed to win much acknowledgement from his father, was delighted. It was part of a process that would continue for years as Monte began to take time to get to know his children.

On the professional front, however, things were not progressing very satisfactorily in San Francisco. The travel and the speeches were engaging; Monte loved the spotlight as much as he loved thinking through the major policy and practice issues he talked about with his audiences. But fundraising ate up the vast majority of his time. He likened it to housecleaning. One did the same things over and over, yet there was always another dust bunny, another dirty dish. There was always a need for more donations. It was not rewarding work.

After a few years, Monte was bored again. He needed a change. His stature put him in the position of choosing among the offers that arrived with regularity on his desk. Once again, he picked something that looked interesting and put him in the vanguard of the nation's health-care delivery system. It required him to learn a whole new set of skills while relying on his experience.

The subject was hospitals. Traditionally, each was an independent and free-standing institution, but a movement was clearly developing in favor of multi-hospital systems. The efficiency of the model explained its growing popularity. The for-profit chains were achieving great economies of scale by centralizing administration, purchasing and other shared functions. Monte knew this well. He'd watched the trend developing with great interest. Now it was time to make it happen in the not-for-profit world, and Monte was being asked to be part of that.

It began with a call in September of 1981 from Edward J. Connors, chair of the board of governors for Associated Hospital Systems. He asked Monte to consider taking over the group.[151] In October, Monte flew to Chicago to meet with Connors, and two other hospital administrators, Stephen Morris and Donald Wegmiller. They wanted him to be the first president of an organization made up of non-profit hospitals. His role would be to make the association a significant player on the national scene. His job would include helping the members compete strategically with the for-profit sector. He would also use his considerable skill and connections to give the group some political muscle. It not only sounded interesting, it also came with a six-figure salary.

In February, 1982, he officially became president of a joint venture of ten not-for-profit multi-hospital systems that represented about 350 hospitals, one of which was Samaritan Health Service in Phoenix. Monte, who'd been told he could set up the national headquarters in any city with a member hospital, did his usual diligent research. He flew to potential locations and made lists of pros and cons. But, Tony Bennett notwithstanding, he'd left his heart in Arizona. He picked Phoenix for the national headquarters and selected a small, but comfortable condominium in Phoenix's Biltmore Estates as his new home.

Shortly after he arrived in Phoenix, he and Carol talked at great length about their life together. Each of them had moved into separate careers. Carol's efforts on behalf of the Arizona Theater Company had been extraordinary; indeed, she had even worked for a while as its business manager. Some – Monte foremost among them – felt the theater survived principally because of her energies and efforts. Monte was moving in an entirely different direction. He was about to launch his second new professional challenge since leaving the medical school. The couple, whose lives had been entwined since the days when Monte used to walk her home from school, had lived apart during Monte's three years in San Francisco and the nearly two years he lived and worked in Washington. The children were grown and on their own. Monte and Carol decided to dissolve their marriage.

• • •

THERE WAS A DRUG STORE on the corner of Country Club and Broadway not far from the home they'd moved into when Monte began building the medical school. They bought a do-it-yourself divorce kit there and took it home. It was the same home where the big cactuses in the front yard had made Carol feel like Alice in Wonderland so many years ago, and where Monte had gazed up through the backyard oleanders wondering if help would come in time to save his life. Now it was the place where they would fill out the forms necessary to end their marriage. They did it over the weekend, assisted by what Monte recalled as "a lot of Scotch." Because he was living in Phoenix and she in Tucson, they split the difference and filed the papers in the grand, old Courthouse in Florence. Some months later, they met there before the judge. He asked if they both agreed the settlement was fair. They both said yes.

"That doesn't happen very often," the judge told them.

With the judge's congratulations and a bang of his gavel, they became separate people. But they did not immediately go their separate ways. Monte bought Carol a cup of coffee and a piece of pie at a nearby café and they chatted in long familiar ways before driving off in opposite directions. Monte went north to Phoenix. Carol went back to Tucson.

Monte was single, living in the city he'd long battled during the development of the medical school. His children were involved in their own lives. Yet, ironically, his job was all about bringing people together. Representatives of the different hospitals that belonged to the association needed to share their experiences and talk about the individual ways they'd solved their common problems. This would lead to association-wide solutions. Shared knowledge would make all the partners stronger. Educational programs and conferences were designed to accomplish these goals. In addition, Monte used his experience and contacts in Washington to monitor what was going on with respect to health care, and to interpret how those trends would impact the association.

He traveled a lot, delivered a lot of keynote addresses and made small talk with a lot of people at head tables. One of those people was a woman named Ruth Behrens. As founding director of the Center for Health Promotion at the American Hospital Association in Chicago, Ruth knew a great deal about the things Monte had been doing. She could also hold her own in discussions about the challenges he was facing. They struck up a conversation that left Monte with the impression that Ruth was "a terribly pleasant person."[152] Ruth was impressed, as well, with the well-spoken, handsome doctor.[153] Ruth traveled to nearly as many conferences, seminars and meetings as did Monte, so they ran into each other regularly. Before long, Monte began to seek her out when their professional lives crossed. He looked forward to those occasions. At one breakfast meeting with Ruth and a group of her co-workers, Monte ordered a shockingly unhealthy plate of bacon and eggs. He met the astonishment of the women whose lives were devoted to promoting healthy lifestyles with a charming bit of advice.

"Everything in moderation," he told them.[154]

It wasn't long before Monte began to see Ruth as more than just pleasant. In 1983, he urged her to join him as his "significant other" in his home in Phoenix. She accepted and they began a relationship that lasted the rest of his life.

• • •

AS RUTH AND MONTE began a life together, Associated Hospital Systems was seeking its own partnership. Another multi-hospital system in Kansas City focused on centralized purchasing of equipment and supplies to achieve the best price for its member hospitals. The leaders of the two groups decided to merge their efforts, and create two new organizations with two new names. One would be called American Healthcare Systems, and it would be focused on purchasing. The other, the American Healthcare Institute, would be located in Washington, D.C., with a focus on the kind of relationship building, education and politics that Monte had been doing. He was invited to become its president and CEO. He, in turn, invited Ruth to join him, and together they moved into a condominium in Georgetown.

Their condo was on two floors at the top of a seven-story building known locally as the Flour Mill. Each level had a small balcony with wonderful views. It was an exclusive address in a great location; their next-door neighbor was Harold Brown, former president of the California Institute of Technology and former Secretary of Defense under Jimmy Carter.

Once again, Monte could walk to and from work, but unlike his time in San Francisco, he did not take his evening walks alone. Despite its size and importance in the world, Washington was eminently livable and he and Ruth spent many nights along the Georgetown waterfront developments. On weekends, the crowds on "M" Street could be excessive, but during the week Ruth and Monte could select dinner at their leisure from a wide range of ethnic restaurants, all a short walk from home.

Ruth worked at the Washington Business Group on Health, located on Capitol Hill. The job gave her professional stature of her own that was obvious when the two went to cocktail parties. Ruth was exacting, specific and hard-evidence based, which gave Monte an invitation to explore the softer side of his personality.[155] She also came with family obligations that helped him experience those relationships in a different way.

Ruth's mother had visited the couple several times during the fourteen months they'd been living together, and Monte had thoroughly charmed her. The ultimate compliment came when he called to ask permission to marry Ruth.[156] Of course, mother said yes. She said she was relieved to know that Ruth would be "taken care of" by someone as wonderful as Monte. But hers wasn't the only sanction necessary.[157]

It was December and when Monte called City Hall to schedule a civil ceremony. He was told there were no appointments before the new year. He didn't want to wait. Typical of Monte, he sweet-talked the woman in charge, and the couple was given a date in mid December. Ruth's father was a minister, so in respect for her religious upbringing, the couple decided to marry in a lovely Lutheran church in Georgetown. It was just the two of them and the minister because no one but Ruth's mother had been told. After a very intimate and memorable service on December 17, 1984, they shared lunch at a Georgetown Inn. Monte returned to work that afternoon and Ruth went home to pack. They met again for a romantic dinner at an elegant restaurant. Early the next morning, Ruth left for the Midwest to see her mother, whose health was failing. Ruth's mother subsequently came to Washington and spent two months with the newlyweds. She returned to her home in February and passed away on April 16, 1985.

Monte and Ruth's relationship was mutually supportive and captivating to those who saw them together.[158] They flirted and joked with each other in a warm and contagious way long after they were newlyweds. Their shared interests resulted in many close friendships.

During their nearly four years in Washington, Monte renewed his friendship with Judith Miller, the brains and energy behind the National Health Policy Forum. Her organization was supported by several foundations and dedicated to educating newly arriving Washington bureaucrats, staff members and politicians about the American health care system. Because her meetings were a lively and informative pivot around which a portion of Washington rotated, Monte and Ruth had professional as well as personal interactions with her. She had married Stan Jones, once head of Sen. Ted Kennedy's health staff. Stan was a partner in a high-powered health consulting firm when Monte and Ruth moved to Washington. Not much later, he decided to follow his lifelong passion and was ordained as an Episcopal priest. The couples became best friends. During the following decades, they shared many meals, memorable vacations and weeks of intellectual and spiritual discussions at the Chautauqua Institute educational center in southwestern New York.

As with all his jobs, Monte would say this one gave him a great many friends and helped him learn a great deal. Among the friends with whom Monte reconnected was Dr. Monroe Trout, who, after a highly successful career as senior vice president and director of Sterling Drug, Inc., became chairman, president and CEO of the American Healthcare Systems. The two men had met years earlier when Monroe was appointed by Elliot Richardson to HEW's malpractice commission, which reported to Monte. These two tall, handsome, white-haired physicians shared the same values and strong work ethic, making them a powerful team on behalf of multi-hospital systems.

But as with every job after he left the University of Arizona, this one paled by comparison. The work was not terribly exciting. The challenges were not on a par with creating a place to train the next generation of physicians. Once again, Monte began looking seriously at his stack of job offers.

One of those offers came from David A. Reed, who was president of Samaritan Health Service in Phoenix. Reed wanted to make Monte senior vice-president of medical affairs at Samaritan. It was a new position, created just for Monte and it was attractive. He accepted and in the spring of 1988, he and Ruth moved back to Phoenix. They bought a patio home in Biltmore Estates. It had a large pool and 2,400 square feet of living space.

Monte's task was to persuade the medical staff of about 2,000 to join forces with the hospital administration and create what was then known as a PHO or physician hospital organization. These were created primarily as a means of writing large contracts with big businesses to provide a full spectrum of medical services to employees. The challenge was significant because Monte saw the demeanor and philosophy of physicians in Phoenix as both conservative and independent. They really wanted no part of formal relationships with the hospital administration, and they said so. Monte warned his future employers that success might prove elusive, but he agreed to try for two years. After that, he planned to retire.

He was successful in terms of getting to know and respect a great many doctors in Phoenix. But in terms of the assignment "I fell flat on my face," he said. The physicians in Phoenix were not ready for what he was selling, and he found that out very soon.

One of his first acts in the new job was to meet with the chief of the medical staff, who invited Monte into the dressing room while he got ready to begin his rounds. Monte watched as the doctor took off his jacket, put it in the locker, then unclipped his six-shooter from his belt and put it in the locker before donning his white coat.

Monte thought to himself: "DuVal, you've just had an education on why you are not going to succeed."

As far as the job was concerned, that may have been true. Although Monte laid the foundation for cooperation in the future, and no one who ever worked with the man would call him a failure, the real success was achieved in another arena.

Monte was, as he had once told his faculty at the medical school, on the verge of greatness in the one area where it had eluded him. His sense of connection with his family was growing. He was rediscovering the same personal warmth and sweetness that made him weep over Lassie's journey and Robert Frost's poems so many years ago. He was making time for people.

He and Carol remained friends. Together with Ruth and Carol's second husband, Jack Whiteman, they spent many pleasant evenings together. What's more, Monte began a concerted effort to get to know his children. It began with phone calls that were often awkward and brief.[159] Barbara said she wasn't sure what to make of his sudden interest. But he persisted. She began to expect the phone calls, and then look forward to them. Before long, the conversations weren't awkward. They had lots to say to each other. Monte made time to get together with each of his children on a regular basis, and he made time for his grandchildren.

Carol said his successful effort to establish deep, meaningful relationships with his children was his greatest achievement.[160] Looking at his resume, the rest of the world might disagree. But as Dr. DuVal became "Monte," he demonstrated that his idea of a completely well human being included carefully nurtured human relationships. He chose to be well.

• • •

CHAPTER TWELVE

My permanent change of fashion

It is an interesting question how far men would retain their
relative rank if they were divested of their clothes.

Henry David Thoreau

I retired in March of 1990, and shortly thereafter I found myself in
a position to explore Thoreau's postulate. It happened during a
trip to Washington. Ruth and I had been invited to attend the 25th
anniversary celebration of the Institute of Medicine, which is a unit
of the National Academy of Sciences. I've always taken a great deal
of pride in my membership in this organization, so we packed our
dress clothes and left for the party with enthusiasm. At the hotel, Ruth
called down for an iron and ironing board to freshen up her dress
and my tuxedo. I took some satisfaction in the fact that I had been
wearing the same tuxedo since my college days. It still fit quite nicely.
But there was a consequence to this sartorial longevity that I had not
considered. As Ruth unpacked the tuxedo in the bright light of that
hotel room, she was horrified to find evidence of moths' handiwork.
The very obvious damage included a scalloping along the bottom
of the jacket and holes in the lapels that revealed a white lining.
Thankfully, the pants were fine. Ruth had brought along a needle and
thread, so she was able to attempt some artful repairs. She turned up
the hem of the jacket to hide the damage along the edge. Sewing was
not an option for the lapels. It would show. I think our solution was
quite clever. We used a black pen to color the white lining so the holes

in the lapels would not be so obvious.

We made a lot of jokes and laughed a great deal during these efforts. We also agreed on two things. First, we would stay in the shadows that evening; our repairs would not withstand scrutiny under bright lights. Second, we would give up black-tie events. I was ready to jump with both feet into the retirement uniform of sneakers and blue jeans. From then on, we sent the appropriate donation to charities that invited us to their "gala" fundraisers, but we did not show up. I have only broken the no-black-tie pledge three times, one of them was Fred's wedding.

I set aside my professional clothes – in addition to the moth-ravaged tux. But I continued to have considerable rank, as Thoreau would have put it. I was regularly asked to take on new tasks by people who insisted that my experience and talents made me the ideal candidate for whatever they had in mind. Some offers were interesting and challenging enough to earn my participation.

The first of those came from the office of Republican Gov. J. Fife Symington III in 1993. The governor wanted me to accept an appointment to the Arizona State Retirement System Board, which oversees the retirement program for public employees. After a lifetime of service to the state, many people, including teachers and college professors, rely on the benefits paid through the system. I took on this responsibility with a full understanding of how important it is to assure the fund is sound and the investments secure. I did my best to learn about the massive investments, asset allocation, annuities, equities and the like. It was engaging and demanding work, and I devoted a great deal of energy to helping assure that the board made wise decisions on behalf of the system's participants. I felt entirely justified wearing an open-necked shirt and casual pants to these meetings because, after all, I was representing a contingent of retired folks.

In addition to overseeing investments on behalf of Arizona's retired workers, I also tried to get the state to use the muscle of those investments for a broader purpose. My model was my own modest stock holdings. As a stock holder, one has a vote. Most people simply go along with the recommendations that come with the proxy they receive in the mail, and vote that way. I always did a little homework. I often found that while the stock was going down, the compensation for the board of directors and CEO was going up. In these cases, I immediately sent my proxy in with votes against every person on the compensation committee. I also called the secretary of the board to explain why I was doing this. I said that if the CEO gets more than 100 times the salary of the lowest-paid worker, he or she should be fired. This was my way of making my voice heard in the board room, and it was satisfying. But my voice was barely a whisper. I knew that. Imagine if the entire state of Arizona, with tens of millions in investments, began making itself heard in a similar manner? I did more than imagine.

I did further investigations and found the state's money managers generally went along with the recommendations that came with their proxies. That's when I made my pitch. Why not use our strength? The companies whose stock I hold can easily write me off as a kook. Nobody would write off an investor like the state of Arizona. We could use our assets to push policy. California does this.

Let me just say that the financial managers of Arizona's retirement system were underwhelmed by my enthusiasm. They weren't going to change. Why? No good reason I could see. They simply wanted to continue to do it the way they had always done it. These were bankers and other conservative-minded money managers who preferred to go along to get along. After ten years on the retirement board, including two terms as chair, I could not get them to take this idea seriously.

I think this is a shame for reasons that go far beyond one company or even the entire portfolio of companies Arizona invests for its retirees. It goes to the heart of who we are as a nation. The for-profit sector of our society is responsible to a large degree for America's greatness. But it has gotten totally out of hand because of the greatness of our greed. One example can be seen in the boards of directors who are paid huge retainers in addition to thousands more for attending each meeting. These are often retired people who are incredibly wealthy; they don't need the money. It makes me angry to see them soak it up. I've asked myself why I feel so strongly about this. After careful thought, I have concluded that it is because there is so much we could do with that money for our society, and even for people in other parts of the world. Instead it all goes into the pockets of a handful of wealthy people. Make no mistake: I believe people succeed in life through hard work. The ones who do succeed deserve to enjoy the comfort they earned through their labor. But the poor don't always fail because of laziness. Oftentimes, they simply don't get a chance to succeed. The failure to recognize this is one of the problems with our for-profit society.

• • •

I THINK one's motive for success should be something other than profit. In my life, the motivation has been the personal satisfaction attained from furthering a worthy goal, whether it be teaching medical students, advancing the understanding of health, helping medical institutions function more efficiently or using the political process to bring medical care to more people. In order to serve our moral evolution as a species, our definition of success should go beyond just personal wealth. In fact, I believe there should be a 100 percent income tax at a certain level. That level could be very generous. But at some point there is no reason to make any more money, you might as well give it back to society. I think this should apply to doctors, as well, though few of my fellow physicians would agree with me on this. In fact, this idea would face strong opposition from most quarters. Yet I think it's worth considering what we become, on a personal level and as a society, when we let greed call the tunes.

Perhaps if I'd made these radical ideas more public, I wouldn't have gotten so many calls from people who wanted to help me fill up my retirement years. But I did get calls and I enjoyed the work I did enormously because I believe it served worthy goals.

One of those goals was to help Maricopa County successfully navigate a financial crisis in its massive health care system. My involvement began in 1994, when I was asked by the Board of Supervisors of Maricopa County to serve on a newly created board of directors for the Maricopa Integrated Health System. My efforts on behalf of the county would continue for nearly a decade. The time and energy I expended were appropriate to the size of the challenge, and they eventually resulted in beneficial changes. But the task was enormous. Maricopa County is one of the biggest counties in the United States. When I began my voluntary service on Maricopa County's behalf, its healthcare system included a hospital with over 500 beds, 11 clinics, a Trauma I Center and the only burn unit between Dallas and Los Angeles. Its educational programs encompassed nurses, medical students and residents in every specialty, making it the second largest health-care educational institution in the state.

The system was struggling financially, and had become an increasing drag on the county budget. The drift into red ink was obvious and unsustainable. The board of citizens on which I served was supposed to find ways to make it operate more efficiently. We did our best. Yet after several years of our intensive efforts, the problems remained. By 1997, the county health system was losing $23 million a year.[161] As a consequence, we began to consider privatizing the institution. We had a bill introduced in the Legislature to permit the sale or lease of the system to a non-profit organization. This effort to privatize was not successful, however, so we went back to trying to provide a safety net for the hospital. We brought in outside management and made striking improvements, including net operating profits for several years.

My involvement in the county health care system was engrossing and I spent a great deal of time educating myself about the situation. I did my research and was in communication with people across the nation who had faced problems similar to those Maricopa County was trying to resolve. I also talked to many people locally who had valuable insights. I attended supervisors' meetings and tried to share what I was learning with politicians and policy makers. But this was not the only thing going on in my life. I was retired, and I engaged in some typical leisure activities that are worth considering here for reasons that will soon become clear.

Up to this point, my hobbies had included repairing clocks, growing bonsai trees and making peanut butter, the latter being the most successful and widely admired of the three. My peanut butter, prepared with specially ordered peanuts that I roast, grind and mix with a few secret ingredients, is better than anything you can get in a store. There's no immodesty involved in saying that. It is simply the truth. Ask anyone who has tried it. If one could consider peanut butter an artistic medium, I am Da Vinci. Ruth, however, persuaded me to join her in attending classes in which more traditional artistic media were used. As a result of the classes, Ruth went on to do pastels so well that her work graces several walls of our home. "Grace" is not a word one would associate with what I produced. Nevertheless, I enjoyed these classes immensely. The effort to view everyday things through an artist's eyes and to see color and light in a different way provided a great deal of pleasure.

• • •

THERE MAY BE a particular reason I got so much satisfaction from dabbling in art at this time, and that is really what makes it worth mentioning here. You'll have to bear with me on this one, though, because it is as hard to explain in purely logical terms as it is to account for the accuracy of that horoscope my mother had drawn up for me when I was born. You see, this foray into art represented a chance to do something I would be unable to do in the future. My eyes were enjoying a last deep look at the world, perhaps with some prescient awareness and appreciation. In a very few years, my eyesight began to fail. I first became sensitive to the fact that I was going blind in 1999. I was told that I had macular degeneration. I would soon be unable to appreciate the gradations of color and the refreshing new view of the world that I enjoyed in that art class. I'm very glad Ruth talked me into taking it.

My macular degeneration is progressive, so it forces me to constantly accommodate myself to the change. I suppose it would be easy to feel sorry for oneself, but one can learn to do other things. The hardest part was being willing to become dependent on someone else's eyes. This became unavoidable after I went to renew my driver's license in the year 2000.

"You know you really did flunk this eye exam," I was told by a wonderful and portly, white-haired lady, "but you seem very nice and you seem to have good judgment so I'm going to tell you that I don't think you should drive. But I'm going to renew your license."

I drove home and never drove again. After that, Ruth took me every place I needed to go. She was a willing chauffeur, so I was able to continue with those efforts for which I felt a real passion. My involvement with Maricopa County's health system was one of those things, so I'll return to telling you about that endeavor now.

To understand the complexity of the matter, consider that we have reached a point nearly a decade after the citizens' board on which I served first began looking at the problem. As I said earlier, the changes we made in the management of the county's health system had delivered some improvement. But there were continuing problems, and the system once again became a financial burden to the county. At this point, the structure of the citizens' board was changed, and a 12-member task force was created to study the entire situation and make recommendations concerning the future of the medical system. I was appointed vice-chair of that Citizens Task Force in 2003. We met every Friday afternoon. I continued my efforts to research and study the issues, a task that was made increasingly difficult by my worsening eyesight. I have a large, closed circuit TV reading machine that allows me to view pages one at a time and "read" despite being legally blind, but it is a painfully slow process.

There are particular problems with operating a healthcare system under the county's umbrella. A government body, such as the county, has legal constraints that hinder the efficient operation of medical facilities. For example, establishing a partnership with other hospitals for complex testing or diagnostic procedures is often less expensive than contracting for those services. But the state prohibited the county from entering such partnerships. State law also prevented the county from offering bonus packages or other incentives to attract nurses and other medical personnel, even though these professionals were badly needed. It was critical to free the system from government bureaucracy that simply didn't work in the field of health care delivery. A most productive part of my research revealed a way to do that.

I found we could establish an independent entity to allow the healthcare system to operate separately from the county, while remaining a public institution. Such entities were in operation in other parts of the country. I familiarized myself with the most effective models and tailored the idea to the needs of Maricopa County. I introduced the concept to the task force and was given credit as the architect of the design that was subsequently adopted. We agreed that a Special Healthcare District should have bonding and taxing authority, and be run by an elected board of directors. It would take voter approval to make it happen.

I worked actively to win support for the Healthcare District. This meant negotiations with those who would be impacted, including private hospitals, physicians, business groups and the faction of Arizona that remains opposed to any sort of tax increase. Ultimately, we had to persuade the voters to go along with the change. The stakes were high. If the voters did not approve the district and the increased property tax to pay for running the hospital and ancillary services, the county Board of Supervisors would be forced to close down parts of Maricopa County's health care system. I made myself available to journalists and explained that there were both moral and practical reasons for making sure the hospital remained open. From a moral standpoint, many people relied on the services the county provided. Practically speaking, other area hospitals would have difficulty handling the increased patient load if the county services were not available. What's more, I saw the county's medical system as integral to offering a package of well-rounded community services that businesses look for when relocating. Arizona was growing, and Arizona needed to maintain and expand its health care options, not close them down. I felt so strongly about this that I wrote an opinion piece that was published in The Arizona Republic to make the case more fully. It appeared shortly before the election in the fall of 2003.[162]

The district was approved by voters, and I was gratified to have played a part in this important effort. But my involvement with the county healthcare system began to ebb. When the reporters called, I did my best to put things into perspective,[163] but I was no longer a major player. My eyesight had deteriorated to such an extent that I felt I could not keep up with the vast amount of reading necessary to do the task well. I am pleased to say that the district has proved successful on many levels, and has allowed the system to reverse the effects of years of chronic underfunding.

I had become involved in other healthcare issues during my service to Maricopa County, however, and these continued. In 1996, several years after I began my long-term involvement with both the state retirement system and the county's health-care system, I received a call from Dr. Andrew Nichols, director of the medical school's Rural Health Office and a state representative from Tucson. Andy had been recruited to the medical school by my dear friend and colleague Dr. Herb Abrams. I regarded Andy very fondly and was delighted to learn he was working on behalf of those who needed the services of the Arizona Health Care Cost Containment System, more commonly called AHCCCS. You'll remember this as the Arizona Medicare plan that I authored years before at the request of Gov. Bruce Babbitt. It had become a success beyond my wildest dreams, having been copied by many other states and cited as a cost efficient and effective way to deliver health care. And why shouldn't it be efficient? Unlike those corporations I wanted the state retirement system to lean on, AHCCCS has no over-paid CEO or board of directors. It does not operate on a profit motive, but exists solely to deliver a service as cost-effectively as possible.

Unfortunately, the program also achieved some of its cost savings by being too stingy. Coverage was limited to people who made less than one-third of the federal poverty level. At the time, the poverty level for a family of four was $15,500.[164] One-third of that was a little over $5,000 per year for a family of four, a ridiculously low standard. Andy wanted to do something about that. He asked me to join him in an effort to expand the eligibility for AHCCCS benefits so those earning up to 100 percent of the federal poverty level would be covered. The Legislature was far too conservative to go along with Andy, who was one of that body's most liberal members. Andy decided to launch a citizen's initiative. It was a large undertaking that required gathering a great many signatures on a petition and then rallying public support for the ballot measure. I gladly agreed to be the chairman of the statewide effort.

The team Andy put together was superb. We raised money for the effort, drew heavily on volunteers, and established offices in both Tucson and Phoenix. The Healthy Arizona Initiative was on the ballot in the fall of 1996, and the people supported it better than two to one. Unfortunately, the Legislature did not take the necessary steps to implement the initiative. It was particularly galling to see elected officials so completely ignore the expressed wishes of the voters in this matter. Andy decided to go back to the voters, and I enthusiastically agreed to participate once again. Healthy Arizona II was also approved by the voters in 2000 by more than 63 percent.[165] As a result, far more of Arizona's working poor are covered by AHCCCS.

The following year, Andy was elected to the state Senate, where he died suddenly at his desk on April 19, 2001. He called me when he began having chest pains at the onset of the coronary that killed him. Of course, there was nothing I could do for my good friend. The state lost a real champion for expanding health care when he died.

My continued commitment to expanding health coverage got me into a bit of an awkward position in the fall of 2006. The previous legislative session, I had supported a bill that would have allowed retired public employees to buy into AHCCCS at full cost. This would have been considerably less cost to them than a private insurance company, but would not have cost the state a thing. Republican Rep. Marian McClure introduced the bill, but it went nowhere because Republican Rep. Doug Quelland wouldn't hear it in the House Health Committee he chaired. That same session, I pledged to support Democratic Rep. Phil Lopes in his attempt to expand healthcare coverage. Over the summer, I was approached by Dr. Eve Shapiro, Dr. Duke Duncan and Dr. Mark Osterloh, who had all been instrumental in the two Healthy Arizona efforts, about crafting an initiative to once again expand health coverage. Their ambitions went far beyond my goals concerning retirees, but I told them I would help. Meanwhile, I contacted Quelland in an effort to persuade him to hear the retiree bill in the 2007 session. He invited me to his office, and before our meeting was finished, he invited me to join a group he had put together to discuss major healthcare reform.

Now I was part of two groups working on ways to expand health care in Arizona, but I was fairly confident that they would not endorse the same approach. My involvement with Quelland had the potential to put me at odds with Lopes and the initiative group because I was sure whatever Quelland came up with – although it might be a very good plan – would be quite different from their approach. The reverse was also true because these two efforts were based on opposing political philosophies. To complicate matters, the group pushing the initiative was asking me to allow myself to be identified publicly as part of its leadership.

It would have required a great deal of tact to balance these interests without alienating either group, but I was ready to make the effort. Quelland seemed very open to innovative solutions to our health care problems, but he faced strong opposition from the leadership of his party. I saw the potential for many of these players to come together in an unusual, but effective, effort to make things happen. Unfortunately, Quelland lost his seat in the Legislature that November. It would have been interesting to try to pursue the goal of expanded access to health care while balancing very divergent political views of how this should be accomplished.

These are not easy choices.

My good friends Herb Abrams and Andy Nichols felt health care was a right. I spent many years weighing the competing values that must be considered before making such a determination. I concluded it should be the highest social aspiration for everyone to have access to medical care. I do not use the word "right" because I feel it makes the issue unnecessarily confrontational by putting patients in conflict with doctors.

If a person goes through long years of higher education to become a doctor, he or she has earned the right of self-determination. A doctor shouldn't be forced to deliver free care, which could be the result of decreeing that a patient has a right to care. Nor should a doctor be forced to deliver below cost care. But the patient also has interests. Those interests must be considered in the context of our national ideals. Our Constitution protects personal liberty and personal property, but one cannot take advantage of those guarantees without good health. This makes access to health care something much bigger than a public policy issue. Taken in the context of our nation's respect for personal liberty and property, health care rises to the level of a fundamental necessity. To deny people access to health care is to deny them the opportunity to pursue the blessings of liberty.

I believe there are ways of serving the interests of both patient and physician without getting entangled in terminology about rights. Under a program like AHCCCS, doctors are fully and fairly compensated and patients get needed care. The solution lies in working with lawmakers and others to expand coverage under AHCCCS with the goal of universal coverage. However, I see no place for private insurers in medicine. The reason has to do with the nature of the service. Unlike homeowners insurance, where a company can expect a claim in maybe eight out of every 100,000 policies, those with health insurance can be expected to make several claims per year, even in a good year. Because of adverse selection, the worst cases will always wind up as public wards and create a drain on the public institutions. This is one of the reasons private insurers can make a profit. That's their business and they are good at it. But I do not think providing access to medical care should be about making a profit. It is the wrong motive. Nor do I believe it is fair to expect American businesses to compete internationally while bearing the burden of providing costly health insurance through private providers. I have thought a great deal about how to balance the competing interests. I believe AHCCCS should be expanded and removed from the government so it can be a non-profit organization into which every physician and every hospital would be invited to join on the same capitation basis. Then health insurance could be both affordable and mandated. Doctors and patients could both have meaningful choices.

Of course, identifying a solution isn't the same as achieving it. One has to convince state lawmakers and/or voters to embrace the solution. There are plenty of energetic people ready to take on that challenge.

• • •

MY RETIREMENT has also given me the chance to explore the last encounter between patient and doctor. It began with a call from Dr. Robert Furman, a friend from Oklahoma City, who retired to Green Valley with his wife Mary Frances. Years ago, he invited me to a meeting in Tucson of the Southern Arizona Chapter of the Hemlock Society. The organization has since – happily – changed its name, but the mission remains the same: to broaden and enhance one's options at the end of life. This led me to some deep introspection and ultimately resulted in my successful effort to change Arizona law in ways that I believe will contribute a great deal to the needs of the dying. It also resulted in my decision not to become involved in another death-with-dignity effort.

Let's begin with the effort I decided not to champion.

Rep. Linda Lopez of Tucson introduced a bill in the 2003 legislature patterned on Oregon's Death with Dignity Act, the physician-assisted suicide law. She asked for my support, and I was happy to discuss the matter. I attended a number of meetings with Rep. Lopez and her advisors, but I could not entirely buy into the concept. I was not convinced that there was a problem in Arizona. I believe a substantial number of physicians increase the pain medication they prescribe to terminally ill patients with the knowledge that death will result. They do so after telling family members the patient is suffering greatly, and that the level of medication necessary to relieve the suffering could result in death. Family members – or sometimes even patients themselves – are asked to authorize these high doses. Most times, the very private decision is to relieve the pain, which results in death. I think this happens far more than people realize. It reflects a well-functioning doctor-patient relationship. I told Rep. Lopez that I would only support her bill if she could show me cases where patients were dying in agony because pain medication was not being given to them. My other reluctance to embrace the Oregon solution was my desire to cling to the conservative medical position that directly aiding in the death of a terminally ill patient is inconsistent with traditional professional ethics.

Yet in spite of my formal education in medicine, I believe that death is not, in most instances, a medical event. While the services of a physician at the deathbed may be helpful, the decisions about the location, circumstances and manner of death should be among the last choices a patient makes for himself or herself. To the extent possible, a patient should have the exclusive and incontestable right to make those choices up to and including self-deliverance.

When it comes to end-of-life issues I see two essential questions: 1) what are the patient's own wishes; and, 2) has the patient chosen someone else to carry out his or her wishes in the event the patient is incompetent or unconscious when the decision needs to be made. That's how my investigations brought me to advance directives, or living wills. This is where I made a contribution that I believe has an unambiguous benefit to both physician and patient.

Living wills outline how you wish to be treated at the end of your life if you are unable to oversee the management of your own care. Arizona's statutes on these advance directives are thoughtful and thorough. The law does not permit assisted suicide, but it allows people to express their wish to decline treatment, and it protects physicians who follow the terms of a living will. Yet there was a two-fold problem to which I instantly became sensitive. First, most people probably did not even know of the existence of these favorable laws. Second, there was no certainty that those who might need access to these documents would know they existed or where they could be found.

That is what brought me to the Arizona Town Hall. For 40 years, this group has convened groups of citizens to discuss issues of contemporary importance. In 2002, I approached the board of directors of the Arizona Town Hall to urge them to look at end-of-life issues. They accepted my recommendation and made this the focus of a Town Hall meeting at the Grand Canyon in May of 2003. One of the recommendations from that meeting was the establishment of a state registry where any citizen could file advance directives, and where physicians and paramedics could easily and rapidly access the information. Almost immediately after the adjournment of the Town Hall I contacted the director of the Department of Health Services to determine her level of interest in having the registry located in her office. She was interested, but she called me back a few days later to say the state Attorney General thought a more appropriate location would be in the office of the Secretary of State. I called Secretary of State Jan Brewer, a friend of several years as a result of our joint appointments to the Board of Directors of the Maricopa Integrated Health System. She was enthusiastic and assigned staff to work with me and others on a bill to set up a registry of advance directives in the Office of the Secretary of State. Legislative leaders wanted this to be accomplished without the use of state funds. The Hospice of the Valley volunteered to help raise the private funding necessary, and our bill was introduced. I testified on its behalf, as did Brewer and Susan Levine, president of the Hospice of the Valley. It was passed and subsequently signed by the governor in the late spring of 2004, barely a year after the idea emerged as a recommendation from our Town Hall.

This is an example of how retirement offers the opportunity to think through issues and begin to do something about them. Retirement also gave Ruth and me time to establish some rewarding habits. It is our custom to have tea at 4:30 each afternoon. We listen to one side of a taped book, usually a mystery, during this delightful interlude. To satisfy my insatiable hunger for non-fiction reading material, I also get recorded books through the Library of Congress, which has a wonderful collection. Reading remains one of my most enjoyable pastimes despite my blindness. Two other retirement traditions that Ruth and I treasure are splitting a beer before lunch, usually on the patio, and our Friday night ritual of martinis and PBS news. We try not to accept any social engagements for Fridays so we can watch The NewsHour with Jim Lehrer, followed by local news on Horizon, then Washington Week in Review and other news shows. Ruth enjoys vodka martinis, while mine are usually made with gin. We eat microwave popcorn with our martinis, usually followed by a very mellow dinner of turkey burgers. These are extremely pleasant evenings, and we look forward to them all week.

Each year, Ruth and I also travel to Chautauqua Institute in New York to meet with our friends Stan and Judith Jones and hear some wonderful programs that lead to long, enchanting discussions about God, the meaning of life and the wonders of the human mind. It was at Chautauqua where I first heard Karen Armstrong lecture. One of her books, "A History of God," is on my list of all-time favorites. Others are "Anatomy of a Murder," by Robert Traver, "American Scripture," by Pauline Maier, "Human Destiny," by Pierre LeCompte du Noüy; and "Democracy in America," by Alexis de Tocqueville.

As I moved deeper into retirement, I have retained the energy and contacts to make a difference in my community. But I have pared away most community activities to focus my remaining time on those directed at providing health insurance for all Arizonans. As a physician, my training and experience provided exactly the right skills for this worthy and challenging goal.

I have also collected accolades. Cornell University Medical College named me distinguished alumnus in 1999, apparently hoping to catch up with Dartmouth College, which had given me its Presidential Medal for Outstanding Leadership and Achievement in 1991. There were plenty of other awards – you can find a list on my vitae if you are interested. I was honored by them all, but I really don't need attaboys at this stage of my life. As I've mentioned, my ego is quite healthy and it has remained intact as I aged. I bring up the Cornell award because my son David introduced me at that event, and what he said does fall into the category of things I need to hear. This is part of what David told the serious men and women at the august occasion of my induction into the ranks of Cornell's Distinguished Alumni:

"My father was an old fashioned kind of physician, he made house calls. Ours occasionally was one of them. Actually it wasn't all that bad. I saw him once in 1957 and again in '71. Both visits were rather pleasant …

"On the first occasion, my mother called him at the hospital and said, 'Honey, David has scarlet fever.' His response, professional and considered: 'No, he doesn't.' He nevertheless made a house call … and after a careful examination and with the full weight of his medical acumen announced, 'he has scarlet fever.' So he bundled me up and took me to the hospital, where, as the son of a famous surgeon, I knew I could expect attention reserved for Olympians, a splendid afternoon of father/son bonding. He put me in a room and left. All was quiet for some time, until I heard what sounded like a horde of elephants coming down the hall. In the course of half an hour, he'd found every medical student in the state of Oklahoma and I suspect several surrounding states to invite them to see a genuine case of scarlet fever …

"Dad surely has spent as much time on the speaking circuit as he has in the operating room, a fact that beckons a famous M.K.D. story. He was addressing a conference of nurses. The gentleman introducing him I'm sure was a nice man, albeit not, perhaps, blessed with a blazing wit. As part of his introduction, he shared with the hundreds of women in the audience that, yes, Monte DuVal did indeed have a 7-inch long Who's Who. The crowd was on the floor. Confused, bewildered and altogether unaware of the double entendre, the gentleman went on: no, no, you don't understand, I've actually seen it and it really is 7-inches long. They were still resuscitating nurses five minutes later, when Monte, who couldn't leave it alone, sauntered to the podium. With a straight face, and a true voice, he told the crowd that in his career many nice things had been said of his credentials, but never had he been so well endowed.

"To this, I have to say, he was right. He is particularly well endowed. Endowed with a magnificent intellect, the most extraordinary integrity I have ever personally known, and as my wife observes, one of the very few for whom the term 'moral authority' finds a true and fitting home. I'll leave it to Cornell to honor my father for his achievements in medicine. For me, and those who wish to join me, the far more important bequeath is to rightfully recognize and honor you, Dad, as one of the most complete, influential and splendid human beings of our time. I love you."

I can't begin to tell you how touched and honored I was by David's words, especially given the truth in what he said about house calls. Seeing him and Fred and Barbara with their children makes me realize what I missed when my children were younger. My great joy is that we became very close and took many wonderful trips together after my retirement. Ruth is most accommodating to these get-togethers, at which I fear she sometimes feels like the odd person out. Her generous spirit facilitates the wonderful times I now have with my children. I'm very proud of their accomplishments, and humbled by their pride in me.

I've sought time to spend with my grandchildren as they grow, and share with them the wisdom I've collected along my 84 years. It is for them that I want this book to be written. Quite simply, I want them to know who I am. Trying to put that down on paper may be no more successful than pointing to the University of Arizona Health Sciences Center and saying, "I built that." There's so much more that went into it than the concrete and steel. There's so much more to a life than you can reduce to words. I want them to know about honor and nobility and the important things you can do with your life that may not make you rich, but may make you happy.

When the Board of Regents announced that a new medical school would be built in Phoenix, I was asked to become involved in the planning required to make it happen. As a member of the advisory board for the University of Arizona Health Sciences Center Phoenix, I can share valuable insights. Experience is a marvelous teacher, and

I can help today's decision makers avoid some of the mistakes we made when we were getting started in Tucson.

• • •

BUT EXPERIENCE can also be a trap. I sometimes hear grumbling from those who were part of the establishment of the Tucson campus. Things are being done differently in Phoenix, they say. The philosophy is not as pure, the emphasis had shifted, they insist. To me, changes in goals and philosophy are entirely appropriate. Decades have passed. The world of medicine is much different. The role and mission of the Phoenix campus will be far different from what was demanded from the Tucson campus when we built it. I'm happy to share my experiences and my wisdom. But I'm not one to cluck because a new era demands new ideas. I can understand the emotion and nostalgia that motivates some to criticize the new ways. But my response is simple: We had our turn.

We did our best and we can polish our accomplishments. Now it is time for others to make their mark and move medical education a little further down the road.

That is what I would say to my grandchildren: I had my turn. I enjoyed my opportunity to move the species a little further along in its moral evolution. I made my life matter.

Now it's your turn.

• • •

Epilogue

Death is the only sure thing in life. It is the one unbreakable promise given to everyone at birth. Yet death so often comes as a complete surprise. It was that way with Monte's death. He and Ruth were packed up and ready to drive south to their newly finished house in Academy Village in Tucson. They had spent weeks saying their goodbyes to their many friends in Phoenix with promises to keep in touch. Monte was wonderful at keeping in touch with the people he cared about, and he cared about a great many people. Now it was time to go. The moving van had left. He and Ruth stopped for dinner before the drive to Tucson. As they were leaving the restaurant, Monte suffered a massive coronary. He died on December 5, 2006.

His memorial service was held in the University Medical Center auditorium that had been named in his honor in 1987. The room was overflowing with people who came to pay their respects. On the wall, an oil painting of Monte looked out over the crowd in absolute composure. White-haired, proud and in full command. Just two months earlier, on September 2, the auditorium had been the setting for a memorial for Dr. Herbert Abrams. Monte spoke in tribute to his old friend and colleague that day.

Now it was Monte's memorial. A string quartet played some of his favorite music: Wagner's "Seigfried Idyll", Samuel Barber's "Adagio", Gershwin's "Lullaby", Ravel's "String Quartet in F Major, Allegro Moderato". Many former founding department heads of the College of Medicine gathered there. Gov. Janet Napolitano was there, too. So were doctors, attorneys, past and present members of Congress and the state Legislature, former students, colleagues and a great many business people. And friends. His childhood pal Graham Harrison flew in to celebrate a remarkable friendship that began when these octogenarians were 11 years old. It was clear that if you were lucky enough to become Monte's friend, you wanted to remain his friend no matter how many years or miles intervened.

After his death, Monte's contributions to Arizona were noted in highly laudatory editorials in the largest papers in the state's two largest urban centers, Phoenix and Tucson. That would have pleased him. The editorial section, with its opinions and ideas and its respect for intelligent argument, was his favorite section of the paper. He preferred being enlightened rather than entertained. Several columnists wrote personal tributes to him.

Gov. Napolitano said at his memorial that Monte's life "reminds us all what it means to build a community, to build a state, to leave a legacy in a human way and a physical way … Monte was a builder-upper."

There are 130 accredited medical schools in the country. Monte built one from the ground up and played a large part in shaping another. That's a remarkable amount of building up. If you consider all the lives touched by the doctors who were trained at the school Monte built – and all the lives touched by those patients, their families, their friends – the ripples reach into eternity. An astonishing accomplishment.

Dr. Keith Joiner, dean of the University of Arizona College of Medicine at the time Monte died, recalled a three-hour lunch he had with Monte in 2004 after he took the job. It was, he said, a captivating afternoon. He said he had two thoughts as they talked. 1) There's nobody else in the world who knows what he's telling me; and 2) Why isn't he telling me what to do? The two men, one who built the medical school and the other who arrived to begin running it decades later, had frequent conversations. Monte would share his experiences and his unique way of putting the pieces of a situation together into a coherent whole. Then he would tell the new dean "this is your show, you decide what to do." He shared insights. He didn't give directions.

Monte's friend Graham Harrison recalled that Monte did offer some advice at one of the high school reunions they both attended. Monte told his old classmates to "avoid anger, anger is the worst illness."

That was the doctor's message: Anger is the worst illness.

It can be comforting after someone dies to imagine that person is looking down from some celestial perch and approving of the depth of one's sorrow or the wisdom of the choices one makes on his behalf. Monte's beliefs precluded such sentimentality. He said he didn't believe in an afterlife. When you die, he said, the body begins to decompose rather rapidly. That's all. No returning in dreams to inspire or chastise the living. No second chance at unfinished business. Yet there remained the kind of ambiguity in his discussion of these things that was both a mark of his intelligence and an invitation to more conversation. He believed in the soul, and even left the door open to some sort of immortality for it.

"You can ascribe a soul to almost anything," he said. "It is whatever makes a person that person or a dog that dog or a river that river. I accept that. I applaud that."

And what happens to that soul when you die?

"My own feeling is that it dies with you because the uniqueness dies with you. The person you were ... that's gone. Pieces of it are in everyone you ever knew. If your daughter takes on your characteristics beyond your genes, if she learns something from the way you choose to live, the way you use your capacity to choose, I think that is the transfer of a piece of your immortal soul. Then a piece of you is in her."

By that definition, it's fair to say Monte's soul is generously distributed among many people, and maybe even a few institutions.

It's not fair to end the story of Merlin K. "Monte" DuVal's life by talking about his death. It's not even honest. His life is what is worth remembering, and he lived it with energy and enthusiasm up to the last minute. What he did with his capacity to choose is what matters. He made his choices with a surgeon's regard for precision and a surgeon's understanding that a carefully calculated risk can yield big rewards. As the Silver Fox, he accepted an invitation to run a medical school that hadn't been funded or built. As the father of grown children, he took a chance on reconnecting with two sons and a daughter who had long ago stopped hoping their father would find time for them.

Many people with the DuVal family history would have wound up estranged, or at least distant. Many people in Monte's position would not have taken a chance on bringing them together. It's risky business, as anyone who has dealt with family resentments can attest. As adults his children had begun to drift away. He made sure they drifted back. Barb went from feeling uncomfortable with ten-minute phone conversations to treasuring the long talks she and her father would share over breakfasts at a local eatery. There had been a time when David asked Monte to dinner, and proceeded to blast him for not being a better father. He blamed Monte for difficulties he was having in his own life. Instead of reacting with anger, Monte simply said "you're right," and the two of them began to connect on a new and better level. Fred had also reached adulthood before he found his father interested in his life. But the three of them – David, Fred and Monte – had gone fishing in Mexico more than once to drink tequila, smoke cigars and catch fish. With Carol, Monte's relationship went from ex-husband to trusted friend. When Carol's second husband, Jack, had the stroke that killed him, Carol's first call was to 911. Her second call was to Monte, who went to the hospital with her. As for Ruth, she was secure enough in her marriage with Monte to encourage his relationship-building with Carol and the children. Monte and Ruth had the kind of marriage people envy. Together, they faced Monte's blindness and found lasting joy in the simple pleasures of each other's company. Monte accomplished more in retirement than some people do in an entire lifetime. He retained such stature that his endorsement could give weight and credibility to health-care initiatives pushed by political activists. Yet, as a man and a friend, Monte was the kind of person whose generosity of spirit inspired others to openness. After he died, his family heard one recurring message from those who'd known him. Many people said simply, "I loved that man."

You have to be willing to take chances to achieve the kind of personal and professional heights Monte reached. When he wanted to do something, he was ready to plunge into the unknown armed only with faith in his abilities and whopping doses of self confidence. He also liked fun. Even at 84, he was very much the boy who used to go away to summer camp and return as champion of every sport he tried.

In the fall of 2006, just a few months before he died, Monte took a vacation with his children and their spouses, as well as Carol and her friend, Terry Hanson, and Ruth, of course. It was one of several vacations they had taken together. Nobody imagined it would be the last.

They rented a private sail boat – six cabins and a crew – and cruised the islands along the Dalmatian Coast off Croatia. The boat had a long plank on the stern that could be lowered to allow passengers to get on and off, and raised while underway. Each evening, the crew would tie the boat up in a quiet cove for the night. Late one afternoon, someone suggested that if the plank were lowered, it would make a wonderful diving board. His kids began leaping into the water. They shrieked about how cold it was and egged each other on. Monte was laughing and cheering with the rest of them. Then he announced he was going to take his turn at diving, too. Ruth told him he had to make the first time a feet-first jump. The crew had insisted on that for everybody. It was the only way to safely gauge the distance to the water, they said. Monte wanted to forego that formality. He'd been swimming since he was a child. He'd been on the Dartmouth swim team. Diving into this peaceful cove would not be a problem. But Ruth insisted he follow the crew's direction. So he did jump in the first time. Then he quickly swam around and climbed back on board.

Now that he'd satisfied the requirements of those who thought this was a big deal, he could do what he wanted. He was vital, strong and able. Monte walked back out on the plank. This time he knew, even if he couldn't exactly see, that the water was about 25 feet below. This time he knew exactly how big a jolt the cold water would deliver to his system as it swallowed him. He paused a moment at the end of the board and stood in the clear air. The sky was growing deeper blue as the sun moved toward the horizon. In the distance, a ridge of white mountains rose along the mainland. Monte sprang into the air. He was in fine form as he arced downward. He sliced the water cleanly and with the efficiency you'd expect from a surgeon. He surfaced to the sound of the people he loved cheering him on.

• • •

Merlin K. DuVal

1 9 2 2 - 2 0 0 6

"The Dive," Croatia, September, 2006

December 16, 2006. Reprinted with permission of David Fitzsimmons and the Arizona Daily Star

Endnotes to the text

1   The Arizona Republic, April 19, 1958, page one news story, "Arizona State Offered Medical School: Harvill Asks for Delay in Action"
2   Tucson Citizen, April 22, 1958, editorial, "UA Victim of Two Coups Before Board of Regents"
3   The Arizona Republic, September 9, 1958, editorial, "Unfortunate Decision"
4   The Arizona Republic, January 2, 1959, editorial, "Tempe is the Place"
5   Arizona Daily Star, December 28, 1958, page one news story, "TMC Offers Its Facilities for U of A Medical School"
6   The Arizona Republic, June 13, 1961, page one news story, "Team Favors UofA Medical College"
7   "A Preliminary Report to the Board of Regents, Universities and State College of Arizona: Arizona Medical School Study," Joseph P. Volker, director, June 12, 1961, Phoenix, AZ. Reprinted as a public service by The Arizona Daily Star and Tucson Citizen
8   Bisbee Daily Review, August 13, 1961, news story, "Vote Okays Medical School – When Funds are Available"
9   Copy of text of John Babbitt's remarks from personal files of Monte DuVal
10 Bruce Babbitt in conversation with Fred DuVal
11 Arizona Daily Star, May 29, 1962, news story, "Phoenix Gets Warning on Med School Issue, Alienation of Other Cities Seen" Also "Full Text of Letter on Med School"
12 Ad ran in Arizona Daily Star on June 25, 1962
13 From the personal files of Monte DuVal
14 University of Arizona Library Special Collections, copy of original correspondence from Merlin K. DuVal to Dr. Richard Harvill, dated March 2,1962
15 University of Arizona Library Special Collections, copy of original letter from J. Leland Gourley to Dr. Richard Harvill, dated March 12, 1962
16 University of Arizona Library Special Collections, copy of original letter from Robert S. Ellis to Dr. Richard Harvill, dated March 14, 1962
17 University of Arizona Library Special Collections, copy of original letter from Ernest Lachman to Dr. Richard Harvill, dated March 9, 1962
18 University of Arizona Library Special Collections, copy of original letter from Hugh G. Payne to Dr. Richard Harvill, dated March 19, 1962
19 From the personal files of Monte DuVal
20 Ibid
21 Ibid
22 The Arizona Republic, March 26, 1963, front page commentary, identified as "An editorial: A Time for Statesmanship"
23 Tucson Citizen, Sept. 27, 1963, news story, "Harvill has Med School Timetable, In Full Swing Within Decade"
24 Information from Kathy Whisman, University of Arizona Budget Office
25 Interview with Carol DuVal Whiteman
26 Interview with Monte DuVal
27 dialogue and information on headline from interviews with Monte DuVal
28 Arizona Historical Society Oral History Project, Medicine and Health Care Delivery in Southern Arizona, Interview with Merlin K. DuVal by Leonard Peltier, June 16, 1994
29 Ibid
30 Ibid
31 Ibid
32 Ibid
33 Ibid
34 Tucson Citizen, February 7, 1964, news story, "DuVal Family Feels Like 'Alice' "

35 Arizona Daily Star, January 15, 1964, news story, "Fundraising Events Televised: Dinners in Two Cities Push Med School Drive"

36 Interview with Monte DuVal

37 Interview with Dan Capps

38 Interview with Dr. Vince Fulginiti

39 Interview with Dr. Philip Krutzsch

40 Winslow Mail, October 11, 1963, editorial, from scrapbook of news clippings at University of Arizona Medical School library Special Collections

41 Arizona Historical Society Oral History Project, Medicine and Health Care Delivery in Southern Arizona, Interview with Merlin K. DuVal by Leonard Peltier, June 16, 1994

42 Arizona Daily Star, December 1, 1963, news story, "Regents Reject Offer of TMC as Med School, Board Decides to Build New Facilities Where Polo Village Now Stands"

43 Ibid and interviews with Monte DuVal and Arizona Historical Society Oral History Project, Medicine and Health Care Delivery in Southern Arizona, Interview with Merlin K. DuVal by Leonard Peltier, June 16, 1994

44 Written commentary provided by Graham Harrison

45 An article on the family history of presidential candidate Sen. Barack Obama that ran subsequent to Monte DuVal's death revealed research that showed one of Obama's ancestors to be a slave owner named Mary Duvall. According to a March 2, 2007 article in the Baltimore Sun by David Nitkin and Harry Merritt, "research traces the Duvalls to Mareen Duvall, a major land owner in Anne Arundel County in the 1600s. The inventory of his estate in 1694 names 18 slaves, according to a family history published in 1952." An Associated Press article published in The Arizona Republic, October 18, 2007, "Cheney, Obama 8th cousins, VP's wife says," reports that Mareen Duvall's son married the granddaughter of Richard Cheney, who arrived in Maryland in the late 1650s.

46 Interview with Monte DuVal

47 The Arizona Wildcat, Nov. 6, 1964, news story, "Medical School: In Gestation, DuVal Reports"

48 Interview with Monte DuVal

49 Arizona Historical Society Oral History Project, Medicine and Health Care Delivery in Southern Arizona, Interview with Merlin K. DuVal by Leonard Peltier, June 16, 1994

50 Personal correspondence of Monte DuVal

51 Ibid

52 Arizona Historical Society Oral History Project, Medicine and Health Care Delivery in Southern Arizona, Interview with Merlin K. DuVal by Leonard Peltier, June 16, 1994

53 Interview with Monte DuVal

54 Interview with Carol DuVal Whiteman

55 Ibid

56 Interview with Monte DuVal

57 Interview with Dr. Jack Layton

58 Personal correspondence of Monte DuVal

59 Ibid

60 Ibid

61 The Arizona Republic, May 2, 1971, news story, "Detention Home Now Health Center"

62 The Phoenix Gazette, November 18, 1967

63 Arizona Daily Star, August 13, 1967, news story, "First Medical School Started with Private Funds on a Tax-supported Campus is a Reality"

64 The Phoenix Gazette, November 17, 1967, news story, "Sciences Building Dedicated at University of Arizona: Medical College 'To Grow Far Beyond .. Hopes, Plans' "

65 Arizona Historical Society Oral History Project, Medicine and Health Care Delivery in Southern Arizona, interview with Merlin K. DuVal by Dr. Leonard Peltier, June 16, 1994

66 Interviews with Monte DuVal

67 Speech to the faculty from the personal files of Monte DuVal
68 Interview with Monte DuVal
69 Interview with Dan Capps
70 Interview with Monte DuVal and news clips
71 Tucson Citizen, August 26, 1965, "UA to get $50,000 marble statue of Hippocrates"
72 Arizona Daily Star, January 19, 1968, news story, "Medical School Threatened by Budget Slashes: UA School Could Lose Accreditation, Dean DuVal tells Arizona Lawmakers"
73 Personal files of Monte DuVal
74 Arizona Daily Star, July 15, 1968, photo
75 Medical World News, June 14, 1968
76 University of Arizona College of Medicine library Special Collections, news clipping identified from "Flagstaff paper," November 20, 1964, "Outlines Plans, Gives Advice to ASC Pre-Med Students: UA Med School Dean Talks Here"
77 Interview with Monte DuVal
78 Ibid
79 Personal files of Monte DuVal
80 Ibid
81 Ibid
82 Ibid
83 Interview with Monte DuVal
84 Arizona Historical Society Oral History Project, Medicine and Health Care in Southern Arizona, Merlin K. DuVal interviewed by Leonard Peltier, June 16, 1994
85 Personal files of Monte DuVal and interviews with Monte DuVal
86 Ibid
87 Ibid
88 Personal files of Monte DuVal
89 Interview with Monte DuVal (Geneva Code)
90 Personal files of Monte DuVal
91 Tucson Citizen, May 14, 1971, editorial, "Good Luck, Monte"
92 Arizona Daily Star, May 8, 1971, editorial, "DuVal leave Justified"
93 The Arizona Republic, May 13, 1971, editorial, "The man for the job"
94 Arizona Medicine, June 1971
95 Medical World News, June 4, 1971, Vol 12, #22, "Why Dr. DuVal Took It: Surgeon plans reviving HEW job nobody wanted to reconcile MD's self-interest and public needs"
96 Interview with Monte DuVal
97 Ibid
98 Tucson Citizen, September 2, 1971, news story, "DuVal Signals He's No Pushover"
99 Ibid
100 Interview with Monte DuVal
101 Ibid
102 Knight-Ridder Newspaper, May 17, 1997, "Tuskegee victims get apology, Clinton calls syphilis study an 'outrage'
103 The Arizona Republic, May 17, 1997, news story, "Arizonan called key to experiment's end"
104 Interview with Monte DuVal
105 Ibid
106 Conversation reconstructed based on interviews with Monte DuVal
107 Interview with Monte DuVal
108 Ibid
109 Medical World News, March 22, 1974
110 Interview with Monte DuVal
111 Letter from Erle Peacock Jr. to Monte DuVal, copy in personal files of MKD
112 Letter from Monte DuVal to Erle Peacock Jr, copy in personal files of MKD
113 Interview with Monte DuVal

114 Dialogue based on interviews with Monte DuVal
115 The Arizona Republic, August 17, 1974, news story, "Fired surgeon made threats on U of A college, jury is told"
116 Interview with Monte DuVal
117 Ibid
118 The Arizona Republic, August 17, 1974, news story, "Fired surgeon made threats on U of A college, jury is told"
119 Personal files of Monte DuVal
120 Interview with Monte DuVal, notes from the personal files of Monte DuVal that include pages of court transcript
121 Interview with Monte DuVal
122 Ibid
123 The Arizona Republic, August 23, 1974, news story, "Fired Surgeon wins $470,000"
124 The Arizona Republic, August 23, 1974, news story, "Committee Endorses UA Firing"
125 Arizona Daily Star, September 26, 1974, news story, "New Trial Ordered in Peacock Lawsuit"
126 Interview with Monte DuVal
127 Arizona Daily Star, Sept. 19, 1975, news story, "Schaefer, DuVal Resignations Sought by Phoenix Legislator"
128 The Arizona Republic. June 27, 1975, editorial, "Just who's in charge?"
129 Los Angeles Times, April 23, 1976, news story, "Feud tears at heart of medical school"
130 Arizona Daily Star, January 29, 1976, editorial, "The Peacock Imbroglio Should Be Ended"
131 Interview with Monte DuVal
132 Ibid
133 Dialogue based on interviews with Monte DuVal
134 Interview with Monte DuVal and subsequent phone interview with Bruce Babbitt
135 Interview with Monte DuVal
136 Interview with Carol DuVal Whiteman
137 Ibid
138 Interview with Monte DuVal
139 Interview with Fred DuVal
140 Interview with David DuVal
141 Interview with Monte DuVal
142 Arizona Historical Society Oral History Project, Medicine and Health Care Delivery in Southern Arizona, Merlin K. Duval interviewed by Leonard Peltier, June 16, 1994
143 The New York Times, October 22, 1985, "Dan White, Killer of San Francisco mayor, a suicide"
144 Dialogue based on interviews with Monte DuVal
145 Personal files of Monte DuVal
146 Personal files of Monte DuVal
147 Ibid
148 Ibid
149 Ibid
150 Ibid
151 Interview with Monte DuVal
152 Ibid
153 Interview with Ruth DuVal
154 Ibid
155 Correspondence with David DuVal
156 Interview with Ruth DuVal
157 Ibid
158 Interview with Jennifer DuVal
159 Interview with Barbara Fenster

160 Interview with Carol DuVal Whiteman
161 The Arizona Republic, September 30, 2003, news story, "Uninsured Rate Rises in State, U.S.; Medical Center's Fate is in Hands of Voters"
162 The Arizona Republic, October 25, 2003, guest column, "Does Proposition 414 Solve the Problem?; Keep Hospital, OK District," by Monte DuVal
163 The Arizona Republic, November 14, 2004, news story, "Health Survey Lists Shortcomings; County Mounts Efforts to Address Inspectors' Concerns"
164 The 1996 U.S. Health and Human Services Poverty Guidelines, http://aspe.hhs.gov/poverty/96poverty.htm
165 Arizona Secretary of State, Election Summary 2000, http://www.azsos.gov/results/2000/general/BM204.htm

Comments by David DuVal at his father's memorial service:

Music was of seminal importance to my father.

In college, he fretted as to whether he should pursue a career in music or one in medicine. In the end, he earned his undergraduate degree in music and then, of course, went on to become a doctor.

And therein, the humanist and the scientist had reconciled in what, for him, would be a pas de deux of arts and science that would last his lifetime.

He was a gentle, sensitive and munificent soul, one given to immeasurable personal and emotional integrity. In the later years of his life, these qualities poured abundantly from him. As my sister-in-law Jennifer says, he is the only person she knew who would start a hug from the other side of a room.

The fact is, in these years, he had found in people what had once only been available to him through his commerce.

In thinking about birth and death, I think of the Taoist view of a tea cup. Lao Tsu wrote that the walls of that cup are incidental. He said what matters is the empty space that those walls create, and the purposes ultimately hosted by it. Perhaps you have asked yourself, as I have, who in your memory has employed that space more remarkably, as purposely, or with such unflagging personal authenticity than he did?

He had what my wife Galyn calls "moral authority."

Each of us is aware of at least some of Dad's temporal accomplishments. The chairs you are sitting in, these walls that contain us, this very house – were all parts of what he did in filling the space of his teacup and we – you and I – are here today in appreciation for what he did with that space, much of which has now become part of our own.

These things notwithstanding, I submit that his greatest life achievement eclipsed the tasks and the tangibles of these walls and vitaes. I believe the music that was his life reached its true crescendo in recent years when he came to know that what he did in life truly mattered, but that love and those that he loved truly mattered even more.

So, as he aged, love was something he gave more and more freely, more and more overtly and more and more generously, and all of it in the same proportion as he had given of his time, his talents and his remarkable intelligence through his career.

The workaholic had become something of a loveaholic.

The Silver Fox had turned to gold. He was utterly accepting; he suspended judgments. He had learned to simply let it all flow. He had become a sweetheart.

Initially, I viewed these changes as unnerving, if not altogether scary, stuff. There was no precedent for it as we grew up, and, for me, it triggered a disquieting alarm perhaps best summed up by the bumper sticker that reads, "may I someday become as good a person as my dog thinks I am."

But when I was with him, I felt that despite my chewed down nails, my unresolved thoughts, my inability to proffer solutions to the mid-East problems, I felt I was nevertheless seen by him – just the way I was – as being perfect.

The ancient Sufis believed that when the morning flowers turn towards the sun, at that moment, the sun comes to know itself. So, as he gave his love and that love grew, and as he accepted life as it was, and that acceptance grew, he concurrently moved deeper into his own being.

As his blindness advanced, it occurred to me once, as I looked into those watery eyes, that he was seeing something younger, keener eyes cannot. He was looking out to that distant place that William Yeats – in his own advanced years – alluded to as a vision that is not about tasks, but about something that informs one – not from the exigencies of the moment – but from the sum of his or her life experience – something that is utterly personal yet concurrently and totally imbedded within the collective human experience.

Yeats symbolized it as an ember in a fireplace; a life that, at its end, pared to an essence.

For this ever-softer man, that essence was the red glowing ember of his love – both for family and friends – the distilled sum of all life's harvests and a poignancy that only one at the end of his life can know as he contemplates its inevitable loss.

The teacup has been taken from the table, but much of what filled its space will continue to flow to us and from our depth perhaps we all hear a bit of that music that leaves us with the task of finding a coda.

For me, it is nothing more than gratitude for an accomplished, soulful and meaningful life, one that was informed by grace and one that sought beauty and all that is humanly perfect.

Comments by Barbara DuVal Fenster
at her father's memorial service:

I'd like to tell you a few of my favorite stories about my dad – and about what I consider some of the defining moments in his private life.

His mother was a singer, actress, model and ice skater. His father was a stock broker – and professional hockey goalie for the Toronto Maple Leafs. As a teenager, he earned money like most teenagers, as a lifeguard and scooping ice cream. He worked this way through college washing dishes at the Dartmouth dining hall.

It was while working at the ice cream shack that he had one of the defining experiences of his life. A man pulled up in a car and honked for dad to come out and serve him. Dad – with teenage exasperation, waved him off. The man honked again – Dad waved him off again. The man parked his car – and as dad watched, he pulled out his crutches and struggled to lift his crippled legs out of the car. As he hobbled his way to the ice cream shack, Dad made a decision that he would never again make assumptions about people. That he would never again be too lazy to go out and help someone who needed him.

That sense of mission defined who he was. It was working toward that mission that gave him such satisfaction all of his life.

This was the man most of us knew. The man of intelligence, determination, charm and caring. The man driven to succeed. The tireless crusader.

The first time I realized that Dad was human was when we lived in Oklahoma – before we moved to Tucson. I was 12 or 13. My best friend's mother had died and her father, who lived in Tucson, was too ill to take care of her. I went to Dad and Mom and pleaded with them to take my friend to Tucson with us. I begged and pleaded with Dad and Mom. I described my friend's pain and begged that we adopt her. I vividly remember Dad, with tears streaming down his face, explaining that you just don't take someone else's child – no matter how much they needed you.

That was the moment I realized that Dad couldn't leap tall buildings

– although he tried – he couldn't fix everything in my world.

But, he WAS my hero – and my teacher. He introduced me to the theater. He got me my own season tickets to the ballet – which he particularly loved. And he took me to the symphony. Did you know that he arranged and composed music? I remember sitting on the floor at home with him, in front of his huge stereo speakers, listening to him explain music to me. How the different instruments came in and out to create certain effects. How Frank Sinatra phrased a song.

He had moments with my brother David. Once when David had scarlet fever, Dad bundled him up gently and took him to the hospital where he paraded every medical student in the place past David, where they poked and prodded him so they could see scarlet fever.

It was different with my brother Fred. When Dad had been in Washington for about six months, Fred also went to Washington as part of model legislature – and met with a lot of congressmen. Dad griped – with great pride – that he'd been working in DC for months – and in two weeks Fred already knew more people than he did! He loved being known as Fred's Dad.

We used to have Sunday dinner together after church. Dad would introduce a topic he knew we felt strongly about – the state of the body politic, or some burning issue of the day or a question of moral or ethical decision. He'd make us defend our position and argue us around the issue, just until we were ready to concede and agree with him. Then he'd switch sides and argue our original position. It was a wonderful way to learn critical thinking and to learn to look at all sides of an issue.

As children, we knew Dad as a workaholic. He was rarely home. When he was home, he was usually in his study working.

That changed at a moment not of his choosing – but when he had a heart attack and he was swacked with the sense of his own mortality. He'd looked at death. Then two weeks later my son – his first grandchild – was born. I remember looking out my hospital door – just upstairs here – and a nurse wheeled Dad down the hall to visit me at the same time another nurse was bringing his new grandson, Adam, into my room. Dad was almost lifting himself out of the chair to see his next generation – and he could see the future.

I believe that that was a defining time for Dad – when he came to see that all of his public accomplishments were given deeper meaning when he had a well of family love to draw upon.

Although he and Mom divorced, they made sure the family stayed in tact. They continued to respect and like each other. Dad fell in love with Ruth – and she became part of the family. Dad called each of us frequently and built new connections with each of his children and grandchildren.

Each year our relationships have gotten closer. For the past two years in fact – Dad, Ruth, Mom, Terry, my brothers and our spouses have taken big vacations together – to Croatia and Alaska. We've had regular family breakfasts – at each one we've argued the state of the world, God and mankind, listened to good music and appreciated how lucky we've been to have each other.

Comments by Fred DuVal at his father's memorial service:

Today we celebrate a life well lived in a marble monument that contains his vision and commitment and in a room that bears his name, but most of all, we celebrate the even more enduring legacy residing in each of us present today.

Some people look back on their lives – and their highlights. We do so on his behalf today and the highlights were many. But he didn't. He looked forward to new and higher summits. He was happier each day and even in his last weeks was plotting an initiative to assure universal health insurance for every Arizonan. Like wine, he got better with age, his passions stronger, regrets fewer, and loves more plentiful and more oft-expressed.

And there are so many things you might not know he truly loved:
- to whistle while he worked.
- a "honey do" list on Saturday morning.
- a well-crafted argument.
- dogs – particularly our family mutt Betsy whose mere mention flooded his tear ducts.
- good Scotch.
- Sinatra, and Goodman and the brothers Gershwin.
- good design and would always note the exact right tool for the right job.
- He loved words, Safire in The Times, good puns and engaging the editorial page, as our friends at The Arizona Republic can surely attest.
- Peanut butter – preferably his own home-made.
- The Constitution, the Federalist Papers and his country.
- He loved his friends.
- And he loved his family.

He was fully alive – and even most happy, of all things, when he cried – something that occurred more often than he would care to admit. He was a music major who believed that human artistic expression awakened the soul. And so he could be counted on to measure the quality of good music, theater, movies – heck, even to well-crafted TV commercials with a good cry. This sweet trait was apparently not always so endearing. One night while in college, Dad went to the movie "Lassie Come Home" with his fraternity brothers, and before it was over was nothing but a mush ball. He was almost thrown out of the fraternity.

Most of all he loved his family. I remember the interminable three-day road trips to, and the sun-filled days in Maine, fishing trips to Mexico and the card games on rainy days. I remember help with math homework, Sunday night Wide World of Disney and the never finished conversations about issues of the day.

Most of all I remember countless pieces of sage and wise advice always available and freely given. Some of it well-worn, some original: Choose to be happy. Money may not always bring happiness, but when it does – spend it. And above all, do the right thing – even when no one is looking.

He could be tough. To displease him meant one was awarded with "the look". Any of you ever get it? You know what I mean: "The Look".

He was at once steel and velvet. Hard as rock, but as soft as drifting fog. He deeply admired excellence – whether in music, art, or in the operating room. It was to do something notably well and to do it with grace, passion and humility. I admit – many of you can no doubt relate to this – it made it harder to please and impress him. But I am a better man for the expectation set. Perhaps we all are, because when affirmation came, it was a genuine and authentic reward.

He was a man of simple and traditional values. Honesty, service, virtue, resourcefulness and honor. His reputation meant everything. His own father Mike was a Wall Street broker who like most, lost his clients' money in the crash of 1929. But unlike most, or probably any, Mike resisted the easy out of bankruptcy and spent the rest of his life repaying every client every dollar they lost. It was not required or expected – but it was right.

Mike left his family with little in the bank but a family legacy of honor and virtue that is priceless. Of every issue or decision, Dad would ask not, "Is it popular?" or "Is it expedient?" but, "Is it right?"

Money actually meant relatively little to him. When he returned to Oklahoma following his interview to be founding dean of this school he said, "President Harvill gave me a private office a phone and a parking space." My Mom asked, "And what will you be paid?" Dad sheepishly replied, "I forgot to ask."

That was the stuff Dad was made of.

Dad engaged possibilities, embraced the life of a larger cause with a thoroughly aroused conscience. And he enjoyed the courage and talent to change the world to his often audacious aspirations.

He was a man of many firsts – first pancreatic surgery technique known, for many years, as the DuVal Procedure, first Arizona medical school, first Arizona professional theater company, first capitated state Medicaid plan, even first medical TV talk show host. Perhaps he ran out of things. So he started a second round. Second Arizona Medical School ...

He knew that most must wait to hear the favorable verdict of history on their careers. Two thousand years ago the poet Sophocles wrote: "One must wait until the evening to see how splendid the day has been." But we don't.

That he would lose his sight was a painful and cruel thing – but he never lost his vision.

He knew his time left was short. He recently said to a friend that at his age he "didn't even buy green bananas anymore."

As in any life there were things that death denied him. He was – as he fell – literally en route, moving back to this city of Tucson and to the friends here he loved. He will not see his memoirs published.

But there is so much he did see and do. In his final months his impending move stimulated him to say good-bye to many friends. He – in the organized, methodical way that was his own – spent meaningful time with each child and grandchild. His daughter and her family returned to Arizona. He witnessed the dedication of the Phoenix College of Medicine which he helped birth. It gave him indescribable pride to see me appointed to the Board of Regents where – we often laughed – I would have been his boss. Thank you, Gov. Napolitano, for the timing and granting of that extraordinary gift.

While we feel the grief of insufficient days, we also rejoice in the extra days granted. Following a massive coronary in 1974 – and the triple bypass that followed – we thought we might lose him at any time. The additional and unexpected 33 years was an incomparable gift and helps to ease the rage I feel against the dying of this light.

In the past 10 days since the phone call every family member dreads, I have been grateful for the words of love, and the many printed and verbalized tributes. I have learned of things he did and the people he touched of which I had no idea. But what as struck me more than anything has been the number of men – peers and friends – who have said simply: "I loved that man." One in particular really got me. Dad's personal doctor was a graduate of an early medical class of this school and has gone on to substantial medical and civic accomplishments. A few weeks ago he told Dad, "To have been entrusted with the care of my mentor is the greatest tribute of my career."

As I said, the tear ducts are genetic. And I am so proud to carry his.

I have spent my life in his shadow and now am comforted by it. You can now go gentle into that good night.

Dad joked, "All my friends who have passed on and are up in heaven just assume I didn't make it."

You made it Dad. You surely made it. We love you and may God Bless you.

Comments by Dr. Vincent A. Fulginiti
at the memorial service of Monte DuVal:

I didn't want to be here this morning. Shirley and I thought we would be at Academy Village welcoming Ruth and Monte to their new home and to his return to all of this where he made such a mark. We thought we would be looking forward, not backward.

I had just spoken to Monte two days before the move and we had just received a lovely note from Ruth, excited about and anticipating their move.

Unfortunately, these messages were followed in too short a time by Carol's call informing us of Monte's sudden and unexpected death. In an instant, we were forced to move from thinking about the future to contemplating the past.

As we began to recall that past, the beginning of Charles Dickens' "Tale of Two Cities" sprang to my mind: "It was the best of times, it was the worst of times…" That phrase summarized for me the more than 40-year personal relationship with Monte. Many others, here today in person, or in spirit, shared those ups and downs. I will not focus on the worst of times, the worst of which was his untimely death, but rather try to bring the man alive in this room in the best of times. His accomplishments are well known. But what of the man himself?

Our first contact with Monte was 41 years ago. Shirley and I were on a Markle Scholars trip to Arizona from Colorado. We were told that the dean of the new medical school in Arizona was to speak to us at the Biltmore Hotel. Merlin K. Duval, MD, was introduced: he was an articulate, dapper man with style and elegance. He displayed great depth of knowledge about medical education and research. He stood before us with that famous head of white hair and gave one of the most sophisticated talks we had ever heard. It was passionate, it was inspirational, and he was very persuasive. He could have sold us the London Bridge that day. At the time, I had no idea that in three years we would join him in that dream he portrayed. We had come to Colorado from Philadelphia, and Monte's slides of the exotic flora and fauna of the desert were both foreign and fascinating. With enthusiasm, he painted a picture of the new medical school and hospital, both in words and with slides. At the time, I didn't realize the photos were based on a model. Three years later, when I came to Tucson for an interview, I discovered that the hospital was actually a hole in the ground and we were issued hardhats for the tour! Monte knew how to use words and images to great effect; that was an outstanding characteristic throughout his life.

Sometimes his enthusiasm was infectious to those who assisted him. For example, in my recruitment in the spring of 1969, Oscar Thorup escorted me throughout the city. On one occasion, I admired the full field of wild flowers fully covering the Tucson Mountains as we drove towards Gates Pass. Between quotes from Thomas Jefferson, Oscar assured me that that lush landscape occurred every year! He was an apt colleague of Monte's!

After we became part of the College of Medicine, we learned of Monte's other characteristics; his intensity, his commitment and dedication to the college and the academic enterprise, his considerable ability at lobbying for that enterprise, his progressive leadership, and his unique mentoring ability. Coupled with his professional zeal, he had a passion for music and drama, a sense of humor, which sometimes he turned against himself, and his keen sense of service to the community in which he lived and functioned both as a professional and a citizen. And above all, his enduring and sincere loyalty to those who worked along with him. Monte was basically a physician skilled in problem analysis and solving; both traits he applied daily to building and managing this institution.

Monte was involved with the arts, from his major in music in college, to his role as a founding member and president of the board of the Arizona Civic Theater, the forerunner of today's Arizona Theater Company. He often yearned to perform on the theater stage, and he wrote poetry…

He gave each of us credit instead of claiming it for himself. His leadership consisted of asking each of us to build the best unit in our area of expertise. His role was to support us, ensure initial adequate financial support, and advocate for us when necessary. At one point, I described his abilities in a letter of support for a position he was nominated for, as follows:

"Monte guided a talented, but contentious group of young

Department Heads/Clinicians/Investigators and Teachers through the founding and development of the College of Medicine.... Monte was able to meld academic ambition, community energy and regional and national support into a unified effort."

As a result of his support for, and confidence in, all of us, his dream of Arizona reaching the elite in academic health institutions was realized a lot sooner than many thought or believed possible.

During our long friendship, we met not only in Tucson and Phoenix, but in San Francisco, in Mexico, in Washington D.C., and even in a variety of courtrooms and lawyers offices.

We watched his children grow and develop into accomplished professionals in various fields: David in television anchoring, advertising, art, and administration; Barbara from a college actress in Peter Moroney's theater group, to expertise in various media, and now working for Gov. Napolitano; and Fred, from a teenager with infectious mono to a career in law and politics and now as a member of the Board of Regents.

We also learned of Monte's personal integrity and humanism. I further wrote at that time: "Monte is one of the more sincere, straight-forward individuals I have known. Despite the need for public pronouncements at various stages in his career, he has remained true to his principles and consistent in his ethical and moral positions. At the core, he never deviated from those principles, even when they nearly cost him his position and his life."

There were also some fascinating and humorous asides during the early years. For example, when the hospital buildings were going up, some UA administrators wanted to know where the wall clocks were to be installed in each room. Monte had to point out the difference between an undergraduate classroom and a clinical setting.

On one occasion the Purchasing Department on the main campus challenged our Blood Bank's purchase of blood from the Red Cross because it violated the dictum that you needed to get three bids and accept the lowest one! Again, Monte and Jack Layton had to explain the single vendor concept when human blood was involved.

And what medical school dean anywhere in the country had to deal with a raccoon that established his home above the hospital cafeteria, relishing the food we so inadvertently and amply provided for him?

And some of us will remember Patrick Henry, who had a troubled academic career at UA, had a dermatology residency, and during those years planned his estranged wife's assassination and wound up in federal prison.

As I've noted, Monte was always the consummate professional, neatly and appropriately dressed, always pressed, always composed and in charge. Well almost always.

Early on, Monte garnered a lot of public notice in an effort to gather community support and financing. He was often pictured in the press and on TV; the image of professionalism and decorum. However, on one occasion he had been working on the house and in the garden wearing tattered jeans, a paint-stained shirt and muddy sneakers. He needed to go out late at night for an urgent purchase, and found a convenience store that was open. As he paid his bill and was about to leave, the young clerk said to him, "Hey, ain't you that dean guy, who's always in the paper?" I think that was the only time that he actually blushed. He told me he knew that his "image" was in danger of being tarnished!

Monte was a mentor; most of us were relatively young at the time and didn't have his experience. He was always available to offer advice if we asked for it, and it was almost always wise advice. There were some exceptions. I remember a discussion with the department heads in which he reflected on reimbursing travel costs. He thought that maybe we shouldn't ask for reimbursement for meals when we were out of town. We had to eat at home, didn't we? So why charge the university for eating away from home? As you've heard Monte was a peanut butter-and-jelly person and this viewpoint possibly reflected that.

Earlier, I noted that Monte was politically astute and so persuasive that he probably could sell us the London Bridge. That created a facade of "slickness" that many perceived as his being sly. That characteristic did not escape our medical students' attention. At our very first Senior Follies, where departing medical students of the first class parodied the faculty and administration, one of our tallest students, Chuck Rolle, appeared with a gray haired wig and a very slick performance as the "Silver Fox," a title most students would not state within his hearing. Nor would anyone call him "Merlin the Great" in his presence. Later in life Monte reflected on these "titles" and said it was better to be remembered than ignored.

Monte continued his mentorship for many of us even after we had departed the College of Medicine. I am very grateful to him for the time and conversations he afforded me at critical points in my career. Monte was always available for sage advice and he ALWAYS answered your phone call or e-mail as soon as possible. The very last bit of advice he gave me was cogent. After retirement and return to Tucson, I was a bit disturbed to learn that "emeritus" meant nobody paid any attention to you. Monte's advice still rings in my ears. "Vince, we've had our turn." Wise advice, indeed.

As we have looked backward today, we can reflect on a passionate, convincing, dedicated, hard-working professional, and on the man whose spirit encompassed his family, his friends, the performing arts and the greater community. Many of us experienced a compassionate and caring friend, and enjoyed an enduring relationship.

Arizona has lost a great man and an accomplished professional; we have lost a true friend, who brought out the best in each of us.

Farewell, Monte, and thank you.

Editorial published in The Arizona Republic, Dec. 8, 2006
"Visionary's drive helped shape state"

Arizona is full of energetic newcomers who look forward, not back.

But that's not new.

It was like that in 1964, when Dr. Merlin K. "Monte" DuVal became the dean of a medical school that wasn't yet built or funded. Through the force of his intelligence, personality and determination, he energized Phoenix and Tucson to work together – no mean feat in any era – and created the University of Arizona College of Medicine in Tucson using donations and federal matching money.

Decades later, long after retirement, he used his stature, expertise and enthusiasm to push for UA's new medical school campus in Phoenix. It was dedicated in October.

A longtime Phoenix resident, DuVal died suddenly Tuesday night at age 84.

The death of one man hardly causes a ripple in a state with a short memory.

But this man's accomplishments are worth remembering because his vision, style and ambition helped shape Arizona.

DuVal was a self-described workaholic, but he was also a man of culture who helped found what became the Arizona Theater Company. He was a community member who became involved with many civic causes. He was a family man who called his children his greatest source of pride.

In 1971, the first class of doctors graduated from the new med school. That same year, DuVal took a leave of absence to become assistant secretary of health for the U.S. Department of Health, Education and Welfare under President Nixon.

In that post, he ended the scandalous 40-year-old Tuskegee experiment in which Black men who had syphilis were left untreated. DuVal returned to UA in 1973, and subsequently wrote the plan that brought Medicaid money to Arizona through the Arizona Health Care Cost Containment System. He remained active in efforts to expand access to health care throughout his life.

A graduate of Dartmouth College and Cornell University Medical College, DuVal brought both a surgeon's love of precision and a sense of humor to his work. He admitted to having plenty of ego, but he was no strutting peacock.

When Tucson's med school was new, he would travel the state to encourage high school kids in rural areas to consider a career in medicine. A principal told DuVal that the minority students in the auditorium would never believe he was talking to them

That's when DuVal designed the Med-Start program to bring ethnic minority, disadvantaged and other non-traditional students to the campus to show them that he was, indeed, talking to them.

DuVal is survived by his wife, Ruth; his former wife, Carol Whiteman; sons David DuVal and Fred DuVal; daughter Barbara Fenster; six grandchildren; and four great-grandchildren.

A fund has been set up to benefit Med-Start in his honor:

UA Foundation/Med-Start, College of Medicine Development Office, P.O. Box 245018, Tucson, AZ 85724.

A memorial will be held at 10:30 a.m., Dec. 16, in DuVal Auditorium at University Medical Center in Tucson.

The place will be full because DuVal was widely respected and loved.

His contributions gave Arizona more reason to look forward, not back.

Reprinted with the permission of The Arizona Republic

Column published in The Arizona Republic, Dec. 10, 2006
"Getting through the broccoli
with Dr. DuVal, a prince of a man"
By Linda Valdez, The Arizona Republic

He had a sorcerer's name and the bearing of a prince.

The attributes of both came in handy when he turned an old polo field full of decrepit Quonset huts into Arizona's first medical school. They came in handy again when he designed the system for indigent health care that brought federal Medicaid money to Arizona.

He told me that they used to call the medical school the Magician's Palace because of his name. People still call the Arizona Health Care Cost Containment System a model because of his skill in crafting it.

He was Dr. Merlin Kearfott DuVal.

Monte.

That's what most people called him.

Monte is what I called him.

The dates and specific details of his remarkable accomplishments are what Monte and I used to call the broccoli.

We had to chew our way through those things for me to do what he wanted me to do. We met once a week, month after month, for most of this past year because he asked me to write his memoir.

After the broccoli or between bites of broccoli – or maybe even instead of broccoli – we'd talk about things that he said he found much more interesting.

Like the dangerous way technology creates its own imperative. Like his philosophy of medicine. Or philosophy in general. Books. Nobility. Old dogs. Politics. Life.

This was the sweet dessert of our discussions.

Like most men of substance and accomplishment, he was remarkably intelligent and well read. He was a surgeon and an academician. He operated on bank robber Willie Sutton and worked for Richard Nixon.

He could quote from a pantheon of philosophers, scholars and politicians

But unlike so many people who use their knowledge as a cudgel, he made a gift of his. He shared ideas in the truest sense of the word "share." A conversation with Monte was an exchange, but it was also a ride on a mental trampoline. You had to pay attention.

We talked about God. He said the universe was too well ordered to have happened by accident, but he wouldn't go so far as attributing it to an "intelligent designer."

It was a mistake, he said, to see God as a personlike entity that could be described with pronouns such as "he" or "she."

We talked of morality and where it came from. We talked of liberty and freedom and the difference between the two.

We talked about babies and what their cries might mean.

"I demand of myself a greater explanation," he said. "I look for it even knowing at the beginning that, when I am through, I will only have an explanation that I needed and I sought and I accepted, and that it has no relevance to anybody else."

I asked him what he thought happened after death. He said the body begins to decompose rather quickly. That's all? Yes. That's all.

We talked about the soul. He said, "You can ascribe a soul to almost anything. It is whatever makes a person that person or a dog that dog or a river that river. I accept that. I applaud that.

"But it does bring up the question: At what stage in life does one acquire a soul?"

It was so much fun talking to him. There was always another question to explore. Another sweet detour.

What happens to the soul when you die? I asked.

"My own feeling is that it dies with you because the uniqueness dies with you. The person you were, whatever made you Linda or me Monte, that's gone. Pieces of it are in everyone you ever knew. If your daughter takes on your characteristics beyond your genes, if she learns something from the way you choose to live, the way you opted to use the capacity to choose, I think that is the transfer of a piece of your immortal soul. Then a piece of you is in her."

We are all born to die. Even sorcerers and princes.

Yet death always comes as a surprise. And so it was with Monte's death last week.

Knowing him enriched my life, and so I choose to keep part of his soul alive as I finish his book without him.

But I also choose to believe that he was wrong about what happens after you die. I like to think that somewhere, in some different reality, Monte and French philosopher Pierre Lecompte du Noüy are sharing their observations about the moral evolution of the human mind.

Reprinted with the permission of The Arizona Republic

News account published in the
Arizona Daily Star, Dec. 7, 2006
"Medical college founder, local icon
Dr. Merlin 'Monte' DuVal dies at 84"
By Carla McClain , Arizona Daily Star

The founder of the University of Arizona College of Medicine, Dr. Merlin K. "Monte" DuVal, died Tuesday night of a heart attack in Phoenix. He was 84.

A former surgeon, federal health official, health-care advocate and longtime community icon in Tucson, DuVal is credited with creating the medical college almost singlehandedly.

"Monte was the College of Medicine as well as the Arizona Health Sciences Center," said Dr. Vincent Fulginiti, a pediatrician and one of the first doctors recruited here by DuVal in the 1960s, who is now co-director of the Medical Reserve Corps of Southern Arizona.

"We have to remember he came here by himself and built the entire faculty. He raised the money to get it going, then convinced the state to fund it and the students to come here.

"This was a man impossible not to admire. Monte had a great vision and a goal to be the best we could be — and he made it all happen.

"We have lost a very great friend, and Arizona has lost a tremendous voice in health care."

DuVal arrived in Tucson in 1963, when he was hired as founding dean of the new medical college by then-UA President Richard Harvill. Charged with the job of establishing Arizona's first school to teach medical students, he launched the massive effort to raise funds, design the buildings and recruit doctors, opening the college in 1967.

Four years later, as the first class of doctors was graduating, the University of Arizona Teaching Hospital — now University Medical Center — opened to patients in 1971.

"Monte was a very clever human being," said Dr. Paul Capp, also brought here by DuVal as the first chief of radiology.

"He was able to get the city excited, he got the newspapers excited, he put on the big campaign, and he built those first buildings for free with the money he raised. He was a team player. He knew what it took to get the medical school off the starting block."

DuVal was named assistant secretary of health in the U.S. Department of Health, Education and Welfare by President Richard Nixon in 1971.

While in Washington, he became a vocal critic of tobacco companies by warning about the dangers of smoking.

DuVal also shut down the notorious and unethical Tuskegee syphilis experiment — a disgraced 40-year study of about 400 black men who were allowed to degenerate and die without treatment, so doctors could see how the disease affected their race.

DuVal returned to the UA in 1973 to serve as acting dean of the medical college for a year, then as vice president for health sciences until 1979.

DuVal's medical career began with his graduation from Dartmouth Medical School in 1944, with completion of his medical degree at Cornell University in 1946.

Following service in the Navy, he completed an internship at Roosevelt Hospital in New York and his surgical residency at the Bronx Veterans Administration Hospital, then joined the surgical faculty at State University of New York in Brooklyn in 1954, where he developed an innovative surgical procedure for treating patients with chronic pancreatitis.

In 1957, DuVal became one of the first full-time faculty members at the University of Oklahoma School of Medicine, then served as assistant director of University of Oklahoma Medical Center until 1963, when he was lured to the UA.

Following his years here, DuVal moved to San Francisco, where he served as president and chief executive officer of the National Center for Health Education from 1979 to 1982. He then returned to Arizona, taking over as president and CEO of Associated Hospital Systems/American Healthcare Institute in Phoenix until 1988, then as senior vice president for medical affairs at Samaritan Health Services in that city until his retirement in 1990.

Active during retirement, DuVal became a strong voice for establishing the UA's new medical school campus in Phoenix and was recognized for that effort during the school's dedication ceremony in October.

UA President Robert Shelton cited DuVal — who was in the audience that day — for meeting with Phoenix Mayor Phil Gordon right after he was elected and urging him to make the medical school a top priority.

"That completed the full circle for him," said his son, Fred DuVal, now a member of the Arizona Board of Regents and a former aide to Arizona Gov. Bruce Babbitt and President Bill Clinton.

"After the fight between Tucson and Phoenix over who would get the first medical school, he was able to see two medical campuses in this state, now in both cities."

Over the course of his life, DuVal was recognized with nine honorary degrees and fellowships and numerous awards for scholarship and public and community service. At the UA, he was given the UA Bobcats Hall of Fame Award in 1978; the College of Pharmacy's Rufus A. Lyman Community Service Award in 1979; and the College of Medicine Dean's Award in 1987.

In 1987, the Arizona Health Sciences Center auditorium was designated "Merlin K. DuVal Auditorium" in his honor.

DuVal's unexpected death occurred just as he and his wife, Ruth, were moving back to Tucson, to live at Academy Village, the development at the base of the Rincon Mountains founded by former UA President Henry Koffler.

After a going-away party in his honor in Phoenix on Sunday night, movers transferred the DuVals' belongings to Tucson on Tuesday. The couple went out for a last dinner in Phoenix that night, where DuVal suddenly collapsed, dying instantly of a massive heart attack, his son said.

DuVal had suffered a previous heart attack in 1971, but had bypass surgery.

"We are so grateful he had three-plus decades of good life since then," Fred DuVal said.

DuVal is survived by his wife, Ruth; his former wife, Carol Whiteman of Tucson; two sons, David of Sonora, Calif., and Fred of Phoenix; and a daughter, Barbara of Phoenix.

The family has established a fund to benefit Med-Start, a UA College of Medicine program established by DuVal that encourages ethnic minority, disadvantaged, rural and nontraditional students to pursue careers in the health professions.

Checks may be made out to the UA Foundation/Med-Start, College of Medicine Development Office, P.O. Box 245018, Tucson AZ 85724-5018.

Reprinted with permission of the Arizona Daily Star.

Curriculum Vitae
Merlin K. Duval

Founding Dean Emeritus
University of Arizona College of Medicine

Post-retirement activities
Arizona State Retirement System Board 1993-2002
    Chair 1994 and 1997
Maricopa County Hospital and Health System Board 1994-2002
Secretary's Advisory Council on Health Promotion and Disease Prevention, DHHS
Founding Director, Arizona Foundation for the Eye 1999-2003
UAHSC Phoenix, Advisory Board, 2004-
MIHS Citizen's Task Force, Vice-Chair

Honorary degrees/fellowships
Alpha Omega Alpha Honor Society 1963
D.Sc. New Jersey College of Medicine and Dentistry 1972
D.Sc. Dartmouth College 1972
Honorary Fellow, American College of Cardiology 1972
D.Sc. Medical College of Wisconsin 1973
D.Sc. Coll. of Osteopathic Medicine & Surgery (Des Moines) 1977
LHD. Ohio College of Podiatric Medicine 1978
Honorary Fellow, American College of Healthcare Executives 1980
Honorary Member, Phi Beta Kappa 1994

Awards/recognitions
Markle Scholar in Medical Sciences 1956-61
Certificate of Commendation, University of Oklahoma 1967
Convocation Medal, American College of Cardiology 1972
Leslie B. Smith Medal for Distinguished Public Service, Maricopa County
Medical Society 1967
Walter P. Patenge Medal of Public Service, Michigan State University 1972
Health Service Award, Charleston (W.VA) Medical Center 1974
Hall of Fame Award, University of Arizona Bobcats 1978
Outstanding Citizen of Tucson, AZ 1978
Maimonides Award, Healing Arts Division, State of Israel Bonds 1978
A.H. Robins Community Service Award, Arizona Medical Association 1979
Rufus A. Lyman Community Service Award, University of Arizona, College of
    Pharmacy 1979
Clarence Salsbury Award for Outstanding Community Service, Arizona Hospital

Association 1979
Dean's Award, University of Arizona College of Medicine 1987
Univ. of Arizona Health Sciences Center Auditorium designated Merlin K. DuVal
     Auditorium 1987
Presidential Medal for Outstanding Leadership and Achievement,
     Dartmouth College 1991
University of Oklahoma Health Sciences Center Research Building Conference
     Room designated the Merlin K. DuVal Room 1997
Distinguished Alumnus Award, Cornell University Medical College 1999
Lifetime Achievement Award, Phoenix Business Journal 2004

Memberships
Alpha Omega Alpha Honor Society 1963-
American Surgical Association 1961-
     Committee on Surgical Education 1966-68
     Committee on Governmental Relations 1970-71
Arizona Town Hall
Association of American Medical Colleges. 1964-
     Executive Council 1967-71
     Chairman, Western Region 1968-69
     Liaison Committee on Medical Education 1968-71
     Ways & Means Committee 1968-71
     Chairman-Elect, Council of Deans 1969-70; Chairman 1970-71
     Task Force on Foreign Medical Graduates 1973
     Task Force on Health Manpower 1974
     Distinguished Service Member 1974-
Institute of Medicine, National Academy of Sciences 1973-
     Health Manpower Cost Study 1973-74
     Board of Advisors, Health Policy Fellowships 1973-75
     Social Security Amendment Study 1974-76
     Chairman, Western Region Advisory Committee 1977-78
     Patient Package Insert Study Committee 1978-79
     Finance Committee 1979-80
     Board on Health Promotion and Disease Prevention 1981-90
     General Council 1983-86
      Chairman, Yr. 2000 Objectives for the Nation Project, 1987-91
Society of Medical Administrators 1972-
     President-Elect 1979-81; President 1981-83
Tucson Literary Club Since 1969
World Organization for Science and Health 1985-

Education/training/certification
College High School, Upper Montclair, NJ 1940
A.B. Dartmouth College, Hanover, NH 1943
Two-Year Certificate, Dartmouth Medical School 1944
M.D. Cornell University Medical College, NYC 1946
Intern (Surgery) New York Hospital 1946-47
Diplomate, National Board of Medical Examiners 1946

Military Duty, U.S. Navy. 1947-49
    U.S. Naval Hospital; St. Albans, NY
    Naval Amphibious Base; Little Creek, VA
Intern (Rotating) Roosevelt Hospital, NYC 1949-50
Residency (Surgery), V.A. Hospital Bronx, NY 1950-54
Certified, American Board of Surgery 1954

Professional and community activities
1954-56   State University of New York College of Medicine, Brooklyn, NY
        Instructor (Surgery) 1954-55
        Attending Surgeon, Kings County Hospital 1954-56
        Assistant Professor (Surgery) 1955-56
        Consultant, St. Albans Naval Hospital, L.I. 1955-56
1957-63   University of Oklahoma School of Medicine, Oklahoma City, OK.
        Associate Professor (Surgery) 1957-61
        Attending Surgeon, VA Hospital, Oklahoma City 1957-63
        Director of Medical Center Development 1960-62
        Vice-Chairman, Department of Surgery 1960-63
        Professor (Surgery) 1961-63
        Assistant Director, University Medical Center 1962-63
1964-71   University of Arizona, Tucson, AZ.
        Founding Dean, College of Medicine; University of Arizona 1964-71
        Director, Southwest Research Foundation 1965-69
        Chairman, Governor's Committee on Regional Medical Programs 1966-67
        Tucson Community Council 1966-71
        Committee on Federal Health Legislation
        Community Survey Committee
        Mental Health Services and Facilities
        Comprehensive Health Planning Committee
        Committee on Impact of Medicare
        Guidelines Committee
        Priorities Committee
        Consultant, HEW Bureau of Health Manpower 1966-68
        Director, National Library of Medicine Study 1966-68
        Air Pollution Control Adv. Board, Pima County 1966-70
        Chairman, Arizona Anatomical Board 1967-71
        Director, Arizona Regional Medical Program 1967-71
        Associate Editor, ARIZONA MEDICINE 1967-71
        Editorial Board, JOURNAL OF MEDICAL EDUCATION 1967-71
        Director, Arizona Kidney Foundation 1968-70
        Director, Nat'l Found. for Asthmatic Children 1968-71
        National Advisory Council on Education for the Health Professions, HEW
           1968-71
        Arizona Health Planning Authority 1968-71
        Health Occupations Advisory Committee, Pima Community College
1970-71
        United Way, Board of Directors 1970-71
        Vice-Chairman/Chairman, Planning and Allocations

Vice-Chairman, United Way Campaign
Advisor, National Alliance of Businessmen, Inc. 1970-71
1971-73 Department of Health, Education and Welfare, Washington, DC
Assistant Secretary of Health
Federal Technology Council
AMA/AAMC Liaison Committee on Medical Education
Chief, U.S. Delegation, World Health Organization, Geneva,
Switzerland 1972
Chief, U.S. Delegation, meeting of Western Hemisphere Ministers of
Health, Santiago, Chile 1972
1973-79: University of Arizona, Tucson, AZ.
Acting Dean, College of Medicine 1973-74
Vice-President for Health Sciences 1973-79
Kino Hospital Advisory Committee 1973-74
Member, Macy Foundation Commission on Physicians for the Future
1973-74
Chairman, Arizona State Committee on Medicaid 1973-74
Chairman, Board of Overseers, Dartmouth Medical School 1973-76
Advisory Committee to the Chancellor, University of Missouri, Kansas
City Medical School 1973-77
National Advisory Council for Professional Standards Review
Organizations, 1973-78, Chairman, 1976-78
Quality of Life Panel, Rockefeller Commission on Critical Choices
for Americans 1974-75
Citizens Conference on State Legislatures 1974-75
Arizona Commission on the Arts and Humanities 1974-76
Advisory Council, AZ Health Planning Authority 1974-79
Member, Advisory Panel on National Health Insurance to Subcommittee
on Health Ways and Means Committee, US Congress, 1975-76
Chairman, Public Policy Work Group, National Commission on Arthritis
1975-76
Consultant to the Director; Lister Hill National Center for Biomedical
Communications, National Library of Medicine 1975-77
National Advisory Committee on Health, American Hospital
Association 1975-78
Arizona Civic Theater
Board of Directors
President 1973-74
Advisory Board
Advisory Commission on Health Care Delivery, Arizona House of
Representatives 1977
National Commission on Smoking and Public Policy, American Cancer
Society 1977-78
Chairman, State Health Coordinating Council 1977-79
Committee on Health Policy, National Association of State and Land
Grant Colleges 1978-79
1979-82 National Center for Health Education, San Francisco, CA
President and Chief Executive Officer

Trustee, San Francisco Regional Cancer Foundation 1979-82
Lecturer, School of Public Health, University of California, Berkeley
    1979-82
Center for Corporate Public Involvement, Advisory Council, Health
    Enhancement 1979 -93
    Chair 1987-93
Editorial Advisory Board, PHYSICIAN'S PATIENT EDUCATION
    NEWSLETTER 1980-81
American Cancer Society Committee on Tobacco and Cancer 1980-82
Board of Directors, Project INSURE 1980-87
Professional Advisor, Health Awareness Systems 1981
Commission on Responsible Health Policy 1981
Professional Advisory Board, Control Data Corp. 1981-83

1982-88 Associated Hospital Systems/American Healthcare Institute,
    Phoenix, AZ and Washington, DC
        President and Chief Executive Officer
    American Hospital Association:
        Special Committee on Healthcare Coalitions 1982
        Hospital Research and Educational Trust Advisory Committee 1982-86
        Human Resources Council 1983-86
    U.S. Chamber of Commerce Health Policy Committee 1982-83
    Director, Westburg Institute 1982-84
    Director, National Center for Health Education
    Commonwealth Fund Task Force on Academic Health Centers 1983-87
    Editorial Board, BUSINESS AND HEALTH 1983-89
    National Council on Patient Information and Education Advisory Group
        1983-88
    Health Executives Round Table 1984-88
    Council, Center for Prepaid Healthcare Research 1985-88
    Board of Directors, National Committee for Quality Health Care 1986-88
    Director, Foundation for Future Choices 1986-90
    H.R.E.T. Task Force on Quality Healthcare 1986-90
    National Leadership Commission on Healthcare 1987-90

1988-90 Samaritan Health Services Phoenix, AZ
        Senior Vice-President for Medical Affairs
    Foundation for Healthcare Quality (Seattle) 1989-90
    Foundation for Burns and Trauma, Director 1989-90
    Governor's Task Force on Head Injury 1989-91

Past memberships
American Association for the Advancement of Science. 1966-90
    Elected Fellow 1982
American College of Surgeons (Fellow) 1958-79
    Member, Board of Governors 1965-68
    Committee on Undergraduate Medical Education 1967-70
American Federation for Clinical Research 1959-63

American Gastroenterological Association 1960-64
American Medical Association 1954-87
    Advisory Committee on Undergraduate Education 1967-71
Arizona Hospital Association Committee on Cigarette Tax, 1996
Arizona Medical Association 1964-84; 1988-91
    Vocational Rehabilitation Committee 1967-68
    Comprehensive Health Plan Committee 1967-68
    Benevolent and Loan Fund Committee 1967-71
    Public Relations Committee 1976-77
Arizona State Hospital Committee to Explore Privatization 1966
Arizona Surgical Association 1967-71
    Committee on Surgical Education 1966-68
    Committee on Governmental Relations 1970-71
Association for Academic Health Centers 1973-79
    Board of Directors 1973-79
    Co-Chairman, Program Committee 1976-77
    President-elect 1976-77; President 1977-78
    Chairman, Committee of Presidents 1978-79
Association of the University of Oklahoma Medical Faculty 1959-63
    President 1961-63
Bergen County (NJ) Medical Society. 1954-55
Brooklyn (NY) Surgical Society 1956
Governance Institute Faculty 1983-90
International Surgical Society 1960-71
Kings County (NY) Medical Society 1955-56
Maricopa County Board Of Supervisors Committee to Privatize the
    Maricopa County Health System 1995-96.
Maricopa County (AZ) Medical Society 1989-91
Medical Care Seminar 1979-96
Medical Society of the State of New York 1955-56
Medical Society of the United States and Mexico 1964-84
National Association of State Universities and Land Grant Colleges 1967-71
    Commission for Education in the Health Professions 1967-71
    Chairman 1968-69
National Health Policy Forum, Development Board 1986-90
Norfleet Forum, National Advisory Board. 1983-90
New York Academy of Science 1958-63
Oklahoma County Medical Society 1958-63
Oklahoma Surgical Association 1960-64
    Vice-President 1961-62
    President-Elect 1962-63
    President 1963-64
Pan American Medical Association 1964-71
Pima County (AZ) Medical Society 1963-84
    Federal Services Committee 1967-68
    Government Services Committee 1968-71
Proposition 203, State Co-Chairman 1996
Rural Health Project Advisory Committee, Chairman 1994-96.

Sigma Xi Scientific Society 1958-63
Society for the Social History of Medicine 1973-77
Society for Surgery of the Alimentary Tract 1962-65
Southwest Surgical Society 1959-71
    Publication and Research Committee 1970-71
Surgical Biology Club II 1960-79
Theresa Foundation (Child Abuse), Director 1991-96
Tucson (AZ) Surgical Society 1964-71
VIM and VIGOR. Editorial Board 1990-96

Founding faculty of the University of Arizona's first medical school

1964
Merlin K. DuVal, MD, Dean
Philip H. Krutzsch, MA, PhD, Anatomy
1965
David Bishop, MSLS, Administration
Donald M. Gleason, MD, Surgery
Thomas D. Higdon, MSLS, Administration
1966
Paul J. Matt, MD, LLB, Community Medicine
John D. Palmer, MS, MD, PhD, Multidiscipline Laboratories, Pharmacology
Oscar A. Thorup, Jr., MD, Internal Medicine
1967
George H. Adams, MD, PhD, Student Affairs
Jay B. Angevine, Jr., MA, PhD, Anatomy
Bill Buchsbaum, MD, Neurology
John R. Davis, MD, Pathology
William F. Denny, MD, Internal Medicine
Samuel Goldfein, MD, Internal Medicine
Donald J. Hanahan, PhD, Biochemistry
Samuel Hodesson, DVM, MPH, Animal Resources
Roy Horst, PhD, Anatomy
Paul C. Johnson, MS, PhD, Physiology
Mark M. Kartchner, MD, Surgery
Jacquelyn Kasper, MSLS, Administration
Jack M. Layton, MD, Pathology
Christopher K. Mathews, PhD, Biochemistry
Hilmi Mavioglu, MD, Internal Medicine
Dermont W. Melick, MD, MSc, DSc, Surgery
Leonard R. Miller, MD, Pathology
David Rifkind, MD, PhD, Microbiology and Internal Medicine
William A. Sibley, MD, Internal Medicine
James F. Stagg, MD, Internal Medicine
Hans F. Stein, MD, Internal Medicine
Douglas G. Stuart, MA, PhD, Physiology
Michael A. Wells, PhD, Biochemistry
John A. Wilson, MA, MD, Internal Medicine
Alexander H. Woods, MD, Internal Medicine
1968
Herbert K. Abrams, MS, MD, MPH, Community Medicine

Harris Bernstein, PhD, Microbiology
John T. Boyer, MD, Internal Medicine
Frederick J. Brady, MD, Community Medicine
Benjamin Burrows, MD, Internal Medicine
Daniel W. Capps, MS, MBA, Hospital Administration
Athol L. Cline, MS, PhD, Biochemistry
William H. Dantzler, MD, PhD, Physiology
Arnold J. Funckes, MD, PhD, Pathology
Charles J. Gauntt, MA, PhD, Microbiology
Raphael P. Gruener, MA, PhD, Physiology
George A. Hedge, MS, PhD, Physiology
Louis J. Kettel, MS, MD, Internal Medicine
Frank I. Marcus, MS, MD, Internal Medicine
Thomas R. McWilliams, BS, Administration
Carter Mosher, MD, Internal Medicine
David W. Mount, MA, PhD, Microbiology
Merle S. Olson, PhD, Biochemistry
Erle E. Peacock, MD, Surgery
R. Neal Pinckard, PhD, Microbiology
Lawrence K. Schneider, PhD, Anatomy
Martin J. Schock, MD, Internal Medicine
Richard R. Willey, PhB, PhD, Social Perspectives in Medicine
Larry Zinn, MD, Surgery
1969
Walter Ahrens, MD, Pediatrics
Robert A. Barbee, MD, Academic Affairs
David Ben-Asher, MD, Internal Medicine
Richard Brown, MD, Pediatrics
C. Donald Christian, MD, PhD, Obstetrics and Gynecology
Harry R. Claypool, MD, Anatomy
H. Allan Collier, MD, Obstetrics and Gynecology
George D. Comerci, MD, Pediatrics
Carl Diener, MD, Internal Medicine
Marshall Dinowitz, ScD, Microbiology
Stuart Edelberg, MD, Obstetrics and Gynecology
Gordon A. Ewy, MD, Internal Medicine
Vincent A. Fulginiti, MD, MS, Pediatrics
John M. Gillette, MD, Obstetrics and Gynecology
Joseph Heinlein, MD, Pediatrics
Robert S. Hoge, DVM, Laboratory Animal Medicine
Douglas W. Huestis, MD, Pathology
Alan B. Humphrey, PhD, Community Medicine
Carol M. Kelley, MSLS, Administration
Arnold J. Kresch, MD, Obstetrics and Gynecology
Charles L. Krone, MD, Internal Medicine
Alan I. Levenson, MD, Psychiatry
Hyok Sang Lew, PhD, Physiology
Elmer S. Lightner, MD, Pediatrics

Martin A. Lohff, MD, Pathology
Eugene M. Long, MD, Obstetrics and Gynecology
John W. Madden, MD, Surgery
Stuart Miller, MD, Internal Medicine
William L. Miller, MD, Pathology
James Morse, MD, Internal Medicine
John Mosman, MD, Pediatrics
David Ogden, MD, Internal Medicine
Charles Pullen, MD, Pediatrics
Youn Bock Rhee, MPH, Community Medicine
Hermann S. Rhu, MD, Obstetrics and Gynecology
Edward Sattenspiel, MD, Obstetrics and Gynecology
William C. Scott, MD, MS, Obstetrics and Gynecology
Milton Semoff, MD, Pediatrics
Katherine Shaffer, MSLS, Administration
Charles Stephens, MD, Internal Medicine
William C. Trier, MD, Surgery
Arie vanRavenswaay, MD, Internal Medicine
Leonard J. Weiner, MD, Surgery
William Willard, PhD, Community Medicine
Charles L. Witte, MD, Surgery
William C. Witting, MD, Obstetrics and Gynecology
Raymond B. Wuerker, MD, Anatomy
Hubert E. Wuesthoff, MD, PsychiatrySteve
Charles F. Zukoski, MD, Surgery

1970

Harry D. Abraham, MD, Community Medicine
Olga Allers, MD, Community Medicine
Ron Almgren, MD, Pediatrics
Fred Alpern, MD, Pediatrics
Norman E. Anderson, MD, Psychiatry
Allan Beigel, MD, Psychiatry
H. Daniel Bodley, PhD, Anatomy
Klaus Brendel, PhD, Pharmacology
Rubin Bressler, MD, Pharmacology
Henry W. Brosin, MD, Psychiatry
Cooley Butler II, MD, Pathology
Duncan W. Campbell, MD, Surgery
M. Paul Capp, MD, Radiology
Edward C. Carlson, PhD, Anatomy
Marian A. Chavez, MA, MSLS, Administration
Walter B. Cherny, MD, Obstetrics and Gynecology
Milos Chvapil, MD, PhD, Surgical Biology
D. Scott Clark, MD, Surgery
William E. Crisp, MD, Obstetrics and Gynecology
Charles P. Crowe Jr., MD, Surgery
Robert J. Cutts, MD, Psychiatry
William M. Davis, MD, Surgery

Murray M. De Armond, MD, Psychiatry
Jack Denlon, MD, Pediatrics
Philip Dew, MD, Pediatrics
George W. Drach, MD, Surgery
Milton Dworin, MD, Internal Medicine
Ernest Eberling, MD, Pediatrics
Hubert R. Estes, MS, MD, Psychiatry
Donald B. Ewing, MD, Surgery
Shirley N. Fahey, MA, PhD, Psychiatry
Thomas Forman, MD, Internal Medicine
Edward S. Gelardin, MD, Psychiatry
Stanley J. Goldberg, MD, Pediatrics
Alan L. Gordon, MD, Internal Medicine
Robert W. Gore, PhD, Physiology
David B. Gurland, MD, Psychiatry
Elliott M. Heiman, MD, Psychiatry
Louis Hirsch, MD, Pathology
John P. Holbrook, MD, Internal Medicine
Raymond J. Jennett, MD, Obstetrics and Gynecology
Helen Johnson, MD, Pediatrics
Marshall W. Jones, MD, Psychiatry
Sidney R. Kemberling, MD, Pediatrics
Charles M. Kerr, MD, Psychiatry
Joel B. Kirkpatrick, MD, Pathology
Ronald Knudson, MD, Internal Medicine
Dale Kreider, MD, Pediatrics
Herbert R. Lazarus, MD, Psychiatry
Alvin R. Leonard, MD, MPH, Community Medicine
Daniel Levinson, MD, PhB, Community Medicine
Tom J. Lindell, PhD, Pharmacology
Vernor F. Lovett, MD, Surgery
David O. Lucas, PhD, Microbiology
Frederic MacCabe MD, Psychiatry
Nick J. Mansour, MD, Internal Medicine
Richard Martin, MD, Pediatrics
John H. McEvers, MD, Obstetrics and Gynecology
Belton Meyer, MD, Pediatrics
Peter D. Mott, MD, Community Medicine
Andrew W. Nichols, MD, MPH, Community Medicine
Milan Novak, MS, MB, MD, PhD, Internal Medicine
Charles A. Nugent, MD, Internal Medicine
Charles Parker, MD, Obstetrics and Gynecology
David Pent, MD, Obstetrics and Gynecology
Herbert Pollack, MD, Obstetrics and Gynecology
Leland K. Reeck, MD, Psychiatry
Newell Richardson, MD, Pediatrics
Clarence Robbins, MD, Internal Medicine
Jacob B. Rudekop, MD, Surgery

Stephen C. Scheiber, MD, Psychiatry
Joseph Seagle, MD, Pediatrics
Shiao-Wei Shen, MD, Internal Medicine
Martin L. Shultz, MD, Urologic Surgery
Otto Sieber, MD, Pediatrics
Jay W. Smith, MD, Medicine
Richard F. Snell, MRCS, LRCP, MBBS, MD, PhD, Anatomy
Mary Ann Sullivan, MD, Community Medicine
William A. Susong, MD, Obstetrics and Gynecology
Stanley Tanz, MD, Surgery
Jesse W. Tapp, MD, MPH, Community Medicine
Hugh C. Thompson, MD, Community Medicine
Leon L. Titche, MD, Surgery
Charles Tompkins, MD, Pediatrics
Gayle Ann Traver, MS, Internal Medicine
Walton Van Winkle Jr., MD, Surgical Biology
John Welsh, MD, Pediatrics
Warren S. Williams, MD, Psychiatry
Marlys H. Witte, MD, Surgical Biology

Names as published in program for University of Arizona College of Medicine 40th Anniversary Celebration

News account on death of Monte's father, Merlin K. DuVal, Sr., published June 10, 1965 The Montclair (NJ) Times "M.K. DuVal, Broker, 68"

A memorial service for Merlin K. DuVal of 10 Crestmont Rd., co-manager of the Montclair branch of Auchincloss, Parker and Redpath, members of the New York Stock Exchange, was held in the Central Presbyterian Church on Sunday. Mr. DuVal died last Thursday in the Mountainside Hospital. He was 68.

Mr. DuVal was born in Winnipeg, Canada, the son of the late Dr. Frederick B. DuVal, moderator of the Presbyterian General Assembly of Canada, and Mrs. DuVal. He attended private and public schools in Winnipeg County and graduated from the University of Manitoba.

With the outbreak of World War I, he enlisted in the First Canadian Division and went overseas in 1914. He is one of the few remaining survivors of the first gas attack at Ypres, Belgium, in 1915.

Mr. DuVal was appointed an officer in the British Army and represented the Central Command in England in the formation of the original training schools in scouting and sniping in the British Army.

When the United States entered the war in 1917, Mr. DuVal reported to the U.S. Army as a part of the British Mission to assist American forces in practical warfare. At the close of the war in 1918, Mr. DuVal came to the United States and settled in Montclair. At this time, he joined the firm of P.M. Chambler and Co., investment brokers in New York. Subsequent to that position, he was vice president of Bond and Goodwin of Boston for twenty years and on sales and research with the Okanite Co. of Passaic for ten years.

Upon leaving the Okanite Co., he was employed by the Crang and Co., a Canadian firm in New York. In 1960, he joined the firm of Auchincloss, Parker and Redpath and was co-manager of the Montclair branch when it opened in April 1960. Highlights of his earlier career included putting natural gas into Edmonton, Alberta, under a company known as Northwestern Utilities. He was also instrumental in forming the first publicly financed grocery chain store combine in the United States, the American Stores of Philadelphia, Pa.

Among companies purchased following the success of this venture was the Charles M. Dreher Co. in Orange and Montclair.

Mr. DuVal was a member of the Huguenot Society of America and in Montclair of the Central Presbyterian Church and Rotary Club. In 1952, he served as chairman of the general fund campaign of the YMCA in Montclair.

He leaves his wife, Mrs. Margaret S. DuVal; two sons, Dr. Merlin K. DuVal Jr., M.D., of Tucson, Ariz., and the Rev. William K. DuVal of the United Presbyterian Church, of Upper Montclair; a brother, retired Manitoba Chief Justice Paul DuVal; two sisters, Miss Lorraine DuVal and Mrs. Robert Guy, all of Winnipeg, and six grandchildren